I Hold
These Truths

by

Don Stott

Editor
and
Cover Design
by
James Van Treese

Northwest Publishing Inc.
5442 South 900 East
Salt Lake City, Utah 84117
801-266-0253

ISBN #1-880416-10-7

Printed in the United States of America

INTRODUCTION

I am not a famous person. If I were an Elizabeth Taylor, sports star, or famous politician, I may be in great demand as a writer, talented or not! As it is, I am only a middle aged, intelligent, free thinking, objective, logical, analytical man, who thinks he has something important to say. Over the years, I have discovered that many hundreds of commonly accepted "truths", are bald faced lies, and have left America in a shambles.

Most take taxes, politics, government, and the corner bank for granted, and never think about their history, honesty, or even necessity. Politics is a matter of habit rather than thought for most. "Hell, I've been a yeller dog democrat all my life and so was my daddy, and grandaddy, so don't talk to me about politics", is too often a philosophy. I've got news for you my friend, politics has done, and continues to do, great harm to America.

I began to have a strange feeling a few years ago. The feeling was that Americans were becoming more and more disgusted with the way things were going in this land. I began to feel that we are sick and tired of the debt, bad schools, huge government, and continual lies by the politicos holding office term after term. So I began to write. I have tried to picture how it used to be, and should be now. I began to pass around the pieces, and someone suggested I assemble them into a book. This is the result.

It is marvelous fun, sifting through lies and deception. I will not bore you with education, writing experience, and a resume. Are they necessary to be able to write and think? I know many college educated idiots. I happen to like plain spoken, "say it like it is" reading, and this is it. No words minced!

This book is totally logical, and is without exaggeration. At first reading, parts of it may be contrary to your upbringing, and customary belief. I hope you will reconsider these chapters, and their consummate common sense.

America is still the most wonderful place on earth, but she's in a terrible rut, and needs to get out quickly before fading from view altogether. What is contained herein as radical, but the idea of freedom from England was also radical 200 years ago. The American Revolutionaries were regarded as "crackpots" by far too many of the Colonists.

Jan Struther, in "A Pocketful of Pebbles" said, "Private opinion creates public opinion. Public opinion overflows eventually into national behavior and national behavior, as things are arranged at present, can make or mar the world. That is why private opinion, and private behavior, and private conversation are so terrifyingly important".

This book is exceedingly important to me. I have tried to say things in a way that may bring much needed change to America. If I can change the minds of people about the subjects considered in the following pages, I will be amply rewarded. America needs to once again be supreme, rather than a declining, debt ridden, has been. America is such a grand, heroic place, and I would give my life to help restore it to its former glory.

I do hope you enjoy and see the logic of it.

TABLE OF CONTENTS

Introduction .... iii & iv

Dedication viii

Chapter

  1. Pride 1

  2. The Postal Service 3

  3. Happy Pigs 5

  4. 535 Men and Women 7

  5. Are guns the Problem? 9

  6. Panama 13

  7. Foreign Aid 15

  8. Dog Catchers 17

  9. The Homeless 19

 10. The Two Most Mispronounced Words ... 21

 11. Robin Hood 23

 12. Shortages & Starvation 27

 13. Why Don't Trucks Have Good Brakes? ... 31

 14. Reporters 33

 15. They Went Broke First 35

 16. The Risen Sun 37

 17. What's Wrong With Being Rich? 43

 18. Corporations 45

 19. Interest 47

 20. Just a Few Cents Each 51

 21. As I Looked About Me 61

 22. Garbo and Her Types 65

 23. Movies 67

 24. Public Art 69

25.	Abortion	73
26.	Police	77
27.	Time Shares	79
28.	The South	81
29.	The Carter Legacy	83
30.	Trash	87
31.	The Great Diesel Fraud	91
32.	Why Use Tankers?	93
33.	Unions	97
34.	Health Care	103
35.	Feed The Children	107
36.	Rewrite?	111
37.	Flag Burning	115
38.	Male Superiority	117
39.	Little Philistines Come From	119
40.	Who Is For Us?	123
41.	Manufacturing	129
42.	Aids	133
43.	Let the Chips Fall Where They May ...	137
44.	60 Years	141
45.	The Mafia	143
46.	Neutrality	147
47.	Who Gives Freedom?	151
48.	Taxes	153
49.	Passing Legislation	157
50.	Race	159
51.	Prejudice	163
52.	Old, Senile, Helpless People	165
53.	Should a Lawyer Defend the Guilty? ..	169
54.	Israel	171
55.	Sophistication	175
56.	Regulators	179
57.	Classical Music	184
58.	Turning Back the Clock	189

59.	The Minimum Wage	193
60.	Limited Terms	197
61.	The Stock Market	201
62.	Insanity and Parole	209
63.	Business	213
64.	Politics	219
65.	Consumerism	225
66.	Run For Your Life	229
67.	Some Advice to Blacks	233
68.	Smoking	239
69.	The 5th Amendment	243
70.	Are They Ever the Same Again?	247
71.	Public	251
72.	Keep 'Em Alive	257
73.	Amtrak and Railroads	261
74.	The Concept of Government	267
75.	Welfare	273
76.	Inflation	283
77.	Public Schools	287
78.	The GNP	295
79.	I Love My Country, But	299
80.	Insurance	303
81.	A Property Tax Proposal	307
82.	They Don't Make Land Anymore	311
83.	Banks	315
84.	Opera	321
85.	The Critics	325
86.	The Media	329
87.	Equality	331
88.	Whatever Happened to Coney Island?	333
89.	What Would You Do?	337
90.	Why Don't Americans Vote?	341
	Epilogue	343
	Conclusion	355

DEDICATION

Dedicated to the Memory of the late Ayn Rand. Her novel *Atlas Shrugged*, and the subsequent reasoning it has generated, has been the strongest influence of my adult life. I first read it in 1972, have re-read it several times, given away countless copies, and urge everyone to read it. *Atlas Shrugged* is a superb example of logical political thought set forth in a novel. Unfortunately, I see *Atlas Shrugged's* horrors engulfing America in what appears to be irreversible slow motion.

Don Stott, December 13, 1991

PRIDE

It isn't difficult to realize that Americans no longer take much pride in anything they do. Be it teaching school, building houses, or a day to day job, no one seems to care much.

Compare buildings built 75, or even 50 years ago, with today's construction. Builders now have wonderful new materials, accurate power tools, and all sorts of mechanization unheard of a few decades ago. The most cursory examination of modern construction, wiring, plumbing, and detail of new buildings readily proves that pride has been replaced by hurry up, cover up, and give me a raise. Builders back then may not have had modern insulation, double glazed windows, efficient heating and air conditioning, but they made the doors fit, the trim match, and they uniformly overbuilt. Any wonder old buildings are coveted?

Cars? Modern cars may have computers, foam rubber, high compression, radial tires, disc brakes, lots of power assists, but they have extremely sloppy construction. No one cares about the fine details of excellent fit, superb finish, and details. Just slop 'em together, fill the gaps with plastic and rubber, and sell them. Pride? Down the drain with the bath water.

Workers who sweep the streets, file the paperwork, type the letters, deliver the mail, or wait on the customers, have little pride or affection for their work. Mailmen deliver to the wrong addresses, clerks are surly, and of course our society is so plagued with errors that at times I think it will all grind to a halt.

Railroaders used to love their engines so much that they would polish them, and develop a whistle blowing technique identifying them as they came into town. They took pride in fast running, and being on time. Today, that is so far gone as to sound ridiculous. Transit drivers and railroaders today usually care not a whit about politeness, schedules, or dignity. It used to be that no matter what job a person had, they would strive to do the absolute best they could do in their field, whatever it might be. No longer.

Contemporary composers and musicians rain garbage on us and our kids with impunity.

Artists deluge us with rubbish, and expect us to laud them, and buy it.

Furniture makers rely on their brand names, which often no longer reflect quality.

Bureaucrats, of course, have never been worth a damn and still aren't, so nothing lost there except a huge increase in their sorry numbers.

Poetry is often a jumble of words, with no rhyme or reason, and of course no talent. No pride or ability.

Where have all the caring, expert, achieving, striving, dedicated, people gone? Read on, and perhaps you may discover, but I'll guarantee you one thing, throwing more money or government at it won't solve it...if it can be solved.

THE POST OFFICE DEPT.

Often characterized by a famous editorial cartoonist as the "U.S. Snail", rather than the U.S. Mail, there can be no question as to the escalating inefficiency of this particular branch of the federal government. This writer had three letters lost in that many months. Letters mailed, but never received. In Philadelphia a few years ago, I mailed a mortgage payment across town 9 days in advance of the payment's due date. It arrived 15 days later, and I had to pay a $50 late charge.

In February, 1991, the U.S. Postal Service put into effect the largest postal rate increase in its history. From 25 cents to 29 cents, first class. The term "first class" has become a non sequitur as applied to the mail service. But I know nothing about delivering the mail. I know nothing of the workings of the U.S. Postal Service. Few, if any of its critics do. So I can't complain about rising costs, unionism, comparisons of foreign rates and quantities delivered, or any other facet of delivering the mail. What I do know is that government never does anything efficiently, cheaply, or timely. My suggestion is not to scream and bellow over the rate increases. Let it happen! Merely go to the root of the problem, which is pure and simple. Government created and protected monopoly.

Before parcel delivery was deregulated, the U.S. Postal Service had 100% of that business. It now has but 3%, and it all came about not with criticism of the post office, but letting the market operate. If delivering the rest of the mail were deregulated, the problem would be quickly solved. The post office knows this, and you and I know it. Everyone knows it! Total deregulation is what the post office bureaucracy fears most. I can see no reason why mail delivered by other than the U.S. Postal Service has to remain a criminal act, nor can I see why the mail box in front of your home, which you bought and erected, has to be for the use of the U.S. Postal Service alone. Eliminate these two outdated, outrageous laws, let the market operate, and presto! All problems will be solved.

HAPPY PIGS

When I was a kid, garbage pickup cost the cities nothing. All homes had two types of refuse containers; one for trash and one for garbage. The trash and garbage were picked up on different days, and with different types of trucks. Trash pickup was with city trucks, and the garbage was picked up by private contractors who charged the city nothing for their service. Sound strange? Lots of things that "used to be" sound strange to young people who can't imagine such things. When I tell my kids there was no TV when I was growing up, they look upon me as prehistoric!

The garbage pickup was free because it was used for something other than landfill, namely, feeding pigs and hogs on rural farms. After all, is there anything happier than a "pig in slop"? In those sensible, "good old days", farmers were delighted to get virtually free feed for their hog operations. What the pigs didn't eat was plowed into the fields as natural fertilizer. There were no garbage disposals then. What happened to such a logical, amazingly simple process of disposing of garbage? Government decided feeding garbage to happy pigs and hogs was dangerous or some such nonsense, so it was banned. Pigs and hogs would thereafter have to be fed commercially produced and expensively bought feed. The producers of such feeds undoubtedly hired lobbyists in Washington D.C. to "educate" the lawmakers on the professional feed vs leftovers that swine had voraciously eaten for thousands of years with no ill effects.

Municipal sewage treatment plants became overloaded

and inadequate, causing hundreds of millions to be spent on new facilities. Sewer, rubbish pickup, administrative costs, and new debt service zoomed into the stratosphere. Pork prices climbed to the neighborhood of beef, making beef producers lyrical, and we all paid through the nose in increased taxes and food prices. Pork used to be cheap, now it's expensive. Poor pigs no longer eat wonderful, tasty scraps from America's dining room tables and restaurants, but must eat artificial food, certainly not a pig's preference. All of this logic, low cost and common sense is a thing of the dim past.

This strange turn of events is known as "progress", but I call it fraud, waste, and absurdity, usually going under the name of "government". Let me know when we reach Utopia, I want to take a picture.

535 MEN & WOMEN

If I told you that 535 men and women control the future of this brave land, would you believe me? If I told you that these 535 men and women have literally bankrupted this country because of a simple selfish desire, would you believe it? John T. Flynn said in his extraordinary book, *The Roosevelt Myth* (1948, Devin-Adir), "... A lot of butter-fingered politicians, two big halls full of shallow and stupid Congressmen and Senators had made a mess of America".

And this was in 1933!

What makes Congress' heart beat fastest of all? It isn't love, consummated; but the prestige and power that comes from membership in the two most exclusive clubs in the world, the U.S. Senate and House of Representatives. These elected lawmakers control the destiny of America. Their greatest dread is losing an election, and they have a very adequate modus operandi for keeping those jobs. So effective, that, 98-99% of these men and women are re-elected each time. These "shallow and stupid Congressmen and Senators", have changed very little over the years. They were re-elected in the 30's the same way they are re-elected today, and that is by voting endless largess from the public treasury. "Vote, vote, vote; spend, spend, spend; elect, elect, elect", goes the famous saying. Voters aren't too discerning about economics, and government money is manna from heaven, with no cost or consequence. "Lets get a government grant". "Get Federal funding". "That's the government's responsibility". "What's Washington going to do about it?" "We need help from the government", etc. In order to stay in two exclusive clubs, politicians gleefully pass appropriation after appropriation, bill after bill, and spend, spend, spend.

Except there **ARE** consequences!

The consequences are a gigantic federal debt which is trillions of dollars, an amount virtually impossible to comprehend. The consequences are high interest rates, low dollar value, huge buyouts of our country by Japan, and becoming the largest debtor nation in the world. The consequences are loss of jobs, loss of industry, loss of leadership and respect from the rest of the world. The consequences are loss of self esteem, and becoming a second rate, bankrupt nation. Those are the consequences, and they are multiplying at an alarming rate, promising eventual total devastation to us, our children, and our land. These consequences are the result of 535 men and women voting endless spending, decade after decade, to please their constituency with a goal of re-election term after term, ad infinitum. Are they stupid? Perhaps. Are they evil? Perhaps. Perhaps both, but that we are being bankrupted by 535 men and women is inarguable. All 245 million of us are suffering from lower life-styles and weakening dollars thanks to those avaricious, greedy, grasping congressmen and senators. Rather than thinking of their country, they think of themselves and show it by continually voting for what will make their re-election a certainty.

Politicians vote for their re-election and statesmen vote for their country, even if they lose an election, knowing they have acted responsibly. America is not benefited by endless spending. If our elected officials cared a whit about America, they would balance the budget instantly, stop the money presses, and be proud as America got back on its feet and again became a mighty nation... the envy of the world. Or has the statesman gone the way of the Dodo?

ARE GUNS THE PROBLEM?

The Stockton, California shooting of children in a school yard by a deranged misfit prompted a national outcry against so called "assault" weapons such as the AK-47, and others of its type. Outlawing these weapons supposedly will cripple psychopathic efforts to maim innocents. A case in Littleton, Colorado resulted in deaths, rape, and injuries by a 20 year old miscreant who used an automatic weapon he had stolen from a home at the beginning of his rampage. In October, 1991 at Killeen, Texas, a man drove his late model pickup through one of the plate glass windows of a Luby's cafeteria, calmly got out and began shooting, killing 22 and wounding 20. He used a legally obtained, registered, non- automatic weapon, was the son of a doctor, and had no evidence of mental illness. All three of these sprees ended when the offenders committed suicide.

The problem is not guns, but criminals. Not machinery, but humans. Outlawing certain types of guns, or all guns, won't eliminate or lessen crime. If the outlaws weren't on the streets they couldn't commit crime no matter how many guns were out there. The problem could be solved by simply replacing inept judges who release criminals, and eliminating parole boards who decide when criminals are "rehabilitated". There should be no parole of any kind, at any time, and the very existence of a "parole board", should be a crime. See the chapter on parole and insanity pleas.

The most troublesome problem is judges releasing criminals or suspending sentences after apprehension by diligent police work. Police work so hard, only to have their efforts totally debilitated by inept, fearful judges. The Stockton and Littleton animals should have already been behind bars with the key thrown away when they committed their dastardly deeds. Outlawing machinery used to commit crimes will not stop crime, or even slow it. Equipment used to commit crime runs from the hands and feet to various sharp objects, rocks, automobiles, telephones, and anything the human brain can concoct, numbers and variations of which are endless. The way to stop crime is to require the citizenry be armed, put away criminals, and eliminate parole.

Are the calamity howlers forgetting the Swiss who are required to own automatic weapons, and where crime is punished? A gun is a compact, ever ready defense needed by civilized people. That old adage really is true: "When guns are outlawed, only outlaws will have guns". Judges have a societal duty and obligation to protect the citizenry from criminals by keeping them put away, and the gun screechers are merely avoiding the real issue which is the judicial system, not guns of any size.

Outlawing certain types of guns is comparable to outlawing certain sizes of cigarettes or whiskey bottles! Might as well blame and outlaw film and videotape as a remedy for pornography. It would help as much. Since a huge number of deaths occur in showers or bathtubs, simply making bathing illegal would certainly save lives. While 50,000 lives are being lost on highways each year, no one is touting legislation making automobiles illegal. A gun is an inanimate object that can only operate when handled, aimed, and shot by a human. In our society, the "good guys" outnumber the "bad guys" probably 100 to 1, and the "bad guys" always obtain whatever they need to be such with little effort. I haven't heard of a criminal who had any trouble getting a gun! Gun control simply makes it extremely difficult for the law abiding citizenry to protect itself from the non law abiding sector.

The certain Midwest town that outlawed all guns comes to mind, and I won't dignify it by naming it, except to say it is the darling of all of the gun haters. Crime there has sky rocketed since criminals know they won't be shot at when they break into homes and businesses. In May, 1982, Kennesaw, Georgia did the opposite by requiring every household to own a firearm. Crime decreased by 16% the first year, something like 60% the second year, and now it is almost non existent! Nothing strikes fear in a criminal's heart more than a nervous householder or shopkeeper pointing a gun at him while he is committing a crime! Laws should REQUIRE owning a gun, not FORBID it.

If gun ownership had been required in Killeen, the chances of a few guns being carried in the crowded Luby's are extremely high. It is almost certain one of these guns would have been used to quickly end the rampage before 42 people were wounded and killed. In just that one instance, required ownership of guns by citizens would have saved lives. If gun ownership were required in America, crime would almost instantly become non existent. What criminal would want to chance a holdup or burglary if he knew everyone had a gun to protect themselves with, even if they were a poor shot. The poor shots would be just as much of a threat as a crack shot. Imagine a burglar suddenly being confronted by a nervous householder holding a loaded gun in a shaking hand. His first sentence might well be, "Now look lady, be careful with that thing, it might go off. Why don't you just call the police and I'll be still".

Government insists on seat belts and all sorts of other protections such as inane E.P.A. rules, but denies us the right to protect ourselves from crime. We should be required to own a gun.

What is the first thing a "would be" dictator does to his

subjects? Look at history and you will see it is to first register
and then collect all guns. Would the Soviet Union have gone
on for 70 years if the citizenry had been armed? Would the
Hungarians and Czechs have perhaps won when the Soviets
invaded them if they all had guns? Would the Chinese be
saddled with sub human vermin ruling over them if they were
armed? Hardly. An armed citizenry is the best possible defense against total government. Nothing is as feared by an
oppressive government and bureaucracy as is a totally armed
citizenry.

Legislators at all levels that continually scream for gun
controls usually are the ones that vote for higher taxes and
more government. These dregs want to remove responsibility
from the people and invest it in government, which they can
control. Power is a terrible thing, and gun control is just
another form of political power. I urge all readers to immediately
become life members of the National Rifle Association, and
obtain several guns. There may come a time when you will
need them. Hopefully not, but it could happen here as it has
happened in every other part of the inhabited world.

PANAMA

The smoke begins to clear in Panama. Noriega is out, and what may become of him is anyone's guess. It would be nice to get the stolen money back to use in the rebuilding process, but it really doesn't matter. Refresh your memory and remember what happened over a decade ago. The vast majority of Americans didn't want the canal given away in the first place. The Treaty was ramrodded through the Senate by Jimmy Carter, and Arizona's disgrace, Dennis DeConcini, over the howls and protests of citizens everywhere. It was never put to a vote at a regular election as it would have failed by an enormous majority. The very idea of giving away the Panama Canal, and even paying them to take it, which is what happened, is similar to paying someone to take away your profitable business you had worked so hard to build into a success. I haven't forgotten. A lot of us haven't forgotten. Even then it passed the Senate by only one vote. It would never pass again. This is one of those rare instances where we may be able to correct a great injustice and make it ever so much better while doing it.

First of all abrogate the treaty. It has been violated repeatedly by Panama, so that is a legal act. Second, make Panama the 51st State. Think about it. We would once again have our canal, and the Panamanians would have protection, security, and democracy once and for all time. Panamanian Statehood guarantees law and order, dignity, prosperity, and freedom to those beleaguered, long suffering victims of Noriega's excesses and brutality. Revenues from the repossessed canal would be welcome to the treasury, and investment by other Americans for resorts, manufacturing, and resource harvesting are guaranteed. Panama is like Hawaii, it never gets cold, and there is no winter. A wonderful place to vacation for millions of freezing Northerners. Obviously citrus and vegetables will grow in profuse quantities with no frost threat. It would make a wonderful 51st State.

Building the Panama Canal was one of the great engineering feats of all time, and cost not only hundreds of millions of sound dollars, (billions now), but extraordinary amounts of lives from yellow fever, malaria, accidents, and disease. The Panama Canal was America's great achievement. A slim connector between the two great oceans, saving thousands of miles for ships. We were the wonder of the world. The Canal's engineering was so sound that little has ever needed to be changed. Most of the world's ships can still fit through its gigantic locks. America created Panama, and nurtured it for 75 years. It was always a wonderful place until the dummies in the Senate and White House betrayed us.

We have watched it go downhill like an out of control railroad train ever since. It crashed, and we can now pick it up, rebuild it, and make it better than ever.... as a State.

FOREIGN AID

America is now the world's largest debtor nation. We owe more money to more people than any other country on earth. A large scale Donald Trump, with little real net worth at all. We owe, owe, owe, thanks to endless deficit spending, printing press money, welfare, and a totally irresponsible Congress and President who grandly sign all those bills each year, driving us further and further into actual bankruptcy, rather than the technical bankruptcy we now have. In just the ten year period from 1981 to 1991, the yearly deficit has gone from $78.9 billion in 1981 to $268.7 billion in 1991, and that's each year, not a collective total. That is also probably untrue, as it doesn't count so called "off budget" and "black budget" expenditures, which run into the tens of billions yearly. Our total indebtedness is in the trillions of dollars, a number impossible to comprehend, it is so high.

Even if we were rolling in money, which we aren't and never have been, why give it away? The $1 million plus per day to Israel alone, plus added millions to other nations is absurd. Congressmen say, "It's only $25 billion a year, and not worth worrying about." Well that's about $100 a year for every man, woman, and child in America, and certainly worth worrying about.

What is supposed to be accomplished by foreign aid? The avowed purpose is to help less fortunate nations, but in reality it is an attempt to buy friends. Ever know of anyone who succeeded in buying real friendship? Some foreign aid is to bribe recipients into allowing us to have bases on their lands. Bases we don't need and shouldn't have. Foreign aid was supposed to "fight communism", but it never worked. Communism failed of its own accord, not because of foreign aid. Foreign aid is a waste of money pure and simple. It buys no friends and accomplishes nothing. We can't afford it. Even if we could, a good example would do far more to influence the world. Our example isn't too exemplary either! Along with that debt, we have a pretty high crime rate, poverty, corruption, and all sorts of other unnecessary problems in America which we will analyze as we go along in this book, but as a clue, most can be traced to Washington, D.C.!

DOG CATCHERS

For many decades now, I have been amazed that this particular part of local government has continued unabated, even though it costs a small fortune, with no hope of ever bringing it into "break even", or demonstrable necessity. The dog catcher will lure loose dogs into his clutches and then hustle them off to a pound or humane society, where they live in fear, awaiting being claimed by loving owners who pay a fine for this "service" rendered by local government.

Locally, I asked the dog catcher if the fines came even close to paying his salary. "Not in a thousand years", was the reply. Now think what would happen to America if there were no dog catchers. If we need a dog catcher system, we must think about what would happen if there were none. Absolutely nothing. If a mad or vicious dog is at large, the police don't call the dog catcher, they shoot the dog. In Suburban Philadelphia, where I lived for many years, there was an entire community of raccoons that lived in the neighborhood. I mean hundreds of them. A few became rabid and vicious and were shot either by police or citizens. Generally they got into trash cans, lived in sewers and vacant garages, climbed trees, and were a delight to behold with their smirky faces and mischievous little hands always getting into everything. Squirrels did the same in the area. When I was a tot in Washington, D.C., my Dad got bitten by a squirrel and had to have tetanus shots. Wild and domestic animals on the loose are nothing new. Yet we have no raccoon catchers, cat catchers, squirrel catchers, or 'possum catchers. We survive and let them go on amusing us, or bothering us.

Not only are dog catchers a total waste of money, but they aren't by any stretch of the imagination a policeman that can be put to use in an emergency. Our local dog catcher is obviously a nice man, living well off a government mistake. That mistake is that unless we have a dog catcher, little kids will be bitten by rabid dogs, and the health and safety will be in dire jeopardy. How absurd. Each dog catcher, (now called "animal control officers"), costs about $50,000 a year, including vehicle cost, fuel, repairs, fringes, salary and other employee costs. That amount of money could blacktop many blocks of street, buy playground equipment, new fire hose, street lights or police cars. Why not eliminate this waste? Everywhere.

THE HOMELESS

In America, there are probably 50,000 homeless. This is after the various estimates from biased and disinterested sources are averaged. They live in subway and bus stations, in cardboard boxes, old cars, and in larger cities over steam vents even. They are smelly, unsightly, disgusting, and often violent beggars that are a scourge on the cities. Many are mentally ill, alcoholics, criminal, or just plain lazy. It's virtually impossible to keep from stumbling over them if you are in a downtown section. What to do? I say arrest them for the Supreme Court rejected law against vagrancy. Congress can overcome the court's rulings.

They invariably have enough money for cigarettes and cheap hootch. Money used for cigarettes and booze could easily buy food or a bath. What right do these bums have to litter the streets and sidewalks, panhandling everyone they see, and in general lousing up the place? The law prohibits dogs from taking a dump on the sidewalks, but human excrement is O.K.? In every city there are many jobs advertised every day in the papers that these loafers could fill. I have a daughter who, with 2 other girls, rents a small house for $450 a month. She makes $3.50 per hour and never gets a full 40 hours. Yet she runs her car, which she bought with her own money, pays her share of the rent, bathes, washes her clothes, and will start college next term. Her parents do not give her a dime, and she is too proud to ask. She wanted to make it "on her own", and is doing it. A source of pride for her, and for us too. The sidewalk bums are no different, so why should I feel sorry for them?

All of us wish we had more of some things. I'd like to have more money, less weight, a lower voice, and be able to play music. Millions lack a tolerable marriage, abhor their jobs, are sick, blind, deaf or old. But they don't live on the sidewalk. Priorities are what counts. The homeless have no priority for a home or job, so they do without. It's really that simple. Anyone can have what they want, to some degree, if they work for it, including having a home. The homeless have no DESIRE for a job, home, cleanliness, warmth, sobriety, or comfort, or they would have them. That's their problem. Don't ask me to feel sorry for them or use my tax dollars to house or feed them!

They are currently the center of media attention, gladly acting out roles the TV cameras and the late Mitch Snyder want them to play. They moan and groan over being homeless, and say they hate society. "You mean I can't live in a cardboard box, beg for food and money, and relieve myself on the sidewalks"? Oh! The outrage! They don't want "low income housing", they want "no income housing", on public sidewalks, living in a disgusting, alcoholic daze. The residents of no income housing have booze, cigarettes and their buddies, and are happy playing their role. As a taxpayer, I demand that this stop.

75 years ago, Charlie Chaplin made himself very rich portraying a lovable bum on the screens of America's fledgling movie theatres. Today's bums aren't lovable, amusing, or entertaining. They are revolting.

THE TWO MOST MISPRONOUNCED
WORDS IN AMERICA

Here in Colorado, we have our own two; Saguache, and Ouray, which have been butchered for years. Ouray (U-RAY) even had a tee shirt with various mispronunciations on it, each one crossed out, with the final correct one at the end. Funny! Saguache (SAWATCH) hasn't produced tee shirts as far as I know.

But in America, two words are almost universally ruined by newscasters, professors, academicians, and housewives. They are PORSCHE and APARTHEID. No other words are more abused than these two. The first, PORSCHE, requires only a knowledge of the German language. German has no silent letters, an ironclad rule. So Porsche is not "PORSH" as far too many call it, but rather POR-SHA, or exactly as the proper name "Portia". Johnny Carson et al please note.

The other is APARTHEID and is not correctly pronounced at all like it appears. It is correctly pronounced "APARTHATE", which makes it easy to remember by thinking to yourself, "keep us apart as we hate them". Apart hate. Tom Brokaw and most of the N.B.C. news staff do well on this one, but C.B.S., A.B.C., CNN etc, all seem to not understand. I remember a CBS interview with Bishop Desmond Tu Tu, who pronounced apartheid correctly. Rather than taking a tip from the person interviewed, the reporter always said "APARTIED". I wanted to pull my hair. Day after day, show after show, these two words are mispronounced by far too many. Now once again, it is "PORTIA" and APART-HATE". Newscasters lead us correctly.

ROBIN HOOD

While Robin Hood and his nights of Sherwood Forest are held in the highest esteem by today's academia and other assorted bubbleheads, I think they certainly are not the apotheosis of civilization. They were common crooks, who robbed from the rich and gave to the poor. Admittedly King Richard was away, and he supposedly left the store in the wrong hands, but that is the trouble with kings. They are human like everyone else, and are not of a higher I.Q., better judgment, or more humanity. They have inherited their position, and for some strange reason are held in high esteem by their mistaken subjects. If a king goes bad, that is tragic, and his people will suffer. But we don't have a monarchy here, so Robin Hood should be no hero in America, in spite of the glorious adulation he gets.

The beauty of America is that we don't have a king, so they can't go bad. That's why we broke away from Mother England, the King had gone nuts and thought the Colonies were supposed to show a huge profit for the royal exchequer. He couldn't even speak English! We disagreed, went to war over it, and won. So forget Robin Hood's reasons, they don't apply here.

What passes for "Robin Hoodism" today, is just as evil, and has no king on which to blame it. Socialism is a nasty word to most, while Robin Hood is wonderful. Both are the same. Rob from the rich to give to the poor. Robin Hood had a king to blame, and we have government. Socialism is leveling every one's incomes. Socialism is taking from the haves, and giving to the have nots. Socialism is government stealing from you, and giving you a pittance back in the form of some food, medicine, or other trinkets. Socialism is taking everyone to the poverty level. Socialism is taking away choice, freedom, happiness, productivity, wealth, health, and prosperity. Robin Hood is no example to follow .

America was made great by having all the things socialism takes away, as explained in the previous paragraph. America is a socialistic country and becomes more so each year, month, and even day. Socialism employs threats from Government to accomplish its will. Socialism hates achievement. Socialism loves failure, because they are so compliant, and willing to follow the current government dictates. Socialism is government of the failures, by the failures, and for the failures.

The achievers that socialists hate so much, achieve not because it is their duty, but a mere outlet for their brain power and creativity. They simply love to do it. The prosperity they provide is a by product of their aptitude, energy, drive, and intelligence. Socialists hate achievers so much that they tax them into submission. Taxation is the most common device socialists use to show their resentment. Regulation is the second. Only achievement can be taxed. Only achievement can be regulated. Nothing else. When something is taxed, you get less of it, namely achievement and prosperity. When something is subsidized, you get more of it, such as poverty and government. We have devolved from a competitive, prosperous, achievement oriented society, into a resentful, guilt ridden, poor, uneducated society.

Socialism's stated goal of raising social classes has the opposite effect. Trying to raise social classes is like trying to raise the water level in a cracked swimming pool. The minute you turn the hose off, the water will begin to go down to its former level. Socialism plunders private property, and the right to property was the cornerstone of America from its humble beginnings.

Socialism places power in the hands of the inept, undeserving, and non achieving. Socialism creates poverty and spends billions trying to eliminate it. The more spent, the more poverty is created. Socialism makes "social work" a career, and issues degrees in that subject. That subject shouldn't exist in the English lexicon.

I hope this has been succinct enough for you. I never liked Robin Hood!

SHORTAGES AND STARVATION

Turn the clock back over 200 years, and think of George Washington and his ragged band of brave freedom fighters freezing and starving at Valley Forge. It was a tough, humid, cold Pennsylvania winter. Soldiers tied rags around their bleeding, frost bitten feet because their shoes were worn out. Everyone was hungry. Visit Valley Forge if you are ever near Philadelphia, and do it in wintertime. Just imagine the terrible hardship these brave souls were suffering for freedom's sake.

Fifteen short miles away, in Philadelphia, the citizens may have been worried about the Redcoats, but they were warm, well fed, and well clothed. Business as usual in Philly, while Washington's troops were freezing and starving. Why? The answer is so simple. The fledgling U.S. Government had decided what they would pay for uniforms, food, and supplies. The prices the government would pay were far under the market price, and even below the cost of production. So no one would sell to the government, Washington was in deep trouble, and we almost lost the war. The British were in fine shape. Between stealing, and their well stocked larders on ships constantly arriving from England, the British weren't hungry or cold, even though they were thousands of miles from home. Washington, on his own turf, was freezing and starving. Good old government!

Most don't realize that the federal government, even 200 years ago, was just about as idiotic as it is today. But this chapter is about shortages, as well as starvation. Washington and his troops, as well as America in the 200 plus years since, lucked out. In spite of the stupidity in Philadelphia, they eventually made it and through Washington's sheer brilliance near Trenton, we became a United States. 85 years later, another moronic federal government action caused the most disastrous war in our history, when the so called "Civil War" was started, which eventually cost over 600,000 Americans their lives.

Shortages are never caused by scarcity of an item unless government attempts to control prices. Is there a shortage of Model A Fords? Nope. Is there a shortage of diamonds, houses, food stuffs, or for that matter, a shortage of anything, if there is no control of prices? Nope. Think about it. If government stepped in and decided in all its wisdom, that Model A Fords should cost no more than $1500, because these antique auto dealers were making huge profits, then immediately there would be a shortage of Model A Fords. No one would sell, so there would be a shortage.

During the 1973 oil crisis, when OPEC was formed, and crude oil prices went from $3 a barrel to $40 a barrel, there were no shortages of gasoline. Prices were high, but no shortages. Government decided that this was hideous, and decided to control prices. Presto! There were long lines at gas stations, stations went out of business by the tens of thousands, lines were everywhere trying to get a few gallons, and America literally shuddered to a halt. No one would sell their gas at less than its cost, so there was an artificial shortage. When controls were removed, prices went up to the point at which everyone could make a profit, and there were no more shortages.

Is there a shortage of water in the desert? Of course not, unless government controls the price of water. Is there a shortage of Picasso paintings? No, unless the price is controlled. No matter what the commodity, there is only a shortage if unhindered trade between willing buyers and willing sellers is thwarted by government, which is the only power capable of making dim-witted laws that violate every common sense principle of economics.

George Washington and his brave soldiers almost lost it because of an ill-advised government policy 15 miles away in Philadelphia. Because of price controls, we almost didn't become the United States of America. Because of price controls in 1973, America almost lost it again, becoming paralyzed without fuel for our cars, trucks, buildings, planes, and locomotives. Next time you hear ignorant politicians speak of "wage and price controls", or "controls" on anything, remember George Washington at Valley Forge.

WHY DON'T TRUCKS HAVE GOOD BRAKES?

Trucks have been around for close to a century, and they have never had adequate brakes. Every year, hundreds run out of control down steep mountain roads, killing and destroying everything in their path. Their smoking, inadequate brakes are always the culprit. Police will blame poor driving skills for the accidents, and a failure to "gear down" on hills. Fine, but all this "gearing down" wouldn't be necessary if the trucks had adequate brakes in the first place!

Railroad trains don't "gear down", but use their brakes all the way to the bottom. Passenger cars likewise, and they never run out of control, careening down hills, and running over everything in their path. Ever see an automobile with smoking brakes? I never have. Automobile brakes are designed to stop the car no matter what skills the driver may possess. Railroad brakes can slow or stop 10,000 ton trains on hills with no burn out, but not trucks, which 100% of the time have terrible brakes, and require drivers to use their engines for slowing on hills. Manufacturers of trucks equip their vehicles with a braking system that is virtually useless, except in stop and go traffic, or at ridiculously slow speeds. With all the protecting government is supposed to be doing for us, why isn't it protecting us from runaway trucks?

Trucks have but a fraction of the braking they should have. I drive in the Colorado Rockies continually, and believe me, those runaway truck ramps are there for a purpose. Trucks with burned out, smoking brakes are a continual sight in any mountainous region, and I think it's time for this to be at an end. How about some legislation requiring trucks to have adequate brakes? Where is Ralph Nader when we need him?

REPORTERS

I am continually amazed at the lack of manners and common courtesy shown by reporters. They will shout silly questions at the President as he walks across the lawn, or attempts to board his plane. Little tape recorders are thrust in the face of a newsmaker. Anyone of any importance will have their way blocked by rude reporters who surround and rasp their inane little questions. Excellent reporters will be digging up obscure material and investigating, while the rest of them are hounding anyone "important", making asses of themselves, and annoying everyone. Public figures rightfully dread reporters.

At any news conference, the least talented are asking the most absurd questions, just to be seen and heard. Questions that have already been asked, questions that have no answer, or questions that simply cannot be answered. And then there are the more well known reporters that love to not only be rude, but to embarrass and humiliate their victim. I would love to see a newsmaker stop dead in his or her tracks, look around and say, "Get out of the way and shut up. I will never answer any shouted questions. Your uncivilized conduct embarrasses me."

Why can't they think of something new rather than rephrasing what has already been asked. Pity anyone obtaining sufficient status to be the object of a reporter's venom and outrageous conduct. Don't reporters have a trade association? If so, why not immediately adopt a "Code of Professional Conduct", and remove credentials from any cretin violating them.

Accuracy is paramount. Inaccurate and exaggerated reporting causes untold agony and harm each year. Viet Nam reporters spent too much time shooting and even staging the most disgusting, and violent footage. Reporters look for scandal that is of no importance. Richard Nixon was hounded out of office by reporters over a matter so insignificant as to be laughable. One of those reporters became rich and famous from a book rich in innuendo, but short on facts. A similar book by him about a deceased official, mercifully was a failure. Reporters, contrary to their attitude, are not the linchpin on which truth and civilization depend. Expert reporters do not shout, never exaggerate, and polemics are not in their lexicon. The profession of reporting has too many lackluster, non achieving, annoying drones getting in the way, befuddling issues, shouting stupid questions, and who need to be summarily fired by their employers who should know better.

THEY WENT BROKE FIRST

Anything written about Europe promises to be outdated pretty quickly, but one thing seems inarguable, and that is that THE SOVIETS SIMPLY WENT BROKE BEFORE WE DID, and as a result of this, millions of Hungarians, Czechs, Poles, and East Germans, have freed themselves from their decades old yoke of slavery. TV cameras recorded hundreds of thousands of rejoicing people, rattling keys, and burning torches, reveling in their newly found freedoms.

After WW II, the Soviets and the West tempted bankruptcy with a frightening tactic called the "arms race", which cost hundreds of billions of dollars, pounds and rubles. The theory of having the most destructive and "first strike" capability, keeping the other side from attempting aggression, seems to have worked. At least we are still here! Nuclear war was actually unthinkable by both sides, because of the total destruction if it ever began.

Ronald Reagan and a compliant Congress doubled the national debt, mostly by huge expenditures for soldiers, rockets, missiles, equipment, and of course the absurd "Star Wars" idea. 400,000 troops in Europe, 40,000 in Korea, plus a few thousand here and there, billions to our allies, hundreds of millions to Central America, Cambodia, and other places, was part of our game plan. The Soviets were blowing their wad on arms, Afganistan, and endless infusions into their puppet states to keep them in line. Both the West and the Soviets were headed pell-mell towards total bankruptcy with this insanity. We outlasted them.

Gorby, unlike previous Soviet heads of State, was an intellect and a pragmatist. He looked at the books and knew the end was at hand. To avoid total bankruptcy and revolution, there was no choice but to withdraw from Afganistan, and stop spending so much on policing and subsidizing the satellites. Jamming the airwaves stopped, Perestroika and Glastnost were "in", and the old Stalinist hard line "out". With that teeny bit of loosening up, the rest wasn't hard to predict. Revolt in the satellites, which came almost immediately.

That revolt bloated like yeasty dough on a warm day. The incentive of being free to choose, brought millions to the squares of Eastern Europe, resulting in the peaceful demise of the communist system. Europe's future looks bright. What will be debated for decades is the question of how it all fell apart. Was it Reagan's build up? Was it a revolt that was long overdue? Was it inevitable? I say it is because they went broke before we did. If we had gone bankrupt first, the world would be entering a dark age that may have required hundreds of years from which to rise. They went broke first because slavery doesn't produce taxable wealth. Our system, as diluted as it is from its original concept, still recognizes freedom and profit. This profit can be taxed by government to spend as it sees fit, in this case on the colossal arms race. Our system made certain that the Soviets would go broke first. This perhaps saved the world.

THE RISEN SUN

The Japanese are buying America. A large part of Rockefeller Plaza, other New York landmark buildings, Los Angeles' Biltmore Hotel, Columbia Pictures, Las Vegas casinos, huge amounts of California, Hawaii, New York City, and unknown to most, millions of acres of American farmlands. Hundreds of billions of dollars worth of purchases. Everyone hates it, and while the British may own more American corporate stock, the Japanese are buying our land and buildings as well as businesses.

It's our own fault. I have called many an embassy in Washington, trying to find out if a non citizen may own property in their country. The answer always seems to be "NO". Why do we allow non citizens to own real property in America? I wish each state would pass laws prohibiting this.

Each year, Americans buy millions of Japanese TV sets, VCRs, camcorders, watches, cars, and other products from the land of the Rising Sun. Profits from American purchases of Japanese products have allowed them to purchase us. Without profits from America, they couldn't buy a garage in North Philly. Why do we buy Japanese, even though every purchase drives another nail in our coffin? The usual excuse is that they build quality. A half truth at best. I would be ashamed to be seen in a Jap car!

A third of the enormous American national debt is usually picked up by the Japanese. They not only buy our businesses, buildings, and land, but we owe them hundreds of billions, thanks to 535 Congressmen and Senators, plus one President, who refuse to rein in their vote buying, spending spree. American products are not welcome in Japan.

We licked the pants off of them in World War 2, which they started, but unfortunately you have to be pushing 60 to remember their atrocities of 50 years ago. I haven't forgotten. They haven't either. Go to Hawaii and visit the Arizona Memorial. The Arizona was one of the U.S. battleships sunk on Dec 7, 1941 by the Japs, and has within it 1177 American bodies. Daily the Japanese tour this memorial, and are seen laughing and snickering about it. They think it is funny, but I don't. I despise them for that action alone. In another sunken battleship, trapped men could be heard tapping from inside the ship's hull, but no rescue was possible. The tapping continued till Christmas.

During World War II, the Japanese were noted for their "Kamikaze" pilots who gave their lives for their emperor and flew their planes straight into their targets, killing themselves naturally, but anything for the good old emperor! Kamikazes were flown right into hospital ships emblazoned with red crosses, killing American wounded being transported to hospitals. The Japanese bombed Pearl Harbor without a declaration of war, which even Noriega remembered to do! The Japanese violated so many international laws and rules of warfare that it was sick. You mean you don't know who built the Japanese Zeros and Kamikazes? It was the American favorite Mitsubishi Corporation, that's who. Now go out and buy a Mitsubishi TV set, why don't you?

When FDR gave his famous "Day that will live in infamy", speech Dec 8, 1941, most overlook another part of that speech when Roosevelt said, "Always will we remember the character of our attacker...". We haven't remembered. A squib in the Rocky Mountain News on June, 1991 says, "Japanese officials are choosing to ignore a confidential CIA funded report depicting Japan as a racist society bent on world economic domination and say it will not strain relations with the United States. Tokyo does not take the draft report, which describes Japan as an "amoral, manipulative culture", as representative of American views, according to analysts. But Japanese officials are worried about extremist opinions in both countries". Over 1 million Americans were killed and wounded in that war.

An extraordinary "FRONTLINE" report on P.B.S. aired on November 19, 1991 gives an even more succinct image of the Japanese character Roosevelt hoped we wouldn't forget. In that report, besides showing three cases of Japanese deliberately attempting to bankrupt American enterprises, the statement was made that "THE LARGEST WEALTH TRANSFER IN THE HISTORY OF THE WORLD IS TAKING PLACE BETWEEN THE UNITED STATES AND JAPAN". It was shown that so called "American Hondas" made in Ohio, have but 1% of their contents made in America. The rest is made in Japan and merely assembled here. 99% of the parts come from Japan, and all the profits go back to Japan. American labor is used merely as a sales tool so that "American Hondas" will sell to foolish, gullible Americans.

The P.B.S. show pointed out that America's largest corporations such as IBM buy huge quantities of Japanese parts for their products, and are forced to say that a copier was "assembled in America", rather than "made in America". A metal stamping company in Ohio that had been in business since 1922, and doing flawless work, was systematically sabotaged by the Japanese, and is now out of business. For the 100,000 Americans hired to "assemble" Japanese cars, many times that amount are out of work because the parts are made in Japan.

After World War II, the Japanese bought a German Leica camera, took it home, copied it to the finest detail, and that was the beginning of the successful Japanese camera industry. Successful, not because of any ability to invent, but to copy, ignore others patents, and exploit cheap labor .

Do you know how many whales the Japs kill each year in violation of international law and agreements? Do you know how much American timber the Japs have removed from our shores over the years, and have buried under water, or in deep, decay proof, underground enclosures for future use? A botanist friend of mine says the entire Sitka Spruce contents of the Tongas National Forest in Alaska has been sold to the Japanese by the Dept. of Interior. Sitka Spruce has been one of the most valuable woods throughout history due to its strong, straight characteristics . It has been used for centuries in masts for sailing vessels. How did the Japs manage that one? Probably through extensive lobbying, and closed door meetings, but American citizens don't know about it, I'll bet! One of the most common occupations for certain ex-government employees, is to become a well paid part of the huge Japanese lobby that daily attempts, and succeeds in swaying American legislators to vote pro Japanese legislation.

Mitsubishi is now entering the American credit card business through a California bank, so Americans can be further drained of assets at the rate of probably 19.8% interest, which will go straight to Tokyo. There are now Mitsubishi elevators, Japanese heavy and farm equipment, outboard motors, generators, and Japanese everything. It makes me want to retch.

Americans are the most innovative people on earth . Everything the Japanese are making a killing on by selling to us, was invented HERE! We are a most outgoing, generous, wonderful people and are being sold into subservience by our own stupidity and leadership! Has this ever happened before in history? Won't YOU stop buying Japanese? American youth thinks this is ridiculous, but it isn't.

Are you familiar with the Japanese plywood industry operating off our shores on huge ships? It buys American timber, converts it to plywood, and then sells it back to us without having to pay U.S. taxes or labor to manufacture it. A group of American rice growers went to Japan and set up an exhibit at a Japanese trade show. They were arrested !

Americans are gradually developing a resistance to Japanese products, regardless of price or quality. It will eventually become a mark of poor taste, and even socially unacceptable to buy or own Japanese. It is coming and they have brought it on themselves. Their insistence on buying us and rubbing our noses in it is arousing the anger of Americans. People will stop buying Columbia Records, Makita tools, Japanese cars, and TV sets. Soon I hope.

In April of 1989, we were eating in a famous restaurant on Fisherman's Wharf, San Francisco. I got to talking with the waiter. He had recently been laid off after 16 years on the job, along with the entire staff of a famous Las Vegas casino. The Japanese had bought 5 major casinos and laid off everyone, installing their own employees. Makes you want to go out and buy a Honda, doesn't it?

Why do Americans buy anything made in Japan, when they are out to economically destroy us, and are succeeding? Why buy American made Japanese products either? Each Jap product we buy sends profits back to Japan, and in turn, these profits are used to buy another thousand acre farm, or a tire company perhaps. Among tire companies owned by the Japanese are Firestone and Bridgestone. Without America as their best customer for the past 35 years, the Japanese would own nothing in America . How can an American, in good conscience, knowingly buy anything that will benefit our economic enemy, Japan? Politicians tell us Japan is our "friend", and we benefit from Japanese products and industry that have invaded our shores. I say that is a crock of you know what.

We have much in common with the British and Europeans. Our languages, architecture, music, heritage, and physical characteristics are remarkably similar. With the Japanese, Americans have absolutely nothing in common. They worship their ancestors, and are not even remotely similar in any physical, religious, historical, or cultural characteristic to Americans. Women in Japan are treated abysmally, and women's liberation in Japan is about where it was in America 100 years ago.

Akio Morita, chairman of Sony, recently tried to wriggle out of a blatantly Anti-American book he co-authored; but it didn't play convincingly. Americans are getting a little tired of watching the Japs buy us, and then writing books telling us how damned stupid we are! I just hope the crumbling of Japanese popularity happens as quickly and surely as communism and the Soviets have self destructed in Eastern Europe. Both deserve to wither and die.

WHAT'S WRONG WITH BEING RICH?

It is very chic now to hate wealthy people, and condemn the old, long dead, super rich, such as the Vanderbilts and Carnegies. It is supposed to be some sort of sin for those people to have had such gigantic mansions, servants, boats, and private railroad cars. I happen to think it was a wonderful time in American history, and one to be cherished, not scorned. Those rich men weren't stingy by any means. They did wonderful things with their money.

Andrew Carnegie built hundreds of libraries, giving them freely to large cities and small towns alike. Few American cities or towns fail to have a Carnegie library. Phoenix, Arizona has one, as does tiny Silverton, Colorado, population 500. Carnegie loved the sound of the pipe organ, and he gave away 6,000 of them to various churches, auditoriums, and halls.

Remember, those rich people got that way by discovering or inventing something, being there first with a good idea, or in some way being an excellent entrepreneur. There were no equalizing taxes then, and when those super rich men built their mansions and railroads, they furnished employment. It took skilled craftsmen to build those edifices, and millions of jobs were provided by the super rich, which unfortunately do not exist any longer, thanks to government's successful leveling of everyone. There are a few left who are living off the old man's legacy, but the wealth has been successfully destroyed by government.

While there are those that complain of the so called "sweat

shops", and child labor in early America, we were still far above any other place in the world. While America was working employees 12 hours a day, in other parts of the world, workers worked 14 or 16 hours, and for lower wages. The industrial revolution and unions took care of that as a natural way for men to invent, invest, and group together for a common cause. No where in the world have more homes been built and owned than in America, even a hundred years ago. It was thanks to those pioneers who got filthy rich, but at the same time raised our entire standard of living.

If the old Commodore had hundreds of servants, those servants had good jobs. If the Astors had a huge mansion, it took lots of people to build it and maintain it for them. The problem is that we resent other people having more than we do, whereas it is far healthier to admire them, and even wish we had more, but certainly not to hate someone else for having more than you. Hatred of those with more, or condemnation of those more successful, is far too common today. Work and improve yourself, don't waste your energy hating others.

I look at those fantastic mansions, and see photos of those grand life-styles and am amazed, not full of animosity. I wish we still had those times with us. I'd rather work for a benevolent Andrew Carnegie, than for a greedy, insatiable government, which taxes me into poverty. Those rich tycoons didn't lower our living standards, but raised them with jobs and prosperity. Government has robbed everyone, virtually destroyed entrepreneurship, and continually lowers our living standard.

CORPORATIONS

As far as I have been able to see, corporations are formed for one of two reasons or both. (1) To raise money, and (2) to avoid liability. The first I am in sympathy with, but the second is pure evil. Here's a corporation that commits fraud, a criminal act, sells poisoned food, operates a dangerous carnival ride, runs up huge debts, or does any of thousands of things that result in liability when the accidents, or failure occurs. The common thing is for the corporation to transfer its assets, and the stockholders to evade responsibility by dissolving, transferring shares, or in some way making the corporation worthless and judgment proof. The perpetrators of the crime get off, and the victim has no recourse. This is shameful and must be stopped.

Why not pass a law, stating that all shareholders are to be held liable for any action, judgment, accident, or debt charged to that corporation. Even if that corporation is dissolved, or its assets transferred, the shareholders will be liable. That is simple enough and would end a lot of shady dealings and fraudulent escaping of debts and responsibilities. Why shouldn't all shareholders be responsible? They own the corporation don't they? It was their corporation that committed the act wasn't it? Why should they be allowed to get off scot free by legal shenanigans? Non corporate businesses and individuals are responsible, why not corporate shareholders? No matter how large or small, the shareholders of a corporation should be fully responsible for their corporation's conduct. It may be radical, but certainly fair!

This sham has been going on for a hundred years, which is about the length of time there has been such a thing as a corporation. Someone starts something, incorporates, runs up bills, and fails. The creditors are left being owed by a corporation that is worthless. Raise money by incorporating? Fine! Avoid liability? Hell no! Why hasn't someone thought of this a long time ago?

INTEREST

Interest is a rental charge for the use of money. Interest is what is paid by home buyers to those who loan the money to buy the home, and the finance charge when a car or washing machine is bought on a time payment plan. Interest is not evil, but a competitive price. High rates for high risks, and low rates for low risks. The "prime rate", is generally the lowest interest charged by lenders to borrowers that are the least risk. "Loan sharking", is an extremely high interest charged borrowers because they are an extremely high risk. The lender takes a big chance lending his money, because he may never see it again. Lending, borrowing, and interest charging is not a violation of the free market principal, nor is it evil. So much for basics.

The prime rate during the Carter Presidency was over 20% due to market factors, and the economy being on the path to collapse. No homeowner, car buyer, or businessman can afford to pay that and remain solvent. As this is written, the prime rate is below 10%, but still too high for real prosperity. Let's assume everyone borrowing money is paying 10% in interest. At 10% a homeowner with a $100,000 mortgage is paying $10,000 per year to the lender. With a $10,000 car finance, and maybe another $10,000 in other debts, Mr. and Mrs. America today are paying $12,000 per year, or over $230 per week for the use of someone else's money. This is $12,000 per year that could go towards buying $12,000 worth of consumer goods. If interest were at 5% instead of 10%, they could buy $6,000 more of consumer goods each year, and if that figure is multiplied by 100 million families, that is $600

BILLION more worth of consumer goods such as cars, TV sets, dishwashers, houses, lawn mowers, vacations, and clothes each year.

If $600 BILLION more were available for consumer spending every year, America would once again be the envy of the world, rather than a laughing stock. How could interest be reduced from an average of 10% to 5%? If the Congress and Senate would reduce government spending by half, and the surplus applied to a reduction of the national debt, government would have to borrow no money, and be paying off the principle, meaning that money to lend would be plentiful, rather than commanding high rates, reducing the prime rate by at least half, maybe more. No more government debt would be available for investors to buy.

Government is the largest borrower, and supposedly the borrower with the least risk, so all interest is directly pegged to the rate government pays. When Ford has to pay high rates, it is passed on to the purchasers of Fords in the form of increased prices. This means Fords cost more to make, and cost more to buy, making the total price perhaps double. As a result, fewer Fords are sold. This same phenomenon goes on throughout the entire country, meaning fewer jobs, fewer purchases, and a lower standard of living for everyone.

Congress and the President refuse to cut spending, and the government is such a risk that no one will lend money to it at low rates. These high rates are passed along to the consumer and manufacturer. The economy is stagnant, and recession threatens constantly because of high interest. When my parents bought their first home in 1935, they paid 3% interest. Home buyers were paying under 5% interest into the mid 1960's. Interest rates reflect the financial risk of the biggest borrower, the U.S. Government. If the budget were balanced, government would have to borrow no money, and we would be prosperous again.

The highest interest charges in America today are the credit card companies, who usually charge close to 20% interest on unpaid balances. If everyone paid their credit cards off, the issuing banks would quickly be in a bidding war to see who could attract the most business with the lowest interest. Credit card companies are actually "loan sharking" to millions of Americans. The way to stop it would be for everyone with credit card debt to take lower interest loans on their homes, and pay off those credit cards. Home interest is deductible from your taxes, whereas credit card interest isn't, so it makes sense. Credit card rates do not reflect federal spending, but private spending. Maybe Americans got into this bind because they copied Uncle Sam rather than a good example of how to manage money.

A balanced budget probably won't happen, most can't afford to pay off their credit cards, interest rates will undoubtedly remain high, and prosperity will continue to be elusive. Sad? You bet!

JUST A FEW CENTS EACH

A long, long time ago, a mythical community was totally free. It had virtually no taxes, a tiny government, and everyone prospered and was happy.

Eventually it was observed there were some people in the community that had less than others. They were poor. A vote was taken to increase taxes to build housing for these poor people. It would only add a few cents to each tax bill. There were vigorous objections by some in the community, who warned that it was not the job of government to care for anyone, only to protect them. The public housing issue barely passed. It was then discovered that these poor were hungry. Food stamps were passed out, so they wouldn't starve. It only cost a few cents tax increase for each person. The same people as before strenuously objected, saying that things were getting out of hand, poor people had always existed, and the best remedy for hunger and homelessness was work, pointing out the low paying jobs that were continuously advertised in the local paper. The objectors lost again, and taxes were raised a few more cents. Then it was discovered the poor had no money to pay for doctor bills, so the voters again raised taxes a few cents for each citizen, to pay for the poor people's doctor bills. The objectors howled that it was becoming very profitable to be poor! They were drowned out in the clamor that said, "surely we can afford to care for those less fortunate than others, it will only cost a few cents each".

The once tiny government had grown very large, and was building new buildings to administer all these benefits, and collect all the taxes. Lots of government employees were now on what had become known as "the public payroll".

Then it was discovered that some of the elderly were poor, because they hadn't saved for their old age, and were profligate. Another vote was taken to increase taxes a whopping 15% to pay for old age care. The same protesters objected again and again, but to no avail. The 15% increase passed. Crime, by this time, had risen appreciably, and the protesters said this was because it wasn't necessary to care for yourself any more, or to work. "Government" did it for you. More prisons and courtrooms had to be built, and more police and prison guards hired.

Then the farmers decided they wanted a piece of the action, and complained that they weren't making any money. Interest rates were too high, taxes too high, and they needed help. By this time, no vote was needed, as government had grown so big, it did just as it wanted, and raised taxes as it pleased. More taxes for the better off, harder working populace, and little or none for the untalented or lazy. The farmers got their subsidies, and food prices went up. With all the lopsided subsidies to farmers, there was too much of one kind of food, and too little of another. Government bought what there was too much of, and set minimum prices on what there was too little of, building huge storehouses, and hiring more employees to store the extra foods, and decide what foods needed to be subsidized. Government employees were by then known as "bureaucrats", and their number grew greatly.

Then government decided regulations were needed over what could be broadcast over the newly invented radio and television, and who was to be allowed to do the broadcasting. Government also decided that the poor were being treated unfairly, so it decided to make laws setting minimum wages and fair treatment. Crime increased and unemployment increased, especially among the poor who were supposed to be helped.

So the government had to increase their subsidies, food stamps, and housing allowances. Taxes of course went up. Government had become so large by this time, that people who wanted something....anything....went to the government, and usually got it. Taxes went up again. Government decided that it should regulate what types of signs businessmen could erect, what their buildings should contain, what they could sell, how much they should charge, and how much profit was "fair". Government then decided to tell the farmers what to grow, how much they could sell it for, how many acres they could till, and what types of fertilizer and insecticide they could use. Government then decided that it should tell land-owners what they could do with their land, and hired many planners to oversee this monumental project. All of this, of course, was deemed to be "for the public good".

Government then decided some factories were not safe, and it began telling manufacturers what the sizes and shapes of their tools, products, and factories could be. Even the stairs and bathrooms in their factories came under regulation. Inspectors came regularly, and didn't even have to knock to gain entrance to inspect the businesses. Of course bribes and payoffs were common to avoid the harsh hand of the bureaucracy. Government decided that more highways were needed, so taxes were raised again to build multi-laned "freeways", as they came to be called. The road builders took whatever land they wanted, and cut through neighborhoods and parks with their superhighways. Mass transit operators, who had rail systems and bus lines, threw up their hands and went bankrupt right and left over the unfair competition. Government took their properties, raised taxes again, and ran the systems at huge losses. The air became polluted because of the freeways, but government decided the cause wasn't the millions of cars, but the crooked businessmen who furnished the electricity. They were forced to install "anti-pollution" devices on their generating plants, but the air didn't get any better. The price of electricity went up to pay for government ordered pollution devices on power plants. It was decided to build more freeways, so motorists wouldn't have to sit in traffic with idling motors. But the more freeways that were built, the more cars were bought, and the air kept getting worse and worse.

By this time, not only was the air unbreathable, but crime was enormous, medical costs were out of range of most, interest rates were quadruple what they had been 50 years before, and life in general was miserable. The politicians had discovered that the less intelligent the voter, the better chance they had of keeping their plush jobs in government. They regularly went about getting everyone they could to register to vote, even those who couldn't read, telling them that it was their "patriotic" duty to vote. Nothing was more important than for everyone to vote! "It doesn't matter who you vote for, but vote!", was the slogan. So politicians kept their offices and high salaries, voting for more government, and more promises for these newly registered voters. As the number of voters increased, usually from poor or semi literate population sectors, the quality of politician went down until it was a commonly understood fact that the politician handing out the most from the government treasury was sure to be elected. Taxes kept going up, of course.

Occasionally, the citizen voters became upset at the taxes, so the politicians quickly voted various "tax cuts" into law, which were really tax raises, but the language was cleverly worded so people thought they were being handed yet another freebie from government. By now, government was regarded by most as a source of wealth which anyone could tap by merely passing more laws or hiring more government employees to dispense the wealth. No one thought for a moment that government couldn't create wealth. After all, government takes care of us, and prints all the money, so all it has to do is pass it out, and my Senator will see to it that I get my fair share, because I am (1) old, (2) minority, (3) sick, (4) insane, (5) female, (6) homosexual, (7) middle income, (8) fat, (9) skinny, (10) have AIDS, (11) member of a union, (12) other.

Finally government got so big and overpowering that everyone was sick of it, only no one knew how to stop it. It was as if it had its own life system that came from some horror movie. The more people tried to stop it, the bigger it got. Government bureaucrats were everywhere meddling in everyone's business, and telling everyone what to do...for their own good of course. But people were tired of it. The voters voted for politicians who promised to rein in government, but it just kept growing. It fed upon itself, and there was no known way to stop it. It just grew, printing money as it went, paying itself, and telling more and more people, more and more things to do, how much to do, how long they could do it, how it must be done, and how much they had to pay government to care for them.

The little community had blossomed into a dragonlike monster, eating everything in its path, and unhappiness was on everyone's face. Everyone talked about how to stop government, but they kept voting for politicians who didn't slow government expansion. It was a lost cause, so everyone decided just to live with it. The little community, grown into a large, impoverished land, now bought its cars, watches, TV sets, cameras, and other things from other lands. Fear was on the faces of the citizens because they knew that if they got sick, they would be unable to pay for their medical bills, and medical insurance was already unaffordable, since government had taken over health care.

The citizens got to taking drugs, and disobeying laws because they were so silly. Government held out shallow hopes of riches by starting government lotteries, complete with flashy advertising, so the poorest could waste their money on false hopes of riches. Each week a new millionaire was put on TV, and had their pictures taken, so the hope of undeserved riches could be kept in front of the poorest folk who kept hoping against hope. Occasionally some private person would start their own lottery, guaranteeing a higher return and the entire winning at once, rather than over 20 years with no interest. They were thrown into jail by the government. Now and then, a brilliant scientist discovered a new cure for a disease, and he tried to sell it without waiting 8 years for the government to approve it, and he went to jail. Once in a while, a businessman would forget one of the government's thousands of laws, and he would go to jail. Sometimes a person would be caught by government doing something that government thought he shouldn't, even in his own home, and he would go to jail. Government could now break into people's homes without warning, and take evidence of real or imagined "crimes", and those people would go to jail. Many accidents happened because of all the shortages, and people took a lot of short cuts to stay alive and ahead of the government agents. They would go to jail if they were caught.

The government had made it difficult to live, because it had its own secret police to ferret out anyone not paying their full share of the ruinous taxes government laid on the citizens. This secret police became known as the IRS, and it could take everything a citizen owned, break into his home, sell it from under him, and destroy anyone they chose to hurt. This was to keep the citizens in constant fear of the government that helped them so much. The government had printed so much money that it had lost its value over the years, and those who had saved for their old age had lost their savings through a process known as "inflation", which was basically government printing money to pay the bills for helping everyone so

much. There were hidden government taxes on everything.
Food, gas, wages, land, profits, beverages, cars, appliances,
clothes, and even telephone calls. Everything had lots of
hidden taxes. Hundreds of taxes that no one even knew about,
were on all the things a person had to have to barely exist. It
became illegal to own a gun to protect yourself, illegal to do
just about anything that was not within the narrow guidelines
set by government. Occasionally, a man or woman would
protest and print something, telling everyone how big and
unruly government had gotten, but the possibility of over-
throwing it was remote. Too many people were indebted to
government for their job, a handout, or a check every month,
and they wouldn't want to rock the boat that was keeping them
afloat, even though their flotation was of the most meager
type.

Some pointed out that ancient Rome fell because of
massive welfare, massive government, massive corruption,
and massive waste, coupled with outrageous tributes, which
were what they called taxes back then. But by then, a large
percentage of the citizens couldn't read because the government schools didn't teach, and those that could read didn't do
it very much. Most people had become totally unthinking,
robotic types of voters, who went to work every day, came
home at night, and watched inane TV, never even thinking
about issues or problems. Others, who tried to think about
issues, had been warped in their thinking by their former
teachers and professors who, being on the government's
payroll, were against individualism and free thought. Judges
mostly ruled against those who would try to change things,
because they were also on the payroll of the government, and
they didn't want to lose their nice job of judging, by finding
against the government or for a protester or thinker.

The unusual thing is that while the little community had
become a monster of virtual slavery and total government, the

rest of the world seemed to be much worse! Other countries had higher taxes, more severe government, dictatorships, monarchies, and even slavery! The entire world seemed to some, to be descending into a total darkness of government, government, government. Everyone seemed to be getting poorer, more enslaved, more unhealthy, and very sad.

The previous dark ages, as they were called, came about because everyone put their trust in religion, which kept them poor and uneducated. Now it was governments in all lands that kept people poor and uneducated!

The only bright spots were from a few little nations who had recently thrown off a most severe government called communism. They were starting afresh, with virtually no government, but unfortunately they seemed to be copying the already degraded lands that had oppressive, all powerful governments, which was every land on the earth. As this closes, we all hope these tiny little countries that have recently thrown off the yoke of total government, will not fall prey to it again, as our mythical little land has done......and every other land on earth!

AS I LOOKED ABOUT ME

I recently sat in my favorite chair, and looked around, thinking of the origins of all the things I know so well. The furniture, wallpaper, building materials, carpet, kitchen, windows, furnace, laundry equipment, water softener, plumbing, garage doors, concrete, cars, trucks, art, refrigerator, TV sets, VCRs, records, C.D.s, tapes, telephones, computers, food, beds, dishes, silver, jewelry, clothing, shoes, newspapers, light fixtures and bulbs, wiring, lumber, nails, screws, roofing, landscaping, and literally hundreds of items right here in my home in Colorado.

Who manufactured, installed, delivered, invented them, or even fixes them when they break? Is it government? Or is it the private sector? Did government make any of the above listed items, or in any way is it responsible for them? A hearty NO!

Well, who did it then? Obviously it was the private sector. Private individuals, businesses, or corporations invented the above, risked capital on their manufacture, and provided the jobs required to make, sell, and distribute them. Our entire life, property, food, housing, clothing, and possessions, have nothing to do with government. Yet, we pay perhaps 95% of our income to government in the form of hundreds of direct and indirect taxes. Am I exaggerating? No! Let's examine the total tax bill we pay, on say a loaf of bread.

The direct tax on the bread is first. There are property taxes on the bakery, grocery store, gas station that fuels the delivery truck, farm that grows the wheat, railroad that delivers the wheat, grain elevator that stores the wheat, garage for the delivery truck. Property taxes on the contractor that built these buildings, and undoubtedly more that haven't been thought of, such as property taxes on buildings housing repair services, utility companies, and companies supplying the grocery store, bakery, and farmer. These property taxes increase the cost of that bread tremendously. Then there are the taxes on the wages of the entire chain, which are well over 50% of each member of the chain, including the manufacturers of the trucks, tractors, trains, railroad builders and repairmen. There were wage, property, and other taxes on the manufacturer of the steel and the employees that built the railroads, trucks, tractors, ovens, cash register, pipe to carry the gas and fuel, generators that provide the electricity to power the entire chain, etc. There are taxes on the telephones, fuel, and transportation. There are taxes on every facet of that loaf of bread that some say are in excess of 95% of the cost of that bread. There are taxes on profits at every level as well.

Government had absolutely NOTHING to do with the chain

of production of that loaf of bread, other than taxing everyone in that chain directly or indirectly. Taxes so massive that it boggles the mind if you stop to think of the actual amount Americans are taxed on every single thing we own, use, buy, or eat. It is probably more than 95%. What has government, at all levels, done to deserve about 95% of our income? Let's see. It has provided us roads, for which they have extracted 36 cents per gallon of fuel here in Colorado. It has provided us with various levels of government which are supposed to protect us from our enemies and administer justice. But basically, government has no link in the production chain of any product. Government rather has provided thousands of roadblocks to that production which makes that consumer goods cost many times what they should.

Government requires permits and licenses for just about everything, and millions of inspectors to administer them. It limits what you can do, tells you how big the toilet seats must be, how much you can grow, and has specifications for just about everything. Government has hidden its taxes and interference so ingeniously that most are not aware of its insipid, cancer like intrusion into our lives. It has convinced most of us we need it! A classic case of a wolf in sheep's clothing.

At a used book store, I found an old book entitled "Barnes' Federal Code", published by Bobbs-Merrill Co. in 1919. A sub heading of the title says, "Containing all federal statutes of general and public nature now in force". It is a wonderful book, bound in leather and has literally every single federal law in existence in 1919. It contains 2,512 pages, and covers everything from "white slavery" to "national defense", to even the complete internal revenue code. There were a total of 2,512 pages, containing ALL federal laws in existence in 1919, a mere 72 years ago. That's it! 2,512 pages. Today there are probably 2,512 MILLION pages of federal laws, if not more. I am certain that state, county and local statutes have increased at the same ratio over the past 72 years.

Now think about 1919. Prosperity was everywhere. People were buying millions of homes each year, and unemployment was microscopic. Manufacturing, inventing, farming, building, and selling, were in full stride. There were microscopic amounts of bureaucracy, laws, or other obstacles to our prosperity. Henry Ford was making cars that sold for about $300, and a new house cost $2,000. The dollar was 50 times more valuable that it is now, and fully backed by gold. Our coinage was silver. America was respected everywhere in the world, we had no national debt, income taxes only if you made over $20,000 per year, and then it was 1%. That $20,000 in 1919 was the equivalent of $1,000,000 today. Then you paid 1%. America was free from government, and loving every minute of it. We were prosperous, happy, and the envy of the world. Americans were taxed barely at all. Now we are taxed probably 95%, and government continues to grow. Everything else is shrinking, including prosperity, education, and self esteem.

We have millions of rules, regulations, laws, and bureaucrats enforcing them. We look at the Soviets and tell them their problem is "central planning", and "central government" ruining everything. Are we any better? Our direct taxes for just income and social security are over 45% if you include employer contributions. If you figure in unemployment, and workmen's comp. it is close to 60% and that is direct taxation. Then you pay directly gas tax, property tax, sales tax, state tax, excise tax, and personal property tax to name a few! Perhaps our real taxation is close to 98%!

I looked around me to see what part of my possessions were provided by, made by, delivered by, sold by, or invented by a government that charges us so much. I could find nothing.

GARBO & LIKE PERSONALITIES

I have watched most Garbo movies, and am amazed at the eternal worship of her by legions of critics and film fans around the world. Recently I viewed what is supposed to be her crowning achievement, a 1933 epic where she plays the Queen of Sweden. The film is given 4 stars by critics, along with the recommendation, "don't miss this one". She is touted as beautiful, a splendid actress, and a sexy siren. She was none of the above. She was a cold, aloof, wooden woman, who certainly was not any great actress. When "Ninotchka" was released, an ad man thought up the phrase, "Garbo smiles", which was a wonderful new attribute of this glum, dour, plain woman who had captured the film world with her eternal sour puss, and stilted acting.

If you think about it, most of the world's most "desirable" men, women, actresses, actors, sex symbols, and idolized characters do have this characteristic of being cold and distant. Garbo was no actress, nor was she beautiful. She was slim, foreign, and detached. Garbo lived alone in a New York apartment, and steadfastly refused to be seen by anyone till her death.

Clark Gable, who inflamed the throbbing hearts of millions of women, made his mark by saying in a totally unconcerned tone to poor wretched Scarlet O'Hara, "Frankly my dear, I don't give a damn". This screen attitude throughout his career made him a big star. Look at the long procession of actors and actresses who made it big by being aloof and uncaring in their screen roles.

This foolishness carries forward into real life all too commonly. The surest way to a man or woman's heart is for the object of attention to be indifferent, uncaring, cold, and have the old Clark Gable, "I don't give a damn" attitude. It is as if the proprietor of this frosty disposition has something so wonderful and rare, that he or she is just not interested in sharing it with the rest of us commoners of the world. Be it sex, knowledge, or power, the aloof attitude is the certain way to success in matters of love and other affairs of the personality. Usually the possessor of this reserved bearing is nothing more than an insecure individual with little to offer other than a haughty attitude.

Count me out. I regard an aloof, disinterested, indifferent, diffident personality as an inferior personality, not that of a superior or "sophisticated" person. Nuts to you, oh elevated one!

MOVIES

50 years ago going to the movies was a wonderful experience! It was cheap, and the theatres were literal palaces, festooned with architectural renderings of wondrous far off places. Stars and fleecy clouds often floated across the ceiling, and a wonderful concert was presented from the "Mighty Wurlitzer", whose console would magically appear from the depths of the orchestra pit. The sound was of the highest fidelity, the picture was perfect, and tremendous in size. In larger houses, there was a stage show, orchestra, and always a short subject, newsreel, and cartoon besides the feature. The entire affair was a splendid experience, with uniformed ushers, scented, refrigerated air, several sets of velour curtains, colored light sequences, and always impressive cleanliness, spit and polish.

Today's theatres are tiny, austere, unattended matchboxes, with sticky floors, and astronomical prices. Couples make out, people talk, babies cry, kids come and go through the exit doors, smoke, and not a single attendant on duty in the auditorium. They're all out in the lobby telling jokes or gossiping with each other. The main interest is selling stale, pre-popped corn, with a poor chemical imitation of butter, plus candy and drinks for prices that seem to make the entire movie going experience cost as much as the average week's groceries. No one cares about the picture or comfort of paying customers. No more ushers or projectionists.

The minimum wage killed off the ushers, and automation the projectionists. The projectionist was replaced by the candy girl or manager who pushes a button, walks out of the projection booth, slams the door and that's it! It's all automatic. The house lights go down, the picture starts, and when it's over, the house lights go up. If a film breaks, the entire thing shuts down and the house lights come up. Usually a member of the audience has to go out to get some help when this happens. Wonderful! When is the last time you went to a theatre and found the volume and focus to be correct? I virtually never find it so. It's either too loud, too soft, or out of focus.

If I were once again in the theatre business, as I was for 11 years, I would have a projectionist and usher on duty at all times, not sell soda pop, and have the most comfortable state of the art rocking chair type of seating. My theatre would be clean, quiet, and comfortable. The projection would be perfect at all times, and I'll bet my theatre would out perform all competition. It costs big bucks to go to the movies today. Admission and refreshment prices have gone up about five times faster than inflation, and the movie experience has degenerated from Lincoln to a war surplus jeep. What do all these movie moguls do for entertainment? I'll bet they never go to the movies in one of their theatres!

What will eventually kill the theatre is "pay per view" TV, the VCR, and the comforts of home. At home, the VCR shows film clearly with no baby sitters, sticky floors, or dirty restrooms. Show time at your convenience, and an adjacent kitchen provides whatever refreshments you wish, at a fraction of theatre prices.. The film cost may be $3, and that includes all who watch, not per person. No driving the car to risky parking lots, looking for a seat, bad projection, uncomfortable seats, interference with your enjoyment by others in the audience, dressing up, or abiding by show times. Bigger and bigger screens, HD-TV, stereo sound, and the comforts of home will lure more and more away from theatres, eventually killing them...I think.

PUBLIC ART

The very title of this indicates almost total ineptness, now doesn't it? After all, a successful artist doesn't need to beg government, at any level, for funds to do "his thing", for all to see, sniggle at, deride, and ridicule. Is there any such thing as even moderately good public art, in say the last 50 years? If so, I haven't seen it, or heard of it. A talented artist does not have to eat at the public trough.

We live near a very successful artist named Jerry who makes a very comfortable 6 figure living from his art. For many years he starved, but wouldn't do any begging. He just kept working till he got really good. He sells originals for many thousands of dollars, and prints even can go for over a hundred dollars. Jerry is smart, talented, and even a pretty good businessman. A few doors from Jerry lives another artist who teaches art at a public school. He often goes to Europe to paint in summers, and he is proud of his work. But no one else seems to be, as he can't get published, or even exhibited. I think his work is awful. If he were good, he wouldn't be teaching art at a public school. Next door to us lives yet another artist who teaches art in a private school. I have never seen Alice's work, but since she teaches in a private school, she is probably better than the public school teacher.

In Philadelphia, there is a piece of public art that is so bad, and so lacking in anything artistic or cultivated, it is the laughing stock of the City. It's at the west end of the Ben Franklin Bridge, and is supposed to be a lightening bolt. Yuk! Paid for with tax money, of course. In Center City, at 15th and Market, across from the magnificent Philadelphia City Hall, is another piece of public art shaped like a giant clothes pin. Need I say more?

Poverty ridden "artists", aren't good artists, or the market would have made them affluent. Anyone needing a handout has no talent, and will only deface the location where their subsidized work is placed.

When chimpanzees throw paint at a canvas and "experts" claim it is good, then we have a problem right here in River City my friend. When teachers of art in high schools discourage students from painting pictures that make sense, and tell the kids ugliness is art, and splotches of paint is talent, we need to do a lot of teacher and program replacement..

Government commissioned art, music, and architecture, will always be hideous because of the nature of government. No person with any talent or self esteem would ever work for government or accept a handout. Those who draw pictures, design buildings, or compose music for government are of necessity the lowest in the talent department, or they wouldn't be working for government in the first place!

Would a great artist teach art in a public school? Would a great architect work for a government salary? Would a great man waste his time working for government? Would a great sculptor depend on government handouts for a living? Nope.

We of course have the N.E.A., (National Endowment for the Arts), which passes out millions to the non talented, vulgar, and obscene in all fields of artistic endeavor. This would be the first on my hit list of government departments. The great artists, composers, and sculptors have never had to depend on government for success. Beethoven, Liszt, Mozart, Bach, Brahms, and the great artists all made excellent livings from their works. I don't think the "impressionists" were good artists, no matter how much their works now sell for at auctions. They starved and deserved to starve. Subsidy of art causes non talent to rise where it ought not be. Public, subsidized art is always a disgrace.

ABORTION

One of the most debated issues in America today is the abortion controversy. Conservatives and strongly religious people insist it is murder and should be outlawed. The more fanatical lay down in front of abortion clinics and even start fake ones to fool the unwary into entering, where they are forced to see grisly films and listen to lectures.

The "pro choice" set are often the liberal leaning citizenry, insisting a woman should have control over her own body, that abortion is a "right", and should be paid for by government. The argument further states it is inhumane to bring unwanted children into the world where they will be unloved, a burden on society, and even the prison system. Both are partially correct, but neither logical.

First of all, abortion is murder. That tiny fetus is alive and has a heart beat. From the second of conception, it is alive. If you kill a living thing, it can technically be called "murder".

What may be murder to one, may not be murder to another. I would kill an intruder in my home, or a robber in my store. I would kill my enemy if I were threatened. I am not a woman, so I cannot say whether I would kill an unwanted fetus. But that woman should be free to decide for herself. It is her body, and she can do with it what she wants. Is it murder to abort an innocent fetus? I am certain it is. I am also certain life begins at conception. But it is also murder to step on an ant or shoot a robber. It is just as murderous to abort a deformed fetus as a normal one, or a fetus that is the result of rape or incest. Where do you draw the line?

It is also wholesale murder to kill thousands of cattle and sheep each day to feed the world's population. It is murder, according to some, to kill trees and plant life, as they are also "alive". It is murder when soldiers kill hundreds of millions, as has happened throughout history.

Abortion laws are just like drug, prohibition, or adultery laws. As impossible to enforce as anti gambling, and prostitution statutes. Worthy efforts perhaps, but doomed to failure. Might as well make a law against bad thoughts or lust. What possible good can such laws do? Absolutely none. If a woman feels strongly about abortion, and she finds herself pregnant with an unwanted or unplanned child, let her own conscience be her guide, not the law. The reverse is also true. A woman who feels that abortion is not against her conscience should be free to have one. It just has to be a matter of individual choice, because any other way is totally unenforceable, and a waste of time and money.

Free abortions are certainly not a "right". Abortion must never be government funded, sponsored, encouraged, or performed. It has nothing to do with government. Abortion is an operation performed on the female body to rid it of a pregnancy, and nothing more. It is a moral issue with each individual female, not the nation as a whole. Are you against abortion? Fine, but don't interfere with someone who is not against it, and wants one. The reverse is also true. I hate squash, and George Bush hates broccoli. I don't mind stepping on a bug, but lots of humans think it is a mortal sin. So they won't use pesticides, and I will.

The current rage is the Roe vs. Wade Supreme Court decision which legalized abortion. The Constitution says nothing about murder, abortion, robbery, incest, or any of today's crimes. The Supreme Court is to determine what laws are Constitutional and not Constitutional, not decide what is "good" or "evil". Abortion has absolutely nothing to do with the Constitution, and laws passed by the individual states regarding what they may, or may not consider crimes, have nothing to do with the Constitution. Abortion should be an individual decision, not a governmental one, at any level.

Abortion is no different than a religious or political belief. Are you a Republican or Democrat? Catholic, Protestant, or Atheist? Do you like Victorian or modern architecture? Do you like the Yankees or the Dodgers? North or South? East or West? It is your business and no one else's. I honestly do not know how I would feel about killing a fetus if I had one in me, but every woman knows. It is her business, not government's. Consciences are different for everyone. Differences make the world go round. Forcing your opinions on others, and doing it by means of law, is pointless and futile.

Suppose cursing was made illegal? Suppose cigarettes were made illegal? I hate both, but would never be so silly as to suggest such a law. A law against abortion, which can be done in secrecy is impossible to enforce, so why put such a law on the books in the first place? Just keep government, subsidies, laws, and bureaucracy out of it, and everyone will do just fine with their own conscience; doing as it dictates.

Smoking is going away rapidly, but not because of laws. Anti smoking laws would only drive cigarettes underground, like it has drugs, prostitution, and gambling. Anti abortion laws will do exactly the same thing, causing hideous, painful deaths from filth, ineptness, and secretive, "back alley" abortions, which will be performed some way, no matter what such laws may say.

Carrie Nation went about breaking up bars with her trusty ax, but accomplished absolutely nothing. She was an ancient absurdity. Today we have the abortion pickets laying down in doorways, blowing up clinics, picketing, and campaigning for a Constitutional amendment against abortion. They are just as absurd as were the "demon rum" calamity howlers and the

WCTU, (Women's Christian Temperance Union). Just the "lunatic fringe" out on a campaign, trying to garner publicity and the spotlight. If the reporters, photographers, and TV cameras weren't there, they might not be either. Of course they're sincere in their fervor, and they really do believe that abortion is murder, which indeed it is. Murder that is impossible to stop or detect. Don't try to legislate the impossible. Remove all abortion laws from all books.

POLICE

Every civilized society needs law and order. When violations occur, police apprehend, and hopefully, the courts try to punish offenders. Unfortunately, crime is on the increase and the police seem ever less effective. It's gotten so bad that sections of major cities now have private police forces carrying guns, patrolling beats, and using their own equipment. Early results show these private police, not under control of "city hall", have cut crime considerably. Wonder why? Curious why the cops aren't as effective as they used to be? Try this theory on for size.

American police seem to be acting more like their movie counterparts than in an effective manner. Picture a typical situation. A robbery, murder, or burglary has occurred. Perhaps 5 police cars come roaring to the scene with lights flashing and sirens screaming. Cops jump out of their cars and rush up with drawn guns. Now I ask you, what the hell good does this do, the crime has been committed, and the perpetrator is long gone. The only thing accomplished is a big show, and big money wasted. Crimes are rarely solved, nor criminals caught like the movies insist. It's just exhibitionism.

Detectives normally solve crimes, and cops driving around in cars can never observe what is really going on in a neighborhood. That sentence should be read over again before you proceed. For a police department to be really effective, the night shifts should be larger than the day shifts, most cops should walk beats, and non police should do the paperwork, court appearances and research. Detectives should be increased in number, and probably half of the police cars should be sold. Read that one again too!

Police driving around in sealed, air conditioned cars are about as much of a crime deterrent as were the Keystone Cops. A burglar will hide in the bushes, enter the rear of houses or stores, cut through yards, go in through roofs, ride bikes, and be totally invisible to a cop in a car. Police spend most of their time racing to scenes of crimes and filling out reports, rather than preventing and solving crimes. Preventing them by walking a beat, knowing their beat, and being unpretentious, quiet, and protective. Eventually the good ones are promoted to detective, where they can solve crimes using the elaborate electronics now available. With modern technical devices, crimes should be going down rather than up. Police riding in cars spend hours giving tickets to traffic offenders, while homes are robbed, women raped, and stores burglarized. How absurd. Why not totally rethink the modus operandi of all police departments? A cop on a beat with a radio, billy club, gun and flashlight is worth 10 lazy bums endlessly riding around in air conditioned cars, doing nothing.

Naturally, our Constitutional guarantee of privacy has been violated millions of times, thanks to the narcs who can, at will, break into your home with guns drawn, and a specious "warrant" in their anxious hands. This chapter isn't on drugs, but another is. The "drug war" has violated the Constitution millions of times, and the police have run wild over our liberties with this useless "war". Without the "drug war", the crime rate would be about half or less, and we would all be a lot safer.

TIME SHARES

Of all the American sales schemes, the time share condo is perhaps the cleverest. The sales pitch is almost irresistible. "Luxury condo time share. The ultimate in luxury for your vacation every year. Buy your dream vacation villa for $10,000, with 5% down, and easy low payments and terms. Own it forever or sell it. A vacation get away that belongs to YOU!" The spiel goes on to tell you the interest is deductible, all maintenance is furnished, full facilities are free for your week's vacation, including pool, tennis courts, beautiful views, golf, etc. sound great? Let's analyze it.

For that $10,000, you own this admittedly beautiful condo, but for only one week a year. Prices depend on the season, but that's a good average. The developer can sell a condo costing $50,000, including land and extras, for 52 times $10,000, or $520,000. If you build a 200 unit time share resort, for $10,000,000, you can sell it for more than ten times that, or $104,000,000. That's a hefty 94 million profit for the builder before sales expenses. Sell them for 5% down, and carry the balance at interest, and you have the entire thing paid for with a receivable of $90 million plus perhaps $9 million income a year in interest. A developer can easily afford to put on hefty promotions, free weekends, lavish advertising, and big name sponsorship!

For the buyer, this seemingly wonderful bargain really isn't. $10,000 isn't the final bill, because there is an average of $200 per year in "maintenance charges", which includes taxes, utilities, and repairs. This is for a one week stay, or about

$30 per day. You can't rent a motel room of this high quality for $30 a day, but if you took your $10,000 and put it in the bank at 8%, that's an additional $115 per day for that week, plus the $30 a day in maintenance for your dream condo, or $145 per day! And who wants to go to the same place every year for a vacation, and especially at $145 per day? The developer has $10,400 per unit to maintain the place, and pay the taxes and insurance, which I can assure you is more big profit...in the hundreds of thousands per year for management. Don't forget, each unit's price and maintenance must be multiplied by 52. There are 52 of these weeks in each year.

Some ads proclaim that you can exchange your week with other owners who might want to go to your location, and you go to theirs. Even if that works, $145 is an outrageous price to pay on a per day basis. Some time shares sell for less and some sell for a lot more. I use these figures from a location close to me, and they are accurate. And lastly, if you ever want to sell, you can practically forget it!

America is getting wise, and what sales there are, are pennies on the dollar. If you walk away from it, you might ruin your credit rating, as it is an official default on your credit sheet. Time shares are not for the smart investor. If you just have to have one, select one of the millions that are for sale, and take over the payments. The owner will usually be delighted!

THE SOUTH

A PBS special on the civil rights movement showed vivid details of the first Negro student attempting to register at "Old Miss" over 20 years ago. During this one incident, 35 U.S. Marshalls were shot and history repeated itself as the South was once again invaded by the North, just as it had been 100 years earlier. In 1989, 20,000 "peace" marchers over ran the all white county of Forsythe, Georgia. The specter of masses of people swarming over a quiet, unassuming place to protest what they felt was an injustice, even though there had been no transgression, is simply appalling. Forsythe's crime was not having a single Negro resident. The Civil War wasn't fought over slavery, but the right of a state to secede from the union because of an irreconcilable difference of opinion. It happens every day when marriages break up, friendships cease, or business affiliations change due to differences in opinion or practice.

Until the 1960's, the policy of the South was "separate but equal". Negroes said their facilities weren't equal to that of whites. Whites said they often were better. But then my house isn't as good as a lot of other houses. On the other hand, it may be a lot better than some. I'm not as good looking or as rich as some. Equality cannot be legislated because equality does not exist between men. We all have our own set of personal assets and liabilities, and we do as well as we can with what we have.

A man's freedom of choice allows him to choose his own friends and associates. It allows him to select his own job, wife, and raise his children as he sees fit. He can strive for financial success, or be a lazy bum, sit on a river bank all day and fish.

If the South had been left alone in the 1860s, the slavery issue would have eventually resolved itself. Slavery could not have continued much longer because the industrial revolution and farm machinery made slavery obsolete. It was a bankrupt system in the process of self destructing even as Lincoln was starting the war. We still feel the effects of this bloody division between the North and South 125 years later. The animosity continues to exist, and even more so now that the South's low taxes and wages have lured many Northern businesses and manufacturing plants.

Just imagine the 620,000 dead from that War between the States. The "war of northern aggression" is what Southerners rightly call it. A horror never to be forgotten.

The hatred between the races is far stronger now than before L.B.J.'s infamous resolve to "integrate" and it shows no signs of abating. School bussing and forced integration has not made the races like each other, but increased the hatred, jealousy, and desire for separatism. The entire United States would be much better off if the South had been left alone to solve it's own problems in it's own way. Without the force of guns and troops, white Southerners would have logically worked their way free of their prejudices.

Force has only fortified hatred.

THE CARTER LEGACY

Jimmy Carter hasn't occupied the White House since January, 1981, but the effects of his Presidential term are far from over. The Carter Presidency hangs over rural America like a black cloud. When Jimmy Carter, with a stroke of his pen stopped farmers from selling wheat to the Soviets, a catastrophic series of events began which has cost the taxpayers hundreds of billions of dollars, and the end is not yet in sight. Carter instituted this embargo as a "get even" move after the Iranians captured the American Embassy and held 72 hostages. They wouldn't have done that if Carter hadn't allowed the Shah to enter America for medical treatment, against the sound advice of the entire State Department and his cabinet.

Before the Carter grain embargo, American farmers were prospering. Grain sales-were gradually increasing to the hungry Soviets, who liked the product and the price. A long time business relationship had developed, which was mutually beneficial. The American farmer had gradually increased his capacity, enlarged his land holdings, and bought more sophisticated machinery on credit deemed good by responsible bankers in the farm belt. The loans were good loans, given on the basis of actual sales and profits, not projected ones. With the Carter grain embargo, all the hard work, good will, efficiency, and developed markets fell apart in a grand heap similar to Humpty Dumpty's fall off that wall.

The Soviets had no trouble finding grain in Canada and other producing countries, which were delighted to supply millions of tons yearly to a foreign purchaser. The Soviets have maintained these sources over the years, and American farmers have never been able to recoup more than a small fraction of the former Soviet sales. The loss of sales was but a tiny fraction of the damage done by Carter. The farmers had gone deeply into debt, buying land and machinery to produce efficiently for a growing market. The Carter embargo snapped a delicate economic chain.

Unused, unneeded land and equipment went into rapid default. Farmers found themselves with blanket mortgages covering not only newly acquired, but already owned land. Land no longer viable, but with continuing payments and taxes due. Loans secured with titles for equipment no longer used or needed, but whose payments continued to fall due. The farmer's sales were slashed so much, that there was nothing left with which to pay the bills and installments, even with no profit at all. Bankers found they owned a lot of equipment after defaults on secured loans. Farmers who had borrowed, had their credit ruined, and were saddled with judgments that would haunt them for decades. Equipment manufacturers such as John Deere, International, Case, Oliver, and others found themselves with no orders. International no longer exists. Mortgage holders foreclosed. No one wanted the land or equipment, so prices plummeted. Used equipment became a dreg on an overstocked market. When taxes weren't paid on foreclosed lands, local, county, and state governments had problems.

Equipment manufacturers laid off employees and their stock prices and dividends fell, hurting individuals, trusts, and retirement plans which had purchased these stocks as security. The same things happened to seed producers, machinery dealers, fuel suppliers, and fertilizer manufacturers. Unemployment reached intolerable levels.

Towns died.

Farm subsidy programs escalated, until they reached $25

billion by 1988, and the end was not in sight. All as a lasting memorial to Jimmy Carter. Farmers, whose families had farmed the same land for over a hundred years, lost everything, being forced off home and land under an auctioneer's gavel. The bleak, empty faces of homeless farm families seared the 6 o'clock news screens and made viewers cringe with anger and pity. The American Dream gone amok. Hard working, small time capitalists, ruined by a Presidential signature.

Banks failed and continue to fail. The bank bailout in the grain belt will cost billions. Thousands of empty, decaying farm houses dot the landscape...unlived in, unwanted, lonely reminders of what was once so wonderful, and now is so dismal. The incurable chain of events caused by one reckless act of an ill informed, ill advised President carried over during the entire 8 year term of Ronald Reagan. That one act has forever changed the landscape of rural America, and destroyed millions of its former participants. The markets are lost, the farms and farmers are lost, and the small towns are lost. Empty grain elevators sit in solemn silence along dirt paths that used to be the Rock Island Railroad. A miniature "Atlas Shrugged".

When will the mind boggling, catastrophic effects of the Carter grain embargo cease to haunt us? Only time will tell.

During Jimmy Carter's Presidency, the prime interest rate soared to unheard of heights, due to the markets voting "no confidence" in his abilities. Gold soared to over $850 and silver to over $50, all totally unrealistic. The populace was afraid of the Carter dollars and wanted out. When metals prices went back to normal after Carter lost his Presidency, millions had lost hundreds of billions. The disasters of the Carter term can be made into a lengthy book I am sure, but it isn't for me to write.

Isn't it lucky we were subjected to only one term of good old Jimmy? After giving away the Panama Canal, destroying banks, decimating small towns, and bankrupting thousands, what else had he in store for us? Maybe in his second term we would have had a 30% prime rate and had a modern day Hitler take his place.

TRASH

It's all the rage now, making prime time news and the front pages of newspapers. Where are we going to put the ever increasing amount of rubbish being discarded by Americans? We're familiar with the photos of landfills growing like Topsy, trash trucks continually regurgitating tons and tons of newspapers, tin cans, old tires, and the offal of a civilized society. Even if there weren't a space problem, landfills are costing us a fortune .

One of the advantages of being old, (or at least advanced middle age!), is the ability to remember when things which are now problems weren't, and why not. Where did we put the trash 50 years ago? Simple! We burned it! Today, burning trash is an illegal act in most places because of strict laws propagated by the EPA. But is burning trash all that bad? Trash has been burned for literally thousands of years .

The smog and putrid air over major cities is not caused by burning trash, which is EXTERNAL COMBUSTION, but by millions of autos and trucks, using INTERNAL COMBUS-TION engines. External combustion is simply burning something in either an enclosed or open place, but not under compression. Internal combustion engines burn petroleum under high compression, their exhaust combines with ambient air and causes highly toxic and ugly "brown clouds" over cities around the world. Smog from internal combustion engines is decaying priceless buildings, statuary, and even auto paint, besides causing the death of trees and other living things. External combustion causes none of this.

Steam locomotives and coal burning furnaces for 150 years caused dirty cities streaked with soot and grime. Coal burning was, and is, external combustion. Coal smoke does not turn into smog. External combustion causes ash and soot which falls to the ground or seas as a nutrient. Smog ruins things. The point is that burning trash doesn't cause air pollution, other than for the amount of time it takes for the ash to fall to earth. Smog hangs there indefinitely and poisons us.

The fire that decimated Yellowstone Park was more fire than would be created by Cities burning trash for fifty years. Yet there was no smog type air pollution created. It all fell to earth and became fertilizer. The air remained clear. In Kuwait, 6 million barrels of oil burned every day under external combustion conditions, not internal combustion. No smog, and no ill effects, just smoke. The Yellowstone fires, Mt. Helens eruption, Kuwait, and yes trash burning, are simple, natural external combustion causing smoke, with the resultant ash and soot becoming instant fertilizer wherever it falls. Trash has been burned throughout all of recorded history, and no one has ever been the worse for it.

What hasn't been going on for all of recorded history are hundreds of millions of internal combustion engines burning petroleum, and literally ruining the earth with their chemical exhausts. Trash should be burned, householders should once again be allowed to burn leaves in the fall, and we should all stop worrying about external combustion.

There is enough money being wasted each year for landfills, compaction, and hauling of trash from place to place to give every American a nice cash bonus each year which could be spent on consumer goods, helping America's economy. The E.P.A. is probably the most out of control bureaucracy ever conceived by the dim bulbs of Congress and the White House. It is making life unbearable for the citizen as well as the businessman. Burn trash, just exactly as man has done since his beginning. Landfills don't benefit the earth. The earth loves ashes falling on its farms and gardens as enrichment for the soil.

THE GREAT DIESEL FRAUD

For close to twenty years we have been robbed blind by one of America's largest industries, at a huge cost to the consumer, and for some strange reason no one has done anything about it. This hand in American pocketbooks has continued without interruption. No one seems to be objecting. I hereby vigorously protest and I hope the victims do something. We are all victims. If Poland, East Germany, Czechoslovakia, and Hungary can throw off their totalitarian oppressors, surely America can throttle the oil companies!

The plain simple fact is that diesel fuel and #2 heating oil, (which are the same), require but a fraction of the refining of gasoline. Diesel and #2 heating oil not only take less refining, but are less dangerous to refine and require fewer additives. In other words diesel costs a lot less to produce than gasoline. These facts always had the price of diesel about a third lower gasoline, at least until 1973. Diesel has more energy (BTU's) per gallon than gasoline and doesn't explode, so it is the preferred fuel for heavy equipment. A gallon of diesel can move a truck almost twice as far as a gallon of gasoline. Since the shortages of 1973, all oil companies have raised the price of diesel to equal or higher than gasoline. The effects are not hard to observe.

Let's say that the average highway tractor trailer gets 5 miles per gallon, and is paying $1.00 per gallon for fuel. This is a 20 cent per mile fuel cost to deliver America's goods. If the price of diesel fuel were 65 cents per gallon, the fuel cost for the same truck would be only 13 cents per mile. An extremely conservative figure of a quarter billion miles per day being driven by truckers, plus railroad locomotives, farm tractors, and home heating furnaces, means the American public is having several BILLION dollars added each week to the cost of literally everything. The diesel gouge costs you maybe an extra $5-$10 each time you buy a week's groceries, a couple of hundred for each car purchased, and many dollars for everything we buy, day in and day out. Home heating costs are at least a third more than they should be if oil is used. All merchandise requires transportation of some sort, and every food product requires diesel farm equipment to produce. The cost to America is astronomical.

I defy anyone to prove me wrong. The plain simple fact is the oil companies have engaged in a huge price fix for close to 2 decades. Where are all the highly paid bureaucrats in the Justice Department? Why has a literal price fixing, crooked, cartel been allowed to exist in America all these years? Why hasn't the marketplace brought the diesel price down? I just don't know, but I am certainly tired of this and I wish some oil company would compete rather than going along with the fix. America would welcome diesel competition. It would save us billions every year.

If we truly had a free market system in America, this wouldn't happen. As it is there are so many intricate, unfathomable, sticky wicket deals between industry and government that we may never know!

WHY USE OIL TANKERS?

Since the Alaskan Oil Pipeline opened, estimates say 9,000 tanker loads of oil have left Valdez Alaska, unloading at Los Angeles. There has been one catastrophe and a few smaller spills, a more recent one being 400,000 gallons spilled off the coast of Huntington Beach, California, when a tanker ran over its own anchor, attempting to hook onto an offshore pipeline for unloading. The 11 million gallon Exxon Valdez spill will linger for perhaps a century, and maybe more. Exxon has already spent $3 billion on the cleanup and is still not finished. There are no estimates as to the total cost before Exxon is clear of it. The ecologists are having a justifiable field day over the Prince William Sound fiasco. Huge super tankers can split in half in rough seas, and are difficult to stop and steer. In an emergency situation, a large oil tanker can require many miles to stop or change course. The cost of spilled oil, fines, lawsuits, damages, and cleanup, would have many times over paid the cost of a superbly engineered double track railroad between Alaska and the "lower 48". Isn't it time to consider the obvious?

The obvious is that even though part of the terrain is difficult, making for expensive construction and mainte- nance, a few oil carrying, unit tank car trains, could do what the tankers are doing, at less cost, and with a major polluting spill virtually impossible. Consider the possibilities of such trains.

Each train would be semi-permanently coupled, with all tank cars connected with a pipe. Loading and unloading could be accomplished from either end of the train with a single connection. Each train of perhaps 100 tank cars, would carry a barrel of North Slope Crude from Alaska to Los Angeles far faster and cheaper than a sea going tanker. If a train should wreck, the chances of more than a few tank cars rupturing is remote, and of course the spill would be on land, not uncontrollable, as in a water spill. A land traveling, oil tanker unit train is not revolutionary, merely adequate use of current technology. The land tanker train could be sent to any place in the Continental U.S. or Canada with little extra cost, thereby diverting crude to areas where refinery capacity might be less strained or cheaper to operate. The huge Southern California refining operation is arousing citizen and ecological outrage because of its polluting the already foul Los Angeles air. Send it somewhere else in the train! Refineries could be built in low cost labor, low tax, low restriction areas, with a savings of billions due to the versatility of railroad tracks being able to carry Alaska crude virtually anywhere.

Alaska crude, as it gets to Valdez, is not too thick to be easily loaded on the unit trains, and in the "lower 48" would be even easier to pump off with no heating. A roller bearing unit train is the most energy efficient form of transport known to man, whereas a boat is one of the least efficient. A railroad line, double tracked between Alaska and the "lower 48, is a major construction project, but not prohibitively expensive when the greatly reduced cost of transporting the oil, and microscopic chance of pollution is concerned. The insurance costs of railroad vs boat would weigh mightily in favor of a low risk, efficient, train. Unloading the train would require far less pumping energy than for a tanker. Loading would be about the same. The train could deliver the load of oil directly to a refiner anywhere, whereas a boat can only deliver to a coastal port.

Experts say that another major oil spill of the Exxon

Valdez scope is certain to happen again in the future. since Alaska oil can be transported 100% by land to its ultimate destination, why risk tankers any longer? It's bad enough that they have to ply the oceans, but to use dangerous, inefficient, flimsy, tankers where rail transport could be used is ludicrous.

UNIONS

It has been said that "Unions were necessary to help the working man, but they became too powerful, and aren't necessary any longer". Words to that effect have been written and spoken millions of times. I disagree. Unions weren't "necessary", so much as they were natural. Natural, just as it is natural for people of like interests to associate. It is natural for people to pool their efforts and numbers to achieve certain objectives. Unions were, and are, organized efforts to achieve goals, be they higher wages, better working conditions, shorter hours, longer vacations, or sick leave. Unions are people uniting together to force an issue. Sometimes it works, and sometimes it doesn't. Organized people always have more clout than individuals.

Assume you own a factory that makes sweaters. Wages cost so much, machinery costs so much, yarn, labels, boxes, advertising, distribution, and sales cost so much. You, as owner of this enterprise, need to price your merchandise so it is competitive. You must keep your costs under control. You must keep your material, rent, labor, and other costs, as low as possible so you can not only compete and sell, but show a profit. Labor is a major cost in any business. If your labor force walks off, you have no production. If your labor cost is too high, you cannot compete, and may fail in your business. There is a balance between so many factors. This is why it is tough to be in business.

If your labor force walks out, it is difficult, time consuming, and expensive, to train a new labor force, all of which adds to your cost of production. If you, as an employee, can make more elsewhere, you will probably go there for the higher wages. If you can organize the factory, persuade everyone to threaten a strike, form a union, and present your demands to the boss, you may come out O.K. Or you may face the loss of your jobs!

In the history of the union movement, there have been successes as well as dismal failures. One classic case was the Atwater Kent radio. Atwater Kent was a rich, young, Philadelphian, who was fascinated by the new rage of his time, radio. He decided to build absolutely the best radio, in the most modern, efficient factory, and call it the "Atwater Kent". It worked. The factory is still there, 70 years old, and still looking modern and efficient. It is not being used as a factory of course, but it is at Roosevelt Blvd and Fox St., if you want to see the still magnificent buildings. All was going well. Kent was paying excellent wages, and producing a fine product, which is now highly collectible. Workers decided to form a union at the urging of some. Kent warned that any difficulties employees had could be settled amicably, and if a union were formed, he would close the plant, and go out of business. A union was voted, and he kept his word. Hundreds lost their jobs, and there were no more Atwater Kent radios. He could afford it. They couldn't. They lost.

The Florida East Coast Railroad got sick of expensive union "make work" rules about 30 years ago, and informed the unions they would either do a day's work for a day's pay, or they were out. The union called the bluff, and all lost their jobs. After years of sabotage, picketing, and threats, it was determined to be a lost cause, and they gave up. Today, the Florida East Coast Railroad pays high wages on an hourly basis, has no union, and makes a decent profit, as opposed to most railroads, which continue to tolerate union featherbedding.

My opinion of unions is totally neutral. You pay your dues

and you get your benefits....sometimes. Eastern Airlines pilots lost their seniority and jobs while at the same time throwing their airline into bankruptcy when they walked out in sympathy with machinists. Frank Lorenzo, the then president of Eastern, was certainly not a likeable man, and a poor manager as well. Eastern no longer exists. It has been said that steel and auto industry management gave in to unions so much, it ruined their businesses, giving much of it away to the Japanese. Possibly true.

If management and labor bargain freely, with no influence from government, it usually works out fine. Union demands are no different from any other transaction in the marketplace. Far too often, union officers squander funds. Far too often unions on strike resort to violence and sabotage, rather than free bargaining. As I write this, Greyhound bus drivers have been on strike for many months, and are shooting at busses. This I despise. Fair is fair, and this isn't fair.

In the spring of 1984, a supermarket chain in the Midwest told the union if they didn't take a small cut in wages, the stores would have to close. Management opened the books for all to see. Competition was severe, and the chain was losing money in spite of every possible economy measure undertaken by management. Labor voted not to take a cut, the entire chain closed its doors, and hundreds lost their jobs.

Then there is the case of Henry Ford. Ford was a genius in labor-management relations. Ford installed a factory production line, made the factory cheery, gave workers breaks, and doubled their wages. Ford's increased production and profits, is textbook in its results. Workers no longer had to lift heavy objects, strain their eyes, and get dirty. Ford's production costs got so low, that in 1927, Model "T" cars were selling at a mere $275, driving other manufacturers up the wall. Model T Fords became farm tractors, taxicabs, buses, and family cars. "Flivers", as they got to be called, were everywhere, and

America fell in love with the automobile. Previously, the automobile cost 4 times as much, and few could afford them. Thousands of "T"s were rolling off the assembly lines each week. Hollywood used them as props to run off cliffs, and film hilarious comedies in the silent days. Labor and management worked well together in the case of Ford in the 20's.

If you are a union member making $15 an hour, and are offered a pay cut, or a layoff, it is a difficult decision to make. Management has to make a profit, and you have to eat. If you are used to living at the $15 per hour level, your expenses are high. A cut might jeopardize your ability to service your debts. Your life-style would be lowered. Maybe you couldn't make that much anywhere else. It's tough. Management, on the other hand, is losing money, and realizes its costs are too high. Management and labor both have tough decisions to make. Foreign competition has hurt immensely. Korean and Japanese workers work for far less money than do Americans, and they can produce for less. Often times tariffs and transportation don't make up the difference, and wages simply have to be reduced to keep the business going. No choice.

America is no longer "king" in the world. Competition rears its ugly head from every direction, making everyone tighten their belts. Management, for far too long, gave in to union demands, rather than fight. Higher wages meant no modernization of plant, and inefficiencies that have now come home to roost. At a shop I had in Philadelphia, a plate glass window was broken. Union glazers got $19 per hour. The bid from the union shop was $200 higher than from a non union shop. I took the non union bid. The glass cost was identical in both bids. In the northeast, and most large cities, unions have held everyone in an iron grip for so long, manufacturers by the hundreds have moved to warmer, more labor friendly places in the west and south. The northeast has earned the title of "rust belt", thanks to outrageous union demands, causing factories to close, and literally rust away.

Railroad's share of inter-city freight business has gone from 90% to a mere 36% because of union intransigence. The non union trucker has a vastly less efficient mode of transport, but can operate on public highways, deliver to the door, and not have his rig stuck in freight yards, being delayed by crew changes, and other make work, featherbedding rules. Employment on railroads has shrunk to an all time low. Hundreds of thousands of jobs have disappeared because of union stubbornness. Meanwhile, the highways are being slowly destroyed by heavy trucks, whose freight would be moving by rail, except for union insistence that a day's pay for a day's work is unacceptable.

The American auto industry could beat the Japs at their own game if the unions would give a little, and do good work. Monday and Friday cars are legend, thanks to union employee sloppiness. Wouldn't it be nice to see American industry blossom again? If management and labor would both wake up, it could happen. It's better to have a job paying a little less, than no job at all! Without profit, there can be no jobs. Do corporate managers really deserve their millions each year? Both are at fault, and that's why I remain neutral. Neutral, except that I am outraged at the silliness and complicity on both sides, which is destroying American productivity. The vast iron and copper deposits lay idle. Factories are shut, and workers are laid off. It is impossible to buy an American watch, camera, or VCR. Stubbornness, and stupidity have gone hand in hand with both management and labor. Unions think there is no limit on a company's ability to pay, and management thinks it deserves millions in salaries, which provokes the unions....as it should. It is all so catastrophic, and America is failing as an obvious consequence.

"Howdy! My name is Phinius T. Government and do I have a national health plan for you!"

HEALTH CARE

Is there any more prevalent complaint in America today than that health care is unaffordable? It is, you know. I have no health coverage, as it is too expensive for my meager wallet. It is said 37 million Americans have no coverage, and this is an accurate figure I am certain. It is a horrible situation, and the political answer is to copy other countries and have universal health care. No matter that it has failed everywhere it has been tried, universal health care will be the means of getting elected, and you just wait and see. Government provided health care will be a total disaster. The reason health care is so expensive now, is because of government meddling in what used to be a very healthy, available to all, industry, namely doctors, nurses, hospitals, and prescription drugs.

Until Lyndon Johnson, and a compliant Democratic Congress got us into government medical care, all was well thank you. Now, with medicare, and medicaid, the doctor-hospital insurance-bureaucratic-political fraud is almost all encompassing. Medical care was affordable and attainable for all of America till government got into it in the mid 60's. With each year that passes, it becomes more of a nightmare, and politicians have discovered a gold mine of election possibilities in legislating government paid health care for all. What a preposterous fraud! Yet America is in such bad condition medically, it is certain to happen! Why can't we ever learn from the past? Why can't we learn from others' experiences?

England, Canada, Sweden, and all other lands where government provided health care is in effect, has seen care go literally down the tubes. Operations are impossible to get, waiting periods for care are months or years, and everyone is unhappy with it. Naturally they are unhappy. If government can't deliver the mail economically, or efficiently, how can it be expected to provide health care? As I have said before, and will say again, government can do absolutely NOTHING well, efficiently, or timely. Look at other government operations such as the IRS, the brutalized national forests, air traffic control, or even grants to obscene art. Name one single thing government has ever done well. Just one!

Government has gotten itself into the health care for the aged, and caused the entire industry to become lopsided, inefficient, and unaffordable. If government had never gotten into it, health care would still be reasonable and attainable. Our memories are so short! Here's a prediction, and it won't take long for it to happen. By the year 2002, no one will be able to afford child care. Government is just getting involved in baby sitting, and the normal result will be astronomical costs, unaffordability, bureaucracy, and eventually, "universal child care", which will make us even with the Soviets, Hitler, and other wonderful examples.

The way to save America is to GET GOVERNMENT OUT OF BUSINESS, not allowing it to further invade areas in which it has no Constitutional business. This means, as I have said in other parts of this work, Washington D.C. must be made into a ghost town. The fed must be 90% decapitated, and never allowed to ever intrude into our natural prosperity, which has been destroyed with myriads of rules, regulations, laws, subsidies, bureaucrats, and gobbledygook. The best way to make health care affordable, would be for government to be totally and immediately removed from it.

But now that millions of oldsters have latched on to medicare and medicaid, that is impossible. If that were removed, the health care industry would topple, because it depends on government checks. The nursing home industry would collapse, as it also depends on government handouts. The pharmaceutical industry would disintegrate also. Lyndon Johnson, and his Congress, have destroyed the medical industry, and politicians from both parties will finish the deed by voting in socialized medicine for America. It is as certain as sunrise and sunset. America will further lower itself into a socialistic state that will be even more difficult to extricate itself from, if it could ever happen.

Citizens and politicians rush to and fro with various "programs", and "solutions", to every problem that arises, and they all involve more government. Like an alcoholic taking another drink, even though each drink further destroys him. After socialized medicine, and socialized baby sitting, politicians will vote for government to take over some other industry and destroy it with rules, regulations, and bureaucrats. Will America stop this before it succumbs totally? Will we join the rest of the socialists in the world, and together re-enter another dark age? It looks like it is unavoidable!

FEED THE CHILDREN

I do get weary of seeing TV commercials urging a mere $21 per month to be sent to this or that organization that will "feed the children", "save lives", "help the starving", or send help to various people in sundry places throughout the "developing" world. First of all, those places aren't developing, but going down the tubes, thanks to their dictatorial, slave driving, rich rulers. The very word "developing", is a total non sequitur.

I submit that feeding fly infested tykes, who are undernourished and dying anyway, thanks to natural phenomena or tyrannical government, is a total waste of money and assets. • Their brains are probably damaged, and even if they did survive, they would have no place in the world other than to produce more leaches, begging for handouts. It's certainly a big tug at the old heart strings when you see these starving wretches out in the desert, but one must show strength. The strength is in NOT giving in to the commercials, realizing that most of the money goes to administration or advertising, and much of the rest will be squandered some other way. A recent typical happening was 34 truck loads of food being blown to bits by the army in Ethiopia.

Strength is resisting something, be it a cigarette, fattening foods, or giving your money to a lost cause. Look at how your $21 a month COULD be used, with long lasting results. The simplest way would be to put it in the bank, where you would earn interest, and give the bank funds to loan, perhaps to help a new business, which would create employment. One of

Japan's most admirable habits is the fact that they save a huge part of their income, giving the banks money to further expand Japanese strength. Americans save very little, are always in debt, and we are suffering from acute lack of capital with which to buy seeds for our national farm.

Saving helps the community in which the saver lives. But there are certainly more things you can do with your $21 per month that will help your own struggling country. Maybe a local candidate really needs it so he can get elected, and perform urgent reforms in local government. Notice I said local, not national. That's another chapter. Your $21 a month could buy trees for a local park, your own lawn, paint for your house, help your kids with something they need, or save for their college educations. It could go towards buying something made in America, thereby helping your own country. There are so many things $21 a month could do.

Feeding a starving kid in some desolate, arid country, is a waste. Do you think all the kids look like the ones you see? Or didn't they find the absolute worst, ugliest, skinniest, most vermin ridden waif to photograph, causing you to break into tears, and send money immediately. I think they must collect flies for these commercials, and release them on their subject child! I can assure you photographs are available of dirty kids, airplane crashes, highway mutilation, forest fires, and accidents here in the U.S. that will tug at your emotions every bit as much. One of the commercials says, "The first thing you will get is a letter..". For crying out loud, are Americans so gullible as to think some non English speaking kid will personally write them a letter? Can't you imagine the computer generated letters being sent to the saps? Do you really think one dose of vitamin A will prevent blindness? Garbage TV is what it is. Don't fall for it.

What you should do with any surplus money you have, is use it for things benefiting yourself, your family, community or loved ones. After that, save it, and your local banker will loan it to a worthwhile person to begin a business, a manufacturing plant, or do something creative. Your savings will give you security, and result in more prosperity and job creation. You just don't realize how short capital is. One further caution. When you deposit it in a savings place, check to see what they do with the money you lend them. Larger banks sometimes get carried away and make loans to "3rd world" countries, which always means it will be (1) lost forever, (2) misused, and (3) wasted. Banks that ship your money out of America, are not good places to deposit your money. Wouldn't it be nice if one bank decided to never again loan money for a Japanese car? The first bank doing that gets 100% of my business! Keep your money at home, and use it for yourself or your community. Otherwise, don't be surprised if America eventually become a third world nation.

REWRITE?

Rewrite the Constitution? Not meaning to sound flippant, but I think that's a pretty good idea. Of course my ideas for a rewrite might be a bit different than most. The Constitution is over 200 years old, and sets out the basic rules for the most wonderful government ever conceived by man. It tells the Congress what it is to do, but as we can easily see today, it fails to tell Congress what it CANNOT do. The things it tells Congress it CAN do, are a far cry from what it HAS DONE, and especially over the last 60 years, since FDR came into office.

As an example, the Constitution's framers never anticipated the Congress, and even the President, would use their office to buy endless re-elections, using a continual flow of pork barrel programs and projects to make the home folk vote for them, term after term. The Constitution tells Congress what it is responsible for, but they have made a mockery of the entire matter. One change I would make is to limit terms to only one 6 year term for President, one 5 year term for a Senator, and one 4 year term for a Representative. They could never again buy their next election.

The originators never intended America to have a national debt in the trillions of dollars either, so I would add a balanced budget amendment saying, "government shall never spend more than it receives in revenues."

The authors of the Constitution never intended that government issue totally worthless money, as it now is, nor that banks be prohibited from issuing money, which they did for over a hundred years. They intended that it be made of gold and silver, or at least backed by such. A slip of the pen inserted "states" with reference to money, but it is obvious they meant all money, not just state money, to be valuable. I therefore would add that, "government shall never issue any money unless it is fully backed by gold and silver, and be redeemable at any time on demand". No prohibitions on private money. Any vehicle of trade desired by anyone shall be legal.

I don't think the Constitution's writers ever intended for the federal government to own billions of acres, which of course, are hideously mismanaged. I also do not, in my wildest imaginings, think our forefathers ever intended government to build and operate canals, dams, power plants, and thousands of other businesses and enterprises in competition with private industry. I therefore would add that, "The federal government shall own no land except national parks, and land on which government buildings are located. The federal government shall pay normal taxes to city, town, county and state governments, at normal rates, for any land it owns. All currently owned federal lands, businesses, utilities, transport systems, airports, highways, and forests shall be sold to the highest bidder with money realized being used to pay off the national debt. Government shall never again incur any debt at any time. States, as well as individuals and corporations, may bid for federal properties, but only American corporations and citizens. No non citizen, or non American corporation shall own American real property."

When the income tax amendment was passed, Congress never intended it to get out of hand as it has, and further, if it had been carefully considered, a tax would have been levied on spending, not income, which is totally regressive. (See chapter on taxes). I would repeal the income tax amendment and disband the IRS.

Our founding fathers wrote the Constitution as a LIMIT

on government, not a LICENSE for government to expand
endlessly, regulate everything, harass everyone, and tax us to
death. I would limit government by stating that, "Congress
shall pass no law involving government in labor relations,
negotiations, or in any way use force to coerce either labor or
management. It shall not encourage nor discourage labor
unions, boycotts, or any trade practice that is voluntary.
Congress shall pass no law to protect anyone from his or her
own folly. Congress shall pass no law redistributing the
wealth of its citizenry, nor give any subsidy to any individual,
group, corporation, business, race, religion, or organization."

Lots of phrases could be added, but the point is that
Congress has gone totally amok and needs to be reined in
pronto, before we have to declare national bankruptcy. How
about, "The basic duty of government shall be to protect its
citizens from their enemies, and to that extent shall maintain
only a Supreme Court to hear appeals from State courts. There
shall be no federal court or police system. No branch of the
military shall be sent out of the country without a 75%
approval of each House of Congress". Even the federal court
system has become a huge pork barrel, which is needless. The
States can conduct their own justice and punishment systems
for crimes in their own State

"Government shall not interfere with any other country's
affairs, but remain strictly neutral. Congress shall pass no law
regulating prices, agriculture, labor, management, education,
transportation, communication, the arts, industry, health care,
land use, or air quality, and shall not subsidize anything, at any
time, for any reason, under any conditions." In other words get
off our backs.

The Constitution never said how long the Congress should
be in session, nor how much it should be paid. Only when it
was to meet. This has also gotten totally out of control, so I
might add this: "Congress shall receive no pay, other than

expenses, when it is in session, which shall be only 2 months a year. It shall make no law in conflict with this Constitution. The President shall have no salary, but be provided the White House as a place to live, as well as various expenses for food, travel, communications, staff, and correspondence." If only rich men could afford to be a Senator, so what? If they had brains enough to get rich, and couldn't vote themselves or their constituency any largess from the public treasury, the post would be largely honorary.

If we were neutral, and the federal government was again limited to what the founders intended, there would be little for Congress to do!

And so on. The point being that about 90% of federal government is superfluous, damned expensive, crooked, and we need to make Washington, D.C. a ghost town. The more government we have, the weaker our citizenry becomes, due to being unable to care for themselves. The more government we have, the poorer, and less competitive we become. In order to recover our position as the leader of the world, and the example for the world, we need to disband 90% of our federal government. The original intent of the Constitution's framers, and founders of this once mighty land, was for the individual states to form a confederation, and compete with each other.

Freedom and competition are the most wonderful original thoughts man has ever conceived. Our Constitution intended that freedom and competition were to be our national principles; not welfare, subsidy, wealth redistribution, endless controls, mighty bureaucracy, and trampled citizens. A rewrite indeed does need to happen along these lines. The above thoughts are not so much radical as they are getting back to the original idea of America.

FLAG BURNING

It's all the rage now! Burn baby burn! The highest court in the land has said it's O.K.

I beg to disagree honorable Justices.

The Court's opinion is that burning an American flag is simply a way of "expressing ones self", and therefore comes under the purview of the first amendment, guaranteeing free speech. At the same time, even the Supreme Court would probably rule that shouting "FIRE!", in a crowded theatre, is not free speech, but a crime.

I'm all for freedom of speech. But how does burning a flag have anything to do with speech? Lighting a match, and incinerating an American Flag requires no speech at all. The highest court in the land has been legislating far too much. Its job isn't to decide what is good or bad, depending on the political persuasion of the individual Justices. The Supreme Court is to decide what is Constitutional, and not Constitutional...all very simple. Their personal opinions have absolutely nothing to do with it. How far they have gotten from their assignments!

If the Congress wants to pass a law forbidding the burning of American flags, that is a Constitutional act. It has nothing whatsoever to do with freedom of speech, press, religion, or freedom of any kind, as covered in the Bill of Rights. No one being legally denied the right to burn the highest symbol of this land, is being denied the right to free speech. He is being denied an ACT that happens to be offensive to most. Laws prohibit public defecation, nudity, intercourse, incest, and even adultery in some places. Laws prohibit speeding, driving on the wrong side of the road, burglary, theft, fraud, and making a nuisance of ones self by playing a radio too loudly. These actions are prohibited by law, and the Supreme Court has never denied the legislature the right to enact, and enforce such laws or prohibitions.

Burning a flag is an ACT, not a speech, and has nothing whatsoever to do with any amendment, much less the first. Maybe their honors should reconsider the issue. Unless an act can be considered speech in their often befuddled minds.

If it is O.K. to burn flags, is it also O.K. for the Ku Klux Klan to burn crosses? Please rule on this, your honors.

MALE SUPERIORITY

Males are NOT the superior sex. We are stronger, and our bodies are physically more adept at athletics. We are more logical than females, and as a result, often make better C.E.O.'s, and scientists. We are more innovative and even capable of more original thought perhaps, but what a nuisance we are to society! Other than brute strength and logic, is there any other thing that makes a male superior to a female? Not on your life! Who commits 90% of crime? Which is the violent sex? Isn't it males that get into the fist fights, and usually are the robbers, burglars, and blackmailers? Who beats their wives and kids? Which sex is usually the graffiti "artist"? Who robs the banks and is impatient and uncompromising? Males 90% of the time.

Men and boys are the chronically insecure fools who do all sorts of "macho" things to make themselves feel adequate. Males do most of the insane driving, especially in their teens. Rarely do you see a girl driving like a maniac, endangering everyone's life on the highway. Ever see a woman try to outrun a cop or speeding train? Drunken brawls, and preposterous motorcycle riding? Usually males.

Sexual hang ups, requiring the services of prostitutes with chains, coffins and other bric a brac? Males. Braggarts, inhabitants of penitentiaries? Males. Look at the most wanted flyers at any post office. Males, 100 to 1. Which kids give teachers the most grief and are chronic truants? Males. Crooked politicians, muggers, insane egomaniacs, the likes of Hitler and Stalin? Males. Mafia thugs, and murderers? You know the answer!

It's only my opinion, and I am certain my fellow men will disagree, but the facts leave little room for argument.

LITTLE PHILISTINES COME FROM.....

Time: 3:45 P.M.

Place: Supermarket parking lot

Happening: A couple, perhaps in their late twenties, emerges from the supermarket. They are dragging their (approximately) 4 year old daughter. The woman has straight, long, dirty blonde hair, is dressed in dingy dungarees and a tank top with no bra. A cigarette hangs out of the corner of her mouth. The man has shoulder length, greasy hair, a pock marked complexion, beard, and is dirty. He wears dirty jeans that look as if they could stand by themselves. The child is dirty, but with an angelic little face, and long blonde hair. They head towards a small, rusty, dent covered, faded blue, Japanese car, that has a cracked windshield, and hanging tailpipe. As they walk along, the adults take turns screaming obscenities at the little child. Even though I despise this type of language, I am going to give you an almost exact quote. "You little s--- a--, you've had enough f------ candy, and if you don't shut your g-- d----- mouth, I'm gonna kick you in the a-- right here. I'm sick of you, you little b----, now get the f--- in the g--d----- car before I smack you silly. Etc, etc, etc."

The title of this chapter is obvious in its meaning. Little Philistines do come from big Philistines. The Philistines are Biblical characters. They were a bad race of people, whom God decided to punish for being such utter sinners.

Can't you see this little girl ten years from now? By then

her parents will have either divorced, murdered each other, be in jail, have abandoned the child, or in some other way continued their abuse.

Ten years from now, if she is still alive and in school, she will almost certainly be the sleaze of the class. She will smoke, do drugs, drink heavily, and in her desperate search for love and acceptance will have lost her virginity at a very early age. She will be the thorn in the side of her school and community. She will have failing grades, probably never finish school, be insolent, trashy, a liar, and a thief. She may well be a one woman VD epidemic, be unstable, and will most likely give birth to an illegitimate child in her early teens, and begin yet another generation of Philistines, all of whom, of course, will be eating at the welfare trough.

Children mimic their parents' behavior, and grow up like them with the same tastes, even for foods. Children copy language, accents, personal habits, and even posture, unconsciously, and this copying is permanent. My parents were honest, hard working people. I also am honest and hard working. My dad was a nut on punctuality, and I am also. My parents stressed cleanliness and order. I bathe daily and like my house and personal items to be kept in a neat, clean, orderly fashion. I was raised to use good grammar, read books, listen to good music, think, be considerate, and a host of other traits, which are part of my life. My basic values are almost exactly the same as those of my late parents, both good and bad. Heredity is a very important thing, but as far as personal habits and values are concerned, it's environment 100%.

I would like to take that scum in the parking lot and dump them and their car in the river that runs behind that supermarket, take the little girl, and allow her to be adopted by a loving, childless, couple who would give her a good start in life. My heart went out to that little girl, whose chances for a successful career, marriage, or life-style are practically zero. I wish her luck.

The most important thing to realize is that these people continue to exist because they are supported by the welfare system. Head Start and all the other gobbledygook welfare nonsense that our taxes support, is nothing but a waste. By the time Head Start gets them it's too late. The only solution, which is Hitler like, illegal, outrageous, and impossible, is to annihilate those parents, and others like them, take the children and place them in decent homes, and forget it. Sterilize them! Our kindness and benevolence has been misplaced for far too long. Robbing from the rich and giving it to the poor is a terrible idea.

That scene at the supermarket parking lot made my blood boil. As I sit here 15 minutes later writing about it, I realize that the same thing goes on all around the world. In line at the post office in front of me yesterday was a guy with no shirt on and it is the middle of December. Why no shirt? Because he wanted to show off a large tattoo on his back of a snarling tiger with blood dripping from its teeth. Was he proud! He needed to be shot for having such a lousy set of values, but then he was probably raised by parents very similar to those in the parking lot. Yuk!

WHO IS FOR US?

A hundred years ago in India, the Thugs waylaid travelers with impunity, killing thousands of India's teachers, businessmen, intellectuals, and intelligentsia. This went on for so long, and was so successful, that India actually lost most of its people who were capable of governing, operating a business, and leading. Today, India is practically bereft of a class of people who could lead India out of the morass it lies in, even after billions of dollars in aid, dividing the nation in half, and every possible help others can provide. The utter ignorance and hopelessness of India defies description, and any chance it has of ever rising out of this dismal swamp seems doomed because of the almost total lack of a class of intelligent, educated citizens who have even a slight sense of responsibility, justice, or motivation. Naturally, there are brilliant Indians, but not nearly enough.

The same exact thing has been going on in the Soviet Union since 1914, and even with Gorbachev's marvelous actions that have helped the Soviets so much since 1985, the hope of their ever rising is dim. It is the Thugs all over again, only going under a different name. The Soviet rulers have murdered tens of millions of the most able, educated, intelligent citizens since 1914, and although it seems to have stopped, an entire class has been virtually eradicated, perhaps never to rise again.

Communists everywhere have done the same thing. If you have a mind, I.Q., education, or ability, look out under communist rule. The carnage committed under the red flag is simply one of the worst crimes in the entire history of the world. Without a class of motivated, thinking, acting, education thirsty people in a nation, that nation will have big problems.

So I ask, who is on "our side"? By "our", I mean who is on the side of the class that makes America prosper? Obviously the employees, stockholders and proprietors of the businesses are on our side. So are the clerks of the local store, the owner of the hardware store down the street, the producers of film, builders of homes, bankers, bakers, auto makers, and any class that works at, or owns a business is on "our side". Who are against us?

I firmly believe the teachers, who continually denigrate the business community, are against America's prosperity. These are the ones responsible for the shabby 1% approval rating the businessman enjoys. But far more numerous of those who are against us is the bureaucracy. The communists and Thugs murdered and slaughtered the entrepreneurs and business class, because that was the only way they could compete. When you are a mental midget, you have but one redeeming asset usually, and that is rank, physical strength, or a gun. It is common for a not too intelligent person to just love to fight and bully his way into first place. In order for his brutality to work, he must destroy the intellect that can compete with him on a much higher level. With intellect out of the way, a bully can rule. History shows communists murdering anyone who was superior to them, which happened to be the ones that could make a nation work successfully.

Now that communism has failed, and left no business entrepreneur class to restore prosperity, it is practically hopeless. Communist factory workers are totally incapable of realizing anything about profit, cost control, efficiency, quality, or merchandising. So the slave nations need help. Who in America cannot compete, and must harm their competition in order to appear successful? Who in America, as a very good generality, cannot succeed in the business sector, and is incapable of innovation or entrepreneurship? Who in America cannot understand quality, profit, cost control, or the sector that made America great? Which class in America does every single thing possible to make profit, success, and entrepreneurship difficult? In short, who are against us?

It just has to be the bureaucracy at all levels. Where do inept people go to work? Government! Where to stupid people go to work as a last resort, usually after failing in the real world? Government. Who virtually cannot be fired regardless of ineptitude? Government employees at all levels. I have never known a bureaucrat, at any level, who wasn't against the businessman, no matter how friendly they may seem to be. They are our enemies. It is bureaucracy, at all levels, that has caused America to degrade continually since the 1930's. Right now, I can think of dozens of inept, paper shuffling, pompous, bureaucrats that have done all in their power to thwart me in a business endeavor, that would have provided jobs and prosperity. From Philadelphia, to Phoenix, to Colorado, they are all the same.

Since they cannot compete in a mental way, they seek to destroy and hinder, not with fists or guns, but with their entangling bureaucracy, which has millions of rules and forms to be filled out, as well as many dollars to be paid in fees, inspections, and stupidity. Think of any bureaucrat, and I will show you a person, if they had any ability at all, could make far more in the private sector.

Could a building inspector make more as a builder or employee of a builder, if he was worth his salt?

Could any bureaucrat, at any level, doing any thing, make far more in the private sector if they were truly able, intelligent, or energetic? Yes!

So it cannot be unfair for productive people to hate the

bureaucracy, can it? It is so obvious the bureaucracy competes
with the creative sector in the only way it can; by throwing
every single obstacle in the way of anyone who wants to do
something productive. The producer looks bad, and they look
good. Their method of competing and winning is to draw up
complicated, inane rules and laws that are virtually impossible
to obey, and still make a project work successfully. Their
excuse for this action is to "protect the citizen", which is pure
hog wash. It isn't murder and brutality as the communists and
Thugs practiced, but something far more insipid. It is millions
of laws, rules, and requirements, that drive productive people
insane.

On a lesser scale, it is the teachers who haven't the foggiest
idea of what made America great, and who fill student minds
with untruths that make them scorn the productive sector. But
there is a third class also, and those are the people who make
all the impossible rules, and create a hostile environment to the
entrepreneur. This is the legislative class at all levels. The
board of trustees in the smallest town can make business and
success virtually impossible, thereby harming the town. A big
city has its politicians who are invariably inferior people as are
their small town counterparts. These politicians stop at nothing
to make the maze of rules and laws impossible for an entrepreneur to wade through, without bribes to pave the way.

At the federal and state level, legislators never tire of
levying new taxes, new rules, and new laws, that effectively
slow or stop what America does best, and what made America
great. That is business and entrepreneurship. Congress never
tires of hamstringing the productive sector. In Colorado,
where I live, believe it or not, business property is taxed at
twice the rate as other property, surely one of the few states
that has gone this far. Have you ever known of a legislator at
any level that is a truly superior person? There are a few, but
extremely few, and these probably have retired from a suc-

cessful profession and will vote against the nonsense promulgated by most legislators.

This entire chapter is a generalization, but a pretty accurate one. There are bureaucrats who may hate their jobs, but for various reasons can't, or won't quit. There are legislators who are not wealthy, and who vote the right way, but not many. Will Rogers once observed that the country is never in such danger as when Congress is in session!

In a small town in Colorado where, as I write this, I own a couple of businesses, the foregoing holds true 100%. The town council is full of the inept or failures. They do everything possible to stop anyone with any brains or a desire to do something worth while for the town. It is their way of fighting intellect with the one thing they have on their side, and that is law, rules, harassment, and bureaucracy.

I have operated businesses in Maryland, D.C., Pennsylvania, California, Arizona, and of course, Colorado. It is always the same. Those who are against us are the bureaucracy, the legislators, and the uninformed teachers who poison the minds of our youth, the results of which we will see for hundreds of years, just like the ex-communist nations will, and as India still does. If America is the light of the world, as we have been called more than once, far too many Americans are trying to snuff out that light. How tragic if the world were plunged into total darkness as it was a few hundred years ago in the "dark ages". Then, it was religion that turned out the lights. Now it is government.

MANUFACTURING

About 15 years ago, a specious theory surfaced from the bubbleheads in Washington, and it goes like this: "It's O.K. if America ceases to be a manufacturing country, as we can clean up our air, get rid of those filthy factories, mills, and mines, have a service economy and do just as well". This is unmitigated B.S.!

America's genius, history, and wealth, were based on manufacturing. America out produced every nation on earth, invented the production line, and got rich and happy with its factories, inventions, and entrepreneurship. We invented the telephone, electricity, phonograph, computer, light bulb, radio, television, airplane, tractor, and the list can include thousands of patents and revolutionary products that made us prosperous beyond our ancestors' wildest dreams. Inventing, producing, manufacturing, and then selling it, is our own niche in history, and anyone who wants to say it's O.K. to drop the whole thing, is dead wrong!

So called "service industries", won't lead us to prosperity. Information handling, paper shuffling, and commodities trading, is not what made us the most civilized, richest nation on earth. We sit on massive amounts of iron, copper, coal, gas, aluminum, and are the most inventive people on earth. Saying it is O.K. to shut the mines down, shut down the factories, stop making things, and be submissive to the Japs, or other nations, who gladly take over our leadership and loan us money so we are indebted to them for the rest of our lives, is not my idea of America, the Beautiful. As an aside, that song was written in the early 1800's after a visit to my cherished State of Colorado.

For close to 200 years, America made things, enjoyed good salaries, high standards of living, and security. Today it is not supposed to be "chic" to get your hands dirty, pour steel, run a lathe, or make something. Those talented, expert woodworkers, machinists, and makers of things are getting old now, and their kids haven't been taught to take the old man's place on the line. Now everyone thinks labor is old hat. Well it isn't old hat, and America had better get its priorities in line pretty quickly before we are trampled to death by foreign nations who still manufacture things.

Here we are, sitting on massive amounts of raw materials, with the ability to invent, manufacture, develop, and innovate, and our professors, teachers, and advisors say we don't need to manufacture things any more. And America has taken them at their word! We have been befuddled by our political and academic fuzz brains, who have poisoned the minds of our youth with the myth that a successful nation doesn't need to be a manufacturing nation.

Shuffling papers, suing people, leveraged buyouts, futures trading, and various other types of hocus pocus didn't make us the most prosperous nation on earth, with the highest standard of living. Those records are no longer ours. America needs to begin all over again being a productive nation, not a passive one. We need to once again make things the world will buy, not buy from the world the things they make. It is all so absurd, I cannot understand why this isn't shouted from every newspaper in the land, instead of this little guy having to say it.

There are two bridges I must bring to mind. Both are in Eastern, formerly industrial cities, and both are virtually useless now, because it isn't considered fashionable to make things any longer. These bridges have huge illuminated signs on them. One says, "TRENTON MAKES, THE WORLD

TAKES". The other says "WHAT CHESTER MAKES, MAKES CHESTER". One is in New Jersey, and the other is in Pennsylvania. They might as well take the signs down, as neither is true any longer. How pathetic.

AIDS

We have passed the tenth anniversary of the first known case of AIDS in America. AIDS has devastated the homosexual community and is doing much the same with the drug shooters. There have been a tiny number of disease acquisitions due to

poor blood testing. In Africa and other "third world" countries, AIDS is killing them off right and left. It is a disease that
is totally preventable, and so far incurable. It is spread when
bloods and possibly other body fluids of an infected and a non
infected person are mixed. Mixed as when a drug shooter uses
a dirty needle, or a male homosexual screws his "lover" in the
rectum, breaking blood vessels. This is how the queers have
spread it among themselves. Female homosexuals haven't
anything to insert in each others' private parts, so they haven't
gotten the disease. In Africa, it is the norm for males to have
as many women as is humanly possible, so they are spreading
it among themselves like the plague. In more civilized soci-
eties, heterosexual contact does not seem to spread the virus.

There is no known cure. No one seems to know how it
began. I saw one pamphlet that swears it was a C.I.A. ex-
periment gone awry in New Jersey that started it.

Maybe it is nature's way of eliminating a bad sector of its
population, ever think of that? Whether it is nature's way or a
natural phenomenon, I say fine!

Fine, because it is totally avoidable. Only the careless get
it. Cruel or practical? Inhuman? I think not. If you don't want
to get AIDS, practice safe sex, it's that simple. Or else don't
shoot up with dirty needles.

Cancer, other than perhaps lung cancer, strikes people
regardless of their personal habits. Heart disease may possibly
be prevented by exercise or avoiding stress. But like cancer,
no one seems to be immune. There are a thousand times as
many cases of cancer and heart disease as there are AIDS
cases, but it is AIDS that dominates the airwaves and print
media. Nuts! Who the hell cares if all the junkies and queers
die? Who has sympathy for an effeminate male dying of
AIDS? Just the thought of how he got it is enough to make you
retch!. There are homosexual bars and baths by the thousands
in the world where males meet to "do" each other in totally

dark rooms over and over and over. A more disgusting thought I cannot imagine. Yet the weepy, bleeding heart media moan and groan over the lack of a cure for AIDS. The cure is not to engage in the practices that spread it.

In early November of 1991, the world famous basketball star, "Magic" Johnson announced that he had contracted the HIV virus that usually leads to AIDS. He retired from basketball and decided to spend his time being an advocate of "safe sex". The media went wild and Johnson was proclaimed the savior of the world for all practical purposes. Once again, I say NUTS! Johnson has never said how he got it, except that it was from a woman, as he had been extremely active, sexually. He could have had anal intercourse with an infected prostitute, or any number of ways that have nothing whatsoever to do with a normal life style practiced by decent people.

According to health department records, not a single case of AIDS was transmitted between heterosexuals in New York City between the years 1987 and 1990. Can you imagine the amount of sex that occurred in New York City during those three years? Statistics show 90% of AIDS transmissions are between male homosexuals or intravenous drug shooters and others. The remaining 10% could easily be by means of other absurd, animalistic practices never even thought of by a normal person, or downright lying by the remaining 10%. It is interesting to note that Johnson's wife has tested free of the virus. They must have had a lot of sex but she has never contracted it. At Thanksgiving 1991, "Magic's" wife announced her pregnancy. "Magic" Johnson is no hero. He just got caught doing what he shouldn't have been doing, and had plenty of warnings not to do it. How this makes him worthy of adulation I cannot understand.

At the rate it is going now, the world may be pretty well cleaned up in another 50 years because of AIDS.

The tragedy of the innocents getting it through blood

transfusions is undeniable, but tens of thousands of innocents are killed each year by drunk drivers. Innocents are killed by falling down stairs, getting hit by lightening, drowning, suffocation, murder, and mugging, but they aren't the main focus of the professional hand wringers, nor are they turned into instant heroes. I have sympathy for the innocents in any situation, but sympathy for dying faggots, druggies, and the careless who know better? Not me.

LET THE CHIPS FALL WHERE THEY MAY!

I KNOW it sounds heartless, cold, and even uncivilized to most readers, but facts must be faced. According to organizations in the know, the population of Africa is growing at such a rate that by the year 2000, it will surpass the ability of the land to feed them, even if the entire continent had a temperate climate. The populations of most, if not all third world countries, are growing astronomically. No one seems to be concerned about bearing untold numbers of babies because the "government" will always care for them. Or so they think. Government, in any situation, can only provide what it confiscates from those who are "haves", giving it to the "have nots", who are incapable, or not desirous of producing anything.

In America, when cold weather sets in, record numbers of "street people" are rounded up by police when temperatures go below 32 degrees, taken to shelters, fed, and bedded down for the night, at taxpayer expense. New York City, on a typical freezing night, may care for over 10,000 vagrants. Numerous hotels have become "welfare hotels", and are full to the brim with welfare cases, taxpayers paying over a thousand dollars a month for some rooms for these useless tramps. In the Dec 20, 1985, New York Times was the story of a blind, deaf infant who was found on a doorstep in Manhattan, and who died soon afterward. The weeping and gnashing of teeth in the Times was something to witness! I say "so what?".

Eventually we will have to realize that those who will not feed and care for themselves will have to fade from view, either from freezing, starvation, disease or other natural cause of death. The taxes able to be collected by governments at various levels, and used to care for useless people, have finite limits. There can never be enough money to care for all of the so called "needy". The more they are cared for, the more there will be. The needy are like cars and freeways. The more freeways built, the more cars people will buy, thereby maintaining the same level of crowded roads. The more needy you care for, their number will increase at the same rate.

There is no limit to the number of poor, homeless, and sick. According to Donald Mann, president of Negative Population Growth, Africa's population will be over a billion by the year 2000. These Negro Africans have a reproduction rate twice or even quadruple the rate of middle or upper classes in any other country on earth, regardless of race. Middle and upper class people everywhere are concerned about the future of themselves, their families, their cities, and their nation, rather than the instant gratification of lower and poverty classes. Concern for the future, and responsibility for actions committed, rarely cross the minds of lower and poverty classes. They do what feels good at any given minute, which means a lot of copulation, and an endless stream of children who never contribute to society, merely drag it down, with no end in sight.

The bleeding heart, built in guilt complex, liberals will moan and groan at the poor and homeless till the cows come home, sending their money to Ethiopia, and teaching their kids to act the same. But they practice "ZPG", (zero population growth), unlike the objects of their concern, wherever they may be. They give awards to each other for showing the most concern about the poor, but send their kids to private schools, and live in nice neighborhoods. I don't like to pour good soup down the drain, and would never think of pouring money down a sewer, but the comparison is the same. I NEVER give anything to a beggar, but will always hire a kid to shovel my walk, cut my grass or do something for pay. Never will I ever give anything to someone for nothing. It has to be payment for work done.

In short, we have to stop trying to short circuit nature. We must stop the endless wealth confiscation of the doers, merrily doling it out to the bums, lazy, sick, starving, or unfortunate. By supporting and preserving worthless, non contributing people, it is exactly like pouring money down a sewer.

Visit a nursing home and look at the empty faced shells who can't feed themselves, don't know where they are, who they are, or what is going on around them. Look at the nurses changing diapers, and wheeling them around, and think of the billions of tax dollars being spent each year to keep these vegetables technically "alive". Think of the billions spent each year on the thousands of vagrants, euphemistically called "homeless" by the media, and for what? Another day's life? Another week's panhandling? Another month's crime? When I see them, I feel disgust, not pity.

Nature's way is for weak, old, and incapacitated things to die or be eaten. It is nature's way to preserve a species and strengthen it as well. Maybe it was nature's way to have a drought in Ethiopia in the mid 80's, causing millions to die. It was far too overcrowded, and the endless copulating and child production was absurd. Starving people squatting under a shade tree and giving birth to more starving, useless human-oids. Maybe nature realized things were getting a bit lopsided, and she gave us AIDS, and cocaine, to let the weaklings kill themselves. Let the stupid, weak, and useless perish from the earth, and good riddance! Maybe it is nature's way of preserving itself to have typhoons sweep down on India or Bangladesh every decade or so, wiping out a million here, or a hundred thousand there.

Am I being unnecessarily hard? No, but I am a logical person who despises weak sob sisters, and professional liberals who would take from me, a worker, and producer, and give to those who don't. You bet I am hard about that one! It will never stop unless every person is forced to take responsibility for their own actions and situations, or can get someone else to do it other than government, which has no money without stealing it from the productive sector. We now live on loans and printing press money, and this can't go on forever without the entire thing crashing like a sand castle when a wave washes it away.

Is my attitude "uncivilized", as I mentioned in the beginning of this? Absolutely not. A dictionary definition of civilization speaks, in all of its definitions, of a high plain of achievement, culture, and societal living, and not once even hints at giving or having ones wealth stolen to feed or care for anyone else. If anything, this mushy claptrap called welfare and feeding the poor starving Africans or vagrants, is a very uncivilized thing to do. It takes valuable assets that could raise the level of life and brings it down to the level of the lowest of creatures.

Ancient Rome was ruined by this same nonsense. It finally got so bad in Rome that the welfare recipients and bureaucrats numbered more than the workers, and the taxpayers revolted. Rome tried to keep the bums amused with circuses, hoping something would save them. Among the amusements provided, were Christians being thrown into the arena with lions. It finally fell, and Nero did indeed fiddle while Rome burned. Torched by welfare recipients who had nothing better to do! Can we escape this morbid end? Probably not, but we will see.

60 YEARS

The old song titled, "What A Difference A Day Makes", is cute, but 60 years seems to make no difference at all. Look at 1931's headlines.

"JAILS OVERFLOWING". MOBS REAPING HUGE PROFITS". INNOCENT BABIES BORN ADDICTED". "STREET CORNER SALES". "FEDS MAKE HUGE BUST". "FAMILIES RUINED". Etc, etc.

The same headlines could be read in today's papers. Change the words, "demon rum", "hootch", or "bootlegger", to "crack", "cocaine", and "dealer", and the scenario is identical, with only the dates changed. One difference is that there are no Carrie Nations around axing drug seller's cars, there isn't a WCTU for drugs, and the fanatics haven't gotten us to pass a Constitutional amendment. Other than that, it's business as usual. The drug crazies are just as adamant about the horrors of drugs as were the prohibitionists. The alcohol fanatics had their horror stories about ruined men, broken families, hideous addictions, and other exaggerations just as do the drug prohibitionists of today. I have a drink most every day, but have never been drunk, and at my age, I suspect I never will. I am not addicted, can easily take it or leave it, and think that the prohibitionists were absolute nuts. The modern drug prohibitionists probably are too.

Drug "Czar" William Bennett became a raving maniac as he was instructed to do when he was appointed. Poor people are the ones being sucked into deeper poverty because they haven't the will power to say no, while the middle and upper classes take their drugs and keep the profits up for the dealers and cartel. Nothing any different from prohibition days except that the drug "speakeasy" hasn't been invented yet. The rum runners are no different from the drug dealers. It is a repeat of history without a Constitutional amendment. The lunatic fringe is having a field day now, just like it did during prohibition. Instant addiction and other horror stories are usually proven untrue eventually.

Prohibition got us alcohol addicts, and now we have drug addicts, both lured by the thrill of doing something illegal. "Stolen water is sweetest", is the old saying. After the current drug craze has left us, we still have the remaining alcohol weaklings, plus the drug weaklings to cope with, but at least the jails won't be full and it will be safe to walk the streets again. The drug fanaticism will pass, just as communism has, which may be another comparison. America set out on a "fighting communism" binge that cost hundreds of billions. Communism failed of its own inanity, economic impossibility, and sheer absurdity.

THE MAFIA

Wow! What a frightening subject. Just think about those nasty, Italian Mafioso gunning down people in cold blood, extracting money from the innocents, and who are rich beyond tally. Remember those movies such as "The Godfather", where the Mafia brothers allot each other territories to threaten and collect protection money from innocent businessmen? Horrible thing, the Mafia! Here are a few facts for you to think about.

First of all, there was no Mafia in America until we had prohibition. Prohibition was merely denying people the legal right to do what they wanted to do and were accustomed to doing, namely consuming alcoholic beverages. America had been drinking since its founding, and even in Biblical times, the Apostle Paul said that, "A little wine for the stomach's sake", was a nice thing. Alcohol was extremely common in the Bible, and throughout history people have drunk alcoholic beverages of various types. Prohibition did several things besides give birth to the underworld.

First of all, prohibition killed the temperance movement.

Second, prohibition made Canada very rich. Before prohibition, there were no major Canadian whiskey brands sold in America. Billions still goes to Canada rather than staying in America, thanks to prohibition.

Third, it made the Kennedys rich, which is REALLY unfortunate. Old Joe Kennedy was bad enough, but his kids aren't any better. Old Joe Kennedy had a long time affair with Gloria Swanson, and his kids have been absolutely disgusting in their behavior, practically since they were old enough to leave home. I simply cannot understand why voters think the Kennedys are so wonderful. White trash is the best description I can think of as I write this. I would be delighted to write extensively about the Kennedys, but this book is about far more important things.

Fourth, prohibition made what had been commonplace and legal, ILLEGAL, and the natural thing happened. People drank far more, it became a fun thing to visit "speakeasys", and alcoholic consumption increased by huge percentages. The alcoholics that prohibition spawned are still with us, as well as their offspring who inherited the trend. But getting back to the Mafia.

Prohibition gave us the underworld, or Mafia. Since drinking was illegal, the underworld came in from Sicily and took advantage of a wonderful opportunity. It supplied what Americans wanted, made billions off of it, and it has been with us ever since. Whether "La Cosa Nostra" exists is open to question, but the Mafia certainly does! The Mafia continues to exist, because it supplies what people want. Be it prostitutes, gambling, or drugs, they have it for sale. The so called "black market" is in reality the "free market", because it supplies things people want at a price they are willing to pay. Prices are so high because this black market merchandise has huge risks due to its illegality. The Mafia has invested its profits for so many years in legitimate businesses, it is possible they are a permanent part of our society. But if you really want them to fade away, the method of doing it is not difficult to understand.

It involves taking the profits away, that's all. Take profits away from any business and it will disappear pretty quickly. What does the Mafia, or underworld, make huge profits from today? Whatever is illegal, that's what. Now look at what is illegal today, but which people want to buy, and you will find the underworld, be it the Mafia or other opportunists. First of all, we have drugs, which I know nothing about, have never tried, and don't even know what they look like other than TV pictures. People seem to want drugs that are illegal, and all the laws in the world won't stop it. So the underworld furnishes them at huge profits.

The underworld also profits handsomely on prostitution. It is illegal everywhere, although it isn't illegal for a man to seduce a woman with drinks, entertainment, meals, and good times. He's paying for sex, but that isn't illegal. Many men don't want the hassle, and just want sex quickly and with no nonsense, so they want a prostitute. That also goes back to Biblical times, and is called the "world's oldest profession". Since it is illegal, the underworld takes over, and profits from it.

The underworld also makes lucrative profits on gambling. Maybe not as much as they used to, but still a lot of money. Most states have "official" lotteries, which are a first rate rip off. Think about it. Your chances of winning the lottery are less than of being hit by lightening. If you win, you don't get the money. You get it over 20 years, with no interest. For each "million" you win, it is really about a fifteenth that, since your payoff is over 20 years with no interest. If you are old, when you die, that's it. Your heirs won't get a dime. Typical government fraud. It works so well because the various state lotteries do heavy, colorful, untrue advertising, and no one can seem to stop it. The ads make me ill. Anyone who wastes a single dollar on a lottery is nuts. The underworld, for many years, has been writing "numbers" and selling other types of gambling games, and they pay far more, percentage wise, than does the government gambling. It is also paid instantly, not over 20 years. So the underworld still makes a few billion a year off of gambling. They would make a lot more if they were allowed to advertise their better payoffs, but of course the states can do legally what others can't.

As an aside, in November of 1991, a few old men and women were members of a Jewish social club which served a lovely lunch every day, had pool tables, TV sets, and was a nice place to spend a retiree's time. Few were under the age of 65. The Denver cops raided the place because a few of the members were playing poker. The police took all the money on the tables, and even emptied everyone's wallets! Over $13,000 was seized during the raid. Outrageous? You bet! Here were a few old gaffers having a nice time, on private property, behind closed doors, in a private club. They weren't safe because Colorado law says gambling is illegal! Except for the Colorado lottery, of course, which pays off in 20 years with no interest, and no leaving any remainder to your heirs. Technically, those ancient, innocent Jews were an "underworld".

If you want to get rid of the Mafia and the underworld, which incidentally increases their take every year, you must remove their source of profits, which happens to be anything "illegal", but which people want to buy. Very simple!

A flourishing underworld has blossomed in various kinds of drugs, imported illegally from Mexico and other places. Drugs that might cure cancer, or other deadly diseases, but which America's bureaucracy, the FDA has not approved. The FDA takes up to 10 years to approve of a drug, and many people can't last that long, and want to try anything that has a possibility of working. So they give huge profits to the drug underworld, or drive to Mexico to get their treatments. Treatments that may not work, or drugs that may not work, but a black market is created that siphons money by the thousands of buckets full out of America, bankrupts the sick people, but gives them a slim hope of a cure. Big profits for the drug runners, of course. Remember, "illegal" drugs, are not just cocaine and marijuana. Lots of illegal drugs are desired by people who wouldn't dream of getting high. They just want to live.

NEUTRALITY

"Only the dead have known the end of war"....Plato.

I beg to disagree, Plato. First of all, given the choice of your philosophy or Aristotle's, I'll take his anytime. Second of all, you forgot to include in your wise saying that neutral nations never need know even the beginnings of war.

Neutrality. That's a dirty word to our military establishment and sector of society that thinks we should be the policeman of the world. They get rich off of those "police actions", naturally. We would be far better off if we copied the Swiss who haven't had a war in hundreds of years, are rich, peaceful, and have one of the highest standards of living in the world.

Neutrality would have kept us out of Viet Nam, Korea, and even Kuwait, which turned out a lot less wonderfully than initially perceived. Why should we be the big arbitrator, peace keeper, conflict solver, and democracy spreader of the world? What gives us the right to tell anyone what to do? Maybe it is because we have a higher crime rate, consume more drugs, owe more money, burn more fuel than any other nation, and have a higher divorce rate than most other nations. Excellent credentials for forcing our way on everyone else, aren't they? We do humane things, like burying alive thousands of Iraqi troops in the late Mideast war.

There is no better way to spread the word of goodness than setting a good example. If democracy is wonderful, then democratic countries will be copied. If communism is the best way, then communist countries will set the example for all to willingly follow. Everyone follows a good lead. If America's example is worthy, others will follow. Our examples have been pretty pitiful of late.

If we were neutral, we would have but a fraction of the armed forces we now have, all soldiers would be on our shores, we would provide no foreign aid, give no advice, mind our own business, not be a member of the U.N., and undoubtedly prosper more than our wildest dreams could ever conceive.

What happened to the communism that we fought and preached so vehemently against for so many decades? It fell, but only because of its own idiocy, not anything we did. Are Viet Nam and Cambodia better off now that we messed around in them and killed 58,000 of our boys? Of course not. Was Korea, with similar statistics, better off when mighty America entered the brawl? Nope. Has any nation ever loved us for giving them foreign aid? Heavens no!

When my kids were growing up, my constant answer to the continual fights was "MYOB", which of course means mind your own business. If it is good enough for a family, it is good enough for a nation. Wealth doesn't give wisdom, neither does might make right. Our armed forces are scattered about the world by the tens of thousands, and we have bases here and bases there. All a big waste of money. The explanation offered is that we are "protecting ourselves", by maintaining military presence around the world, but in reality we are just making everyone angry. We are separated from our supposed "enemies" by two large oceans. Even if we were threatened by rockets, ours could be based on our soil and go up to meet the enemy's and destroy them.

If we were neutral, and not involving ourselves in other's business, the world wouldn't come apart any more than communism in Europe fell as a result of any efforts on our part. Things will go on without us if we keep the boys, guns, tanks, money, and planes right here in the U.S.A. Take us over? What is there to take if we are neutral? Our farms, which are individually owned? Our cities? What is there to take? If our central government was a tenth of its current size, and we were a peaceful nation, well armed individually, with defenses set up on both coasts, what could possibly happen to us from an enemy? Neutral nations don't seem to have enemies.

Of course, we could do charitable things by sending supplies to other nations if they had a natural catastrophe such as an earthquake, fire, flood, or pestilence. But to forcibly try to alter their political system? Not on you're life! The C.I.A. should be dismantled immediately. That nefarious organization has been responsible for much America caused mayhem around the world. Our State Department has been messing around in everyone's business far too long. Stay home, set a good example, and the world will follow. Try to force our will and everyone will stub up just like they always have. Will we never learn? Why would a politician be afraid to run on a neutrality platform?

WHO GIVES FREEDOM?

Far too many people think government GIVES freedom, rather than taking it from them, as is the case. People with red, white, and blue attitudes, rave about our freedoms, and thank government for them. This is totally wrong, and it is high time someone said so.

Government is a cancer, growing unchecked. Remember the "Thing" in the old horror movie, that kept growing and eating everything in its path? The comparison to government is unavoidable. Government bureaucrats have two main goals. 1) increase their power base by expanding the bureaucracy so they will rise as it expands, having the newcomers under them, and (2) make themselves appear to be necessary and indispensable.

A businessman increases his wealth and importance by increasing his efficiency, whereas a bureaucrat operates exactly the opposite. Bureaucracy expands itself at the expense of efficiency, resulting in less freedom, because as bureaucracy enlarges, government control over us grows.

Our system of government lets voters decide who will represent them. Originally, in order to be able to vote, you had to be able to read and write. Voting was intended to be a privilege, not a duty. It has become a devout belief that voting is some sort of sacred, patriotic deed that must be performed. Voting is not desirable if you are stupid, illiterate, or unread, contrary to the common thought of today. If the ignoramuses didn't vote, it would be a service to their country, because they always vote for the candidate promising the most from the public treasury, guaranteeing eventual bankruptcy, and the worst possible office holders. The ignorant will always elect the ignorant.

How is America helped by an ever larger proportion of voters being of the lower class? How is America aided by college kids invading the slums, getting people registered to vote? Their vote always cancels out an intelligent vote, which would be for a candidate against ever more government spending, and larger bureaucracy. When the poll tax was in effect, it meant that in order to vote, a voter generally had to pay a dollar or so to cover the cost of the election. A pittance that generally weeded out the non beneficial votes. The Supreme Court threw out the poll tax many years ago, unfortunately.

I would prefer no one vote unless he or she had a job, could read and write, and knew something about what they voting for or against on election day. The literacy test for voters was also thrown out by the Supreme Court years ago, although I could never comprehend that decision either. Freedom coasts downhill into a slave state ever so much faster, now that more and more voters with no ability to think, read, write, or reason are added each year to the voter lists. This is not patriotism, but self destruction, from which we probably will not recover.

Freedom is not given by government and the bureaucracy, but ravaged by them. If voters are self registered, they will have proven themselves to be good citizens. If it takes coercion for them to register and vote, they are not worthy of the privilege.

TAXES

Every one hates taxes! Every one hates the IRS. Through-out history, even in Biblical times, the tax collector has been despised. A certain amount of taxes are necessary, but some are so regressive that they actually sabotage our country, rather than support it. There are several, but the most insipid, without question, is the income tax. The income tax defeats several desirable things, such as savings, job creation, and investing.

Taxing what people spend rather than what they earn makes so much sense! The rich obviously spend more than the poor because they have more, and want to live more luxuri-ously. A tax on spending will automatically be a graduated tax with no bureaucracy.

A sales tax means that the money will be collected when money is spent. There would be no deductions, no annual returns, and no IRS for the public, only those in business, who collect the taxes. If taxes were collected only on spent money, people could save and earn interest with no penalty, helping the economy. Banks would then have more money to loan; another boost.

Another regressive tax is the corporate tax. Why tax corporations? They only add the taxes they pay to the cost of what they sell, so prices are higher. If the corporate tax were eliminated, prices would be lower, and people would buy more. Corporations don't pay taxes, consumers pay taxes. Not only that, but America's exports would increase tremendously, because prices would be lower. Our billion in trade deficits would shrink immediately.

The property tax is hideous. The very concept of the property tax means you never really own anything! If you don't pay a yearly tax on what you think you own, you don't have it any longer. You can't count on a debt free retirement, or have any real security to speak of. Once you buy something and pay for it, it should be yours without a yearly tax on it. Property, and personal property taxes apply to every business as well as home. As an example, railroads pay property tax on their rights of way, yards and stations. If there were no taxes on them, or for that matter on warehouses, truck stops, truck garages, boat slips, etc., the cost of everything would be much lower. Property taxes on hotels, motels, grocery stores, auto agencies, and other businesses obviously raise the cost of merchandise. Tax purchases, not property.

Inheritance taxes prohibit parents from leaving the results of their life's work to their children, which is grossly unfair.

Capital gains taxes remove incentives from businessmen and investors who provide the jobs and prosperity to America.

There are hundreds of "hidden" taxes that make an honest

analysis of the actual cost of any purchase impossible to make. The only logical way to tax is to tax WHAT YOU BUY.

Since most government is unnecessary anyway, a tax on purchases ONLY would bring that point home very quickly. Hiding thousands of taxes everywhere, like so many Easter eggs in the jungle, is the ultimate deception by government.

PASSING LEGISLATION

When any incumbent runs for re-election, (unfortunately!) they will usually brag about how much legislation they passed or helped pass. "I was responsible for 25 pieces of legislation", old Senator Blowhard will say in his campaign speeches. I say that is the very reason he SHOULD NOT be re-elected!

As if we don't have enough laws already! We have millions and millions of laws on the books; literally. We have so many laws, rules, regulations, and other claptrap hanging around our necks, that no one has the slightest idea how many there are, what they are or, how they apply, and why they are there. Why, in the name of common sense, is it a thing to brag about to say, "I was responsible for the passage of 37 pieces of legislation in the last session". Ted Kennedy's supporters love to boast about how much legislation he gets passed. Nuts! I say the man for the job is the man who took a thousand laws off the books, fired a thousand bureaucrats, saved a billion dollars, eliminated a cabinet post, and basically voted "NO", to most things put before him.

More laws? We already have several million too many. We are drowning in laws, edicts, regulations and bureaucracy. Next time some legislator brags about how much legislation he got passed, tell him you will pass on him.

RACE

Race problems are ripping America from one end to another. "Black-white" hatreds are increasing in intensity, as well as other racial rivalries. I say that race is of no importance whatsoever, other than racial hatreds as fanned by the Al Sharptons, Jesse Jacksons, and the Ku Klux Klan egged on by the yearly "civil rights" bill that always appears. Of what possible difference can it make if races choose to segregate themselves? Look at obvious comparisons.

In matters of romance, does government try to force certain people to fall in love and marry? Does government try to force you to buy one car over another? Does government try to force you to go to a certain place for a vacation? Does government try to force you to eat only "approved" types of foods? Does government try to force you into buying only one type of TV set, radio, carpet, refrigerator, or tire? So why does government try to integrate races that don't want to integrate? Why does government spend billions attempting to force people to intermingle, live near each other, and for that matter, like each other?

If you have ever raised kids, and I have, the surest way to brew rebellion is to try to force your child to like another child. Or to try to force your daughter to love that handsome boy from that wonderful family down the street that makes straight "A's" in school. The unquestionable way to guarantee it will never occur! The same thing happens to humans of all ages. The most magnificent way to popularize anything is to make it illegal, as witness prohibition and the incessant "drug war".

Tell someone they HAVE to do something, and the chances of them voluntarily doing it are next to zero.

Are races more peaceful now that so called "civil rights" laws are on the books? Of course not. As a matter of fact, race hatred is now reaching new heights. Why? Because it isn't race that is an issue, but force. No where in the Constitution does that sacred document give government the right to legislate social behavior, morality, taste, preference, or choice. So why try?

Hispanics have certain food, architectural, and music tastes. Negroes the same. Orientals prefer certain types of houses, foods, music and clothing. All races have certain characteristics common to them, be they Polish, German, Spanish, Indian, Italian, or what have you. America is one big melting pot, and from its earliest foundings, it has thrived on the differences between its populations, and not tried to force them into a common mold, neighborhood, or school. It is one of the most futile moves ever made by government, as well as one of the most costly. And all for nothing.

It is the upbringing and personal habits of people that makes them desirable, or undesirable, not their race. Would you rather live next to Bryant Gumbel or some poor white trash? Would you rather live next to a wonderfully clean, well educated, Mexican family, or Ma and Pa Kettle? Would you rather live in a neighborhood populated with people of your own economic and social strata, or in a neighborhood far beneath your standards.

In the August, 1946 (!) Reader's Digest, page 176, William Ellery Channing is quoted as saying, "The office of government is not to confer happiness, but to give men opportunity to work out happiness for themselves".

Why attempt to change the natural order of things, which results in harmony among peoples who voluntarily choose to live near each other and associate with each other as best suits their desires and pocketbooks? It is no one's business but theirs. Might as well attempt to force one type of bird to associate with another, or force animals that don't like each other to do so. Why not try to stop the existence of "Chinatowns", where Chinese live, congregate, and enjoy each other? How about an attempt to destroy Greenwich Village or other neighborhoods in various cities where certain people like to be. Do you know how many "Germantowns" there are in America? If the equalizers had their way, there would be no differences or choices anywhere in America. What "rights" are "civil"? As usual, no one knows where to draw the line.

PREJUDICE

Prejudice is a normal, healthy thing, and don't let anyone try to talk you out of it! Prejudice is actually "prejudging" something, either favorably or unfavorably, usually based on an educated guess. Today it is supposed to be a virtual felony to have prejudice.

Is it sinister to think Italians have an uncanny sense of the arts? After all, a great many great painters, musicians, composers, and singers are Italian. I have prejudice that anything made by a German is likely to be superior, well designed, precise, and long lasting. That is prejudice. I have prejudice that when I see a skinny, long haired, bearded, male listening to acid rock in his Volkswagon bus with granny glasses on, that he is probably into drugs.

Jews have prejudices about Germans, and will never buy a Mercedes, even though Hitler has been dead for 50 years. Southerners have prejudice against Northerners, in spite of the fact that the War has been over for 125 years. The poor have prejudice against the rich. When you see a run down house that hasn't been painted for years, the lawn is overgrown, and a rattletrap car is in the driveway, your prejudice will tell you that the homeowner isn't going to be a good neighbor.

When the Soviets have been observed to violate 99% of every treaty they have ever signed, one might be a bit prejudiced about doing business with them. If you have had quite a few Chevrolets, and they have all been troublesome, one might be prejudiced about Chevys. If you have been ripped off by several chiropractors, faith healers, or acupuncturists, one might be a bit prejudiced.

Prejudice can be positive or negative. If all Holiday Inns are clean every time you visit one, you are positively prejudiced. If your prejudice is positive or negative, it doesn't matter. It is normal and healthy as far as I can see. It is only abnormal to those who have no opinions or feelings. Guts, if you please. Am I ever prejudiced about those who have no prejudice! I have an almost unholy prejudice against government, and a marvelous prejudice in favor of freedom from government. Those claiming to be without prejudice are lying, and leave me nauseated. They'll just love this book!

OLD, SENILE, HELPLESS PEOPLE

It is my understanding that in the last 45 years, life expectancy has increased by 4 years. I am sure this is due to medical research, treatment, and the many cures discovered for formerly dreaded diseases that are now virtually extinct. Great! I am all for medical research, and lengthening of life through all types of improvements in diet, environment, and medicine. It does seem to me that 3 of the extra 4 years are given to those whose mind and bodily functions have left them a mere shell of a body, serving no earthly purpose. What has multiplied a hundred fold is a business that uses up the estates of the people who live the 4 extra years. The nursing home.

I speak from first hand experience. As I write this in 1987, my mother is 80, and a vegetable in a nursing home. She has no idea of where she is, who she is, or who I am. She has no control of her body and wears diapers. She is a helpless, senile, wonderful old lady who has shrunk from her former 5'4" to about 4'. She needs a hearing aid to hear, but hasn't the slightest idea of what she hears. She is incapable of thought or memory, and hallucinates constantly. Her nursing home bill is a bit over $2,000 per month.

In her youth, middle, and even old age, my mother was a happy, useful member of the community. She had friends, was independent, lived without the aid of anyone, was self sufficient, drove her own car, shopped, and in general had a happy life. She reared her child well, or at least as well as could be expected. We all have a few gripes about our rearing! She and my dad operated their own business and did it successfully and responsibly for 40 years. They were both honest, clean, trustworthy, and respected members of the community. They owned their home, bought a retirement farm after selling their business, did lots of nice things, and my mom and dad were a credit to America. Dad died in 1963 from lung cancer. He began smoking when he was 15. His one weakness did him in. My mom continued to live by herself for over 20 years. As all good things must eventually end, she is about to die. I don't know when. We have that extra 4 years to contend with you see. Her money will last a year. (She died shortly after this was written).

No matter how useful, intelligent, or active a person is, there comes a time when he or she is no longer that. Most end their lives gazing off into space, with no control over their bodily functions, and are literal vegetables. Yet they continue to live, because we have devised a theory saying, "where there is life, there is hope". This is simply not true.

Dying cancer patients, old, feeble, geriatrics, whose time has come and gone a long time ago are fed intravenously, pushed about in wheelchairs, kept drugged, and oxygenated just to keep them technically "alive". But they aren't alive at all. They are miserable, uncomfortable, and if given a vote, would love to be put out of their misery. Yet those profitable nursing homes thrive on their misery. Their children will never see a cent of inheritance, as the nursing home will consume every available dollar, just keeping them breathing as long as possible.

This nonsense is called "kindness", "benevolence", and "humanity", but it is none of the above. It is crass commercialism. These people, like my mother, have no future and can remember no past. They are living, mindless, skeletons, who are kept alive for the most selfish reasons, profit to the nursing home, and even the doctors who administer these drugs, oxygen, and stimulants.

Karen Ann Quinlan finally died after being kept alive, in a coma, for decades. Her brain was dead, and her body was fed intravenously to keep her alive. My mother will never again have a lucid thought. To see the people in her nursing home is pitiful and gross all at the same time. Babbling old people who can't move, think, or eat by themselves. No one thinks they will "snap back", or ever again be anything but a burden. No one thinks they even know where they are. It is so insane that I hate to even write this. I consider myself a kind, warm, considerate person, but what is happening to my mother is going on in America and the world millions of times a day. It is eating the life's blood out of us, and tormenting the old.

I think it is important for everyone to write a will stating they never want to be sent to a nursing home, never want to be kept alive artificially, and never want to be forced to have endless pain, drugs, and life support systems that waste money, and cause indescribable pain and misery for everyone concerned. I have done so. I want memories of me to be that of a strong, virile, intelligent man, not a vegetable. I want to be remembered as an innovator, contributor, writer, and a lucid thinker. As one famous saying goes, "it is better to live one day as a lion than a hundred years as a sheep". I buy that!

It is impossible to imagine how many billions in federal and state funds are wasted to keep the nursing homes in the black and multiplying, but it is a disgrace. When parents do not have a will and are in the usual helpless, miserable state that is the common condition of nursing home inmates, the children should have the power to painlessly end the tormented life of their loved one for the sake of kindness. This cruelty, in the name of humanity, but translated into the word profit, is a national outrage.

SHOULD A LAWYER DEFEND THE GUILTY?

The right to a fair trial by a jury of one's peers is a guarantee given by the Constitution. In America, a man is innocent until proven guilty, except for the IRS, and that is another chapter. The guarantee of a fair trial, and justice, is one of the great cornerstones of our democracy. I do fume however, when I see crooked, greedy lawyers using all their expertise to defend the obviously guilty. We speak of the ethical standards of doctors, automobile salesmen, and politicians, but what about lawyers? Isn't a lawyer just as immoral when he defends the guilty as a used car salesman turning back the odometer?

Isn't it unethical to defend a client you know is guilty simply because he has the money to pay you for your services? Attorneys who are willing to accept such cases should be branded accordingly. Would this bias a jury? I hope so! A jury should not be befuddled by a slicker whose aim is the acquittal of a guilty client.

It is not a well known fact of law, but a jury can violate the instructions of a judge, finding a defendant guilty or innocent, no matter what the technical requirements may be. Jurors can indeed change things by standing up for principles rather than technicalities.

An attorney should hold as his highest ideal the fact that he would never knowingly defend a person he believed to be guilty. I would have made a damned good trial lawyer, and if I had gone into that profession, I would certainly want to have that reputation. Yet the courts are filled with lawyers defending admitted child molesters, rapists, burglars, thieves, and murderers, using their knowledge of legal technicalities and other assorted mumbo jumbo to free their clients and return them to society. Lawyers should have the reputation of being reasonable, moral, honest people who sleep well at night, knowing they had not "hoodwinked a jury who is not overwise", (Gilbert and Sullivan). How can a lawyer live with himself, knowing he is defending a client he knows is guilty, much less expect the acceptance and adulation of his community? What kind of monster would not be bothered by seeing a twisted child molester or other rabble released back into the community to rape and pillage again? Far too many lawyers dance with their wives at the country club, knowing the scum he freed that afternoon is at large, and perhaps repeating a murder of a little lady for the change in her cookie jar. Sure this is being melodramatic, but so what? Shakespeare might well have been right at least for part of the legal community.

LAWYERS AT WORK

ISRAEL

For over 40 years, America has been pumping over a million dollars a day into the State of Israel. It has been an endless siphon of American taxpayer dollars into a tiny, sun parched land in the middle of no where, that as far as I am concerned, has no raison d'etre, or reason for being. It has been an absurd waste of money, and Israel has been responsible for unrest, hundreds of thousands of deaths, and countless aberrations in the world economic scene. The funniest thing is that Israel proclaims itself a dear, close, inseparable friend of the United States. I'll be your friend too for a million dollars a day! It is said there are only 11 million Jews in the world, most of them living in either Israel or America. It is American Jewish pressure that has continued the transfusion of money from America to Israel.

Shortly after World War II, the United Nations decided to partition Palestine into two states, creating the new State of Israel. The Arabs, who would not agree to this theft of what they believed to be their land, attacked Israel and lost. The prime part of the land Israel captured in this short war, has been retained by them over the protests of the attackers, and the trouble has continued ever since. Israel wins most of the battles with U.S. money and arms. Israel's bravery and skill in battle goes back to Biblical times, only then it was supposedly with God's assistance, rather than America's. The Israelis have taken a barren, desolate land and cultivated it. They have tried and almost fulfilled the prophecy of Isaiah and made, "the desert blossom as the rose". They are an intelligent, energetic, determined, cultured people, with high inflation and almost total dependence on American dollars and strength.

Let me illustrate the situation. Suppose you lived on and owned a rundown farm. It had literally gone to seed, with nothing being produced, weeds in the overgrown fields, erosion taking away the topsoil, crumbling barns, rusting, broken machinery, and a ramshackle house that defied description, due to its poor condition. A farm that was disgusting in every respect. A man comes along and offers you what he considers a fair price for your farm, telling you that he will restore it in every way, make it a showplace, and make you proud. You could even continue living there under his rules. He had a personal interest in it, as his ancestors lived on the farm a couple of thousand years ago, he says. You aren't interested in selling at any price, as the farm had been in your family since revolutionary times, it is none of his business how you live or maintain your property, and there isn't enough money in the world for you to sell. The man goes to the government, has your property condemned, pays you the money, takes ownership of the land, and allows you to continue to live there under his rules, and under the lowest of circumstances. You protest this unjust treatment, and appeal to the highest courts, but in the end you are thrown off your land. Sound fair? That is almost exactly what has happened to the Palestinians under the United Nations decree creating the State of Israel. The Palestinians had lived there for hundreds of years, and did not want to sell or move. They lived in squalor, and merely wanted to be left alone. They were thrown out, and their land was given to the Jews whom they have hated for thousands of years. The resulting violence, bloodshed, and war was just a natural reaction to an unjust land grab. I can't imagine it ever ending.

The Jews have no more business being there than the man who had your farm condemned after you refused to sell it to him. The Palestinian anger is just as normal as yours would be if your land were forcefully sold to your worst enemy. It is admirable that the Jews have done wondrous things with the formerly barren land, but this does not solve the basic injustice found in the fact that Israel exists at all. They have over 2 dozen symphony orchestras, high educational and literacy rates, and enough good things cannot be said about their zeal for success. This just doesn't make it right. I see businesses and properties every day I would love to upgrade, transform, and restore, or make more efficient. But this doesn't give me the right to have these properties condemned and allow me to take over.

As an aside, the so called "right of eminent domain", often exercised by government and power companies is no more right or just than is the existence of Israel. What the Jews did with the land is no justification for their having it. Our continued support of this fiasco is wrong. It was a crude, brutal, land grab under United Nations command, which gives it no legitimacy, nor does the Jews supposed divine right to the land make it any better.

Postscript: The above was written in 1988, long before Israel was attacked by Iraq Scud missiles. Israel not getting involved in the Iraq-Kuwait affair helped its image greatly, and perhaps the Arab community will soften its hostile attitudes towards Israel. Also, tens of thousands of Soviet Jews have immigrated to Israel since this was written. Perhaps, in spite of the unfairness of it all, and because of the Palestinians making asses of themselves on a regular basis, Israel will come out of it O.K. Whatever happens, the main part of this is still my opinion and it is logical to the ultimate degree!

SOPHISTICATION

It is a sad day, but I am about to admit a terrible short coming. I am not sophisticated. After all, I dislike modern art, dissonant music, trendy clothing, strange tasting cheeses, exotic teas, and as a matter of fact, I don't like tea very much in the first place. After years of concerted effort to shape myself into a sophisticated man, I hereby admit defeat.

As an example of my desire to become a true sophisticate, I own several large volumes on wine, and have even read some of them. I once joined a wine tasting group in Phoenix, and remember one evening at a fancy Scottsdale hotel. Firestone vineyards was the supplier. Yes, the same Firestone. Others were cooing and gushing about the "nose" and acid content, swishing it around in their mouths, and smiling in a simply delightful manner. I thought the stuff to be undrinkable, and remarked that perhaps Firestone should stick with tires. Shortly after that, Firestone tires began coming apart, and now they are owned by the Japs, so perhaps the entire outfit had problems. Now I'll take Gallo Hearty Red Burgundy thank you, or a Chenin Blanc ordinare perhaps. I'll never forget a 1959 Nuits St Georges I drank in the 60's which was sublime, but still I can't possibly be counted as a wine sophisticate.

Teas? I tried them. I had at one time close to twenty teas in my cupboard. Everything from Lapsang Suchong to English Breakfast and Earl Grey. I dutifully tried them all, drank them at the correct times, and prepared them properly. I had tea pots, and strainers, gleefully boiled water, and let them steep for the required periods. I tried to be a tea snob but failed miserably, ending up thinking it was all so much colored water. Thanks, but I'll take my coffee black.

And, of course, cheese is a snob's delight. I never could stand those obscure cheeses that taste a lot like Firestone's tires and other assorted bitter, sour, and disagreeable things. And the smell of some of them! Heavens, what a stench. But I did really try. Now I'll take a strong cheddar any day, and you can keep the sophisticate's Brie and other nauseous chunks of unknown fermentation.

Art is the true indication of a sophisticate. One must ooh and aah over strange scribblings and splashes by the likes of the late Jackson Pollock, and other assorted "artists", which includes chimpanzees, who throw paint randomly at a canvas, while the true believers scream in ecstasy. I think good art has realism, detail, and feeling. It isn't strange, like the "impressionists", or childlike. I have seen 3rd graders who can outpaint a lot of contemporary artists. Now there are some who applaud and praise that disgrace, known commonly, as graffiti.

As for music, I just like it to be harmonious and pretty. We recently canceled our season tickets to the world's best orchestra, (the Philadelphia Orchestra), because they are getting far too "sophisticated", playing ever more ugly, dissonant music, that last Saturday included two vacuums and a floor polisher. No kidding! I resent paying $22 per seat to go to a concert when the "music" sounds like a train derailing, or 55 gallon oil drums rolling down stairways. Is this sophistication? Is it sophisticated music when each player seems to be playing a different piece or in a different key?

Apologies are in order for being so unsophisticated as not to appreciate foul tasting foods, ugly art, and senseless music. Real sophisticates love the latest trendy clothes that swish and sway in every way, with clashing colors and designs. When it comes to dress, I'll take sensible shirts and slacks with a good suit for special occasions. If Doc Severinson is sophisticated, count me out.

Sophisticated autos all seem to be capable of 4 times the speed of sound, come from foreign lands, cost small fortunes to operate, buy, maintain, and feed, not to mention being impossible to get in or out of in comfort. I'll pass.

While not meaning to sound boorish, I have observed that the architecture considered to be sophisticated, often has no harmony or beauty. Too often it is clashing cubes, jutting lines, strutting beams, and exposed ductwork. The Kennedy Center in Washington, D.C. is not only ugly, but has poor acoustics, and a perpetually leaking roof. I took photos of the wonderful, eclectic Victorian brewery that stood on the site before it was demolished for the Kennedy Center. It was wonderful, but definitely passe' to the modern crowd. Much of Frank Lloyd Wright's work is excellent, but much of it is appalling such as Taliesin outside of Scottsdale, Arizona. Guess I fail in architecture too.

I am feeling more and more of a loner. I am too old to be "sophisticated", which means too old to put on airs. I did give it an honest try. My desk is large, has drawers and isn't shaped like a teardrop. I don't sit around in a Buddha like trance, and I don't have a mantra. I am just not sophisticated.... and damned glad of it.

REGULATORS

It is "correct political thought" in America that government has an important duty to regulate things. Conservatives and liberals alike delight in establishing new regulatory bureaucracies. Republicans seem to do it more than Democrats of late, but it is perhaps fairly evenly split over the past 60 years. Everyone in America is supposed to be evil, and we will do awful things unless government steps in and regulates us to keep us on the straight and narrow. As a result of this distrust of everything, except what should be mistrusted—government, the federal budget is out of control, and our productive economy is a shambles. Let's examine a few regulatory agencies to see how much they have helped.

Start anywhere you please. Take the SEC as an example. The Securities and Exchange Commission regulates all stocks and bonds. The SEC is the law that the stock and bond markets must adhere to, and fill out forms for, if they want to exist. Corporations regularly diversify, split, go bankrupt, and leave town, with the innocents holding the bag. All approved by the SEC. The bonds that now have the appellation of "junk", and which have cost Americans hundreds of billions, were all blessed and sanctioned by the SEC. Statistics show that the SEC has saved no one a penny, stopped no white collar crime, and cost hundreds of billions in actual cost, not to mention making it extremely difficult to raise money by issuing stocks or bonds. A failure.

The insurance industry is tightly regulated, and now in the process of failing.

The agricultural sector is tightly regulated and subsidized, and not at all healthy. Tobacco farmers do O.K. with the federal subsidies, while government spends millions telling everyone not to use the tobacco they subsidize. The cattle and meat industry receives little subsidy or bureaucratic meddling, and it thrives.

Banks and savings and loans come under the most severe regulatory scrutiny, and are failing by the hundreds. Another agency, the RTC, is trying to pick up the pieces and is already full of corruption, and boondoggles. People bid $20 million on an RTC building, and the agency sold it to another for $4 million. These stories are becoming the usual, just like in any other federal agency. As banks and S&Ls fail, not a single person can say they weren't under the most severe regulation. Of course, the government owned and operated bank and S&L insurance agencies are also bankrupt.

The Federal regulatory agencies are responsible for the "dioxin" fraud that began at Times Beach Missouri, with the fed forcing people out of their town because of this supposed deadly chemical contaminant. Now we find out that it is about 1,000 times less harmful than was initially published. It only cost the taxpayer hundreds of millions. Radon is another federal fraud as is now being proven. Millions have spent good money for radon detection units and been scared to death needlessly.

The asbestos scare of a few years ago bankrupted businesses, cost billions so far, and now the truth comes out that it was as basic an outrage as has ever occurred. Asbestos is harmful to asbestos workers who don't wear masks, but not anyone else. So an industry has collapsed, thousands out of work, and hundreds of millions spent removing a wonderful insulation that never had to be removed in the first place.

Studies have shown that non smoking coal miners don't get "black lung", and non smoking uranium miners don't get cancer, but the regulatory agencies continue to rant and rave, destroying yet another industry.

PCBs will eventually be exposed as another federal fraud, mark my words. In Paoli, Pa, a few years ago, the feds came in with space suits and yellow ropes to cordon off a section of a railroad yard where PCBs had been dumped for years. What a performance! Kids had been playing there for 60 years, and workers had been working there for 60 years. A total hoax, as time will tell.

The swine flu episode a decade ago cost many their life through bad shots to prevent a disease that didn't exist, and not only cost millions, but was a sham.

Now it is the so called shrinking of the ozone layer. Except that no one never saw the ozone layer whole. When it was discovered a few years ago, it looked just about as it does now. It may have had a hole in it for millions of years, but it is a good excuse to ruin the refrigeration industry, making freon a bad item, which also will be found out eventually to be a phony. In the mean time, consumers will pay billions in costs for machinery using another refrigerant, and for no reason.

Is the earth warming? Is carbon dioxide increasing? I doubt it!

It is practically impossible to go into the gas station business now because of the hideous regulations on tanks. It is also almost impossible to go out of it because of the same regulations. It has become a nightmare.

15 years ago, a kiddy pajama manufacturer was told by the fed to use a certain chemical as a fire retardant in the P.J.s or they couldn't be sold. Do kids die from smoking in bed? At any rate, the manufacturer did as he was told and spent thousands of dollars making the Mother Goose jammies fireproof. Then the fed decided that the required fireproofing was a toxic substance and required the manufacturer to destroy a million bucks worth of merchandise that had been treated

exactly as had been ordered by the agency that now required destruction. After he went bankrupt, he was seen in a straight jacket, blubbering some unintelligible fantasy concerning the government.

The regulatory agencies tell the businessmen, housewives, students, farmers, and workers how large the toilet seats are to be, how high the hand railings are to be, how much to plant, how much to water, how much to pay, how much to make, and how much to charge. No one escapes. All of these horrendous costs are borne by the consumer who pays through the nose for purchases, which naturally have the regulatory costs included.

Schools are another chapter, but are a classic as far as regulation is concerned. Highly regulated and almost total failures. The Department of Education is in charge of this fiasco.

Then we have the Department of Transportation which rushes to the scene of accidents to make pronouncements as to their cause. What did we ever do without them? It also reeks with stifling rules, regulations, and an assortment of bureaucracies that costs transportation operators, and in the end the public, hundreds of millions each year. There are just as many accidents as ever. They just cost more.

The FHA loses billions each year, and has literally ruined the cities of America.

There are controls on just about everything in medicine. It takes an average of 8 years to get the FDA to approve a drug, which is absurd, because they are just more know nothing government employees. In 1964 the FDA had reports on the dangers of polyurethane as breast implants, and several times after that, but paid no attention. Now the FDA has decided that it is bad. 27 years later, after how many cancer cases? Thousands I am certain. I have seen huge files on the failure of the FDA to do anything worthwhile.

There are controls on every single facet of our lives. We are never far from a snooping bureaucrat in a government car collectively costing us hundreds of billions every year with their subsidies, regulations, rules, and other roadblocks to prosperity. I can see no value or benefit provided by federal regulations and regulators. Certainly the Constitution doesn't call for them. I call for their prompt removal.

Regulators and government add to the cost of everything, making purchases smaller or eliminated all together. Houses are out of reach of most today, whereas 75 years ago, anyone could afford one. America can buy less today than it used to buy. Maybe 75% less! These fewer and smaller purchases make our life style lower, and cost the jobs of the people who would make these things for us to buy. Jobs are instead going to government which is a totally non productive entity, feeding off of the populace rather than profits realized though manufacturing, selling, and producing. Taxpayers pay for regulating, and the more they pay the lower their life-style becomes. Each government job is paid for by you. Out of your pocket, either directly or through lower value of your dollar. Private sector jobs cost the taxpayer nothing, but are paid from profits.

If someone knocks on your door and says, "Hello, I am from the government, and I am here to help you", you'd better run for your life!

MUSIC

It is November 16, 1987, and I am building bookshelves in the living room. WFMT, from Chicago, is playing at high volume through my speakers. WFMT is a fine arts station that comes in on our TV cable here in Colorado. It has won many Peabody awards for excellence in broadcasting. The small town in Colorado in which I live has no classical music station, so I listen to WFMT. At any rate, the Detroit Symphony concert is being broadcast by delayed tape recording. As usual, the music director thinks it is his duty to insert a "modern" composition into the program. Today's piece is titled Fantas Mada by one Christopher Ruse. I am outraged by the horrendous sounds emitting from my speakers. It sounds like elephants trumpeting, accompanied by lots of percussion. The ugliness is breathtaking!

Modern music, like modern art, is ugly, senseless, and offensive. It requires no talent to create, and a shallow brain to appreciate. I well remember a Philadelphia Orchestra concert during the 1985 season when we were being bombarded by senseless noise. Seated directly in front of us was a man with beard, granny glasses, long hair, and levis. He was an "intellectual", who finds great merit in the works of untalented charlatans. When it was finally over, for the first time in my life, I loudly hissed rather than simply abstaining from applause. The fool in front was instantly on his feet shouting "bravo", cheering, whistling, and shouting loud hosannas to a virtually silent concert hall.

Why has the composition of beautiful music become a lost

art? Even in the pop field, kids today listen to absolute garbage, full of sexual and suicide messages, screeching sounds, deafening guitars, and distortion beyond belief. Youth today, is literally going deaf, due to the high decibel levels of so called "music" they listen to, often in cars, where it is so loud that even with the windows rolled up, the sounds 50 feet away can be offensive. Until the 50's, kids and adults listened to the same popular music, and it was pretty, harmonious, often catchy, but really nice. When I was in high school, my parents didn't refuse to listen to popular music. We all listened to the same music. Glenn Miller, Benny Goodman, Harry James, the Dorsey brothers, and their ilk made kids as well as adults cheer for more when they played.

But classical music is the subject. As the Detroit Symphony concluded the abuse of harmony by Christopher Ruse, the concert hall was virtually silent. The announcer said that the audience gave the new work a, "warm reception". Like hell it did! It gave an absolutely chilling reception by applauding virtually not at all. The sparse applause was undoubtedly given by the likes of the above mentioned man in front of my wife and I in Philadelphia.

All the great composers are dead. Not only the Beethovens, but the Glenn Millers as well. Even on Broadway, "A Chorus Line", can't compete with the South Pacifics, and Oklahomas of decades before. Can Sondheim be honestly compared to Rogers and Hammerstein?

There can be no doubt that modern composers are not appreciated by 95% of the buyers of symphony tickets. We had superb seats for all three series in Philadelphia. Row "E", seats 3 and 4. The grand old Philadelphia Academy of Music is a wonderful concert hall. Tchaikovsky conducted from its stage, and Abraham Lincoln spoke from it. But we gave up our seats and stopped going. The reason was that we didn't need to pay big bucks to listen to ugly music.

Jascha Heifetz, that most wonderful of violinists, is quoted as saying, "I occasionally play works by contemporary composers, and for two reasons. First, to discourage the composer from writing any more, and second to remind myself how much I appreciate Beethoven."

Concert programmers always schedule the dissonance and disgusting stuff before intermission, and the wonderful Bach, Brahms, Beethoven, and Tchaikovsky after intermission. The reason isn't hard to understand. If the beauty and thrills were before intermission, and the junk was after, everyone would leave at intermission! Obvious. My wife and I got tired of sitting through pain while waiting for beauty. So we quit. At $44 for two seats per concert, not counting dressing, traveling to center city, parking and yes, even taking a chance of not getting mugged, the expense wasn't worth it. In 1986, the Philadelphia Orchestra concerts were not sold out in advance with season tickets for the first time in anyone's memory. The reason is described above. Will music directors of symphony orchestras learn? Will they play what people want to hear, or must they continue the crashing dissonance and commissioning of such compositions for future generations?

Is it possible there exists a conspiracy to teach bad things to students? Is it possible that the teachers are so screwed up that they are unable to teach beauty? Is it possible that a gigantic conspiracy exists to poison the minds of our youth with trash music and obscene lyrics? Is it evil or stupid? Is it planned or by accident? When art teachers teach non art, and music teachers teach non music, is it lack of taste, or a mere repeating of what they were taught? I just don't know, but it is scary. Is it possible our civilization has sunk so low that appreciation for beautiful architecture, art, and music is impossible to be taught to our youth, and it is becoming literally lost? Does Trump Tower even remotely compare with the

Chrysler building in New York?

I just wish America would stand up for what is beautiful, and deny an audience or income to creators of ugliness. Perhaps the government funding of hideous public art applies to music as well. Most so called "composers" of trash concert music are heavily subsidized. If classical music devotees would boycott orchestras that play dissonance, perhaps the light would shine through the empty seats. The Metropolitan Opera has similar problems, but seems to be learning. The 1988 season had more ugliness than the 1989 season, and the 1990 season has even less. Of course I have written letters protesting! Of course I have with held contributions as a protest. Have you? Everyone should.

It is our ticket purchases that pay the bills for ugly things. My integrity will no longer allow me to buy a ticket for a symphony concert having dissonance in it. After writing letters, hissing, and walking out, I voted with the ultimate weapon, the pocketbook. I denied them my money. You had better believe the programmers know how we feel. They have gotten away with it for far too long. Symphony orchestras are cutting off their noses with a large pair of scissors. This thing can be turned around if enough people write, scream, boycott, and complain. There is no shortage of beautiful compositions to play. There are hundreds of thousands of magnificent pieces to be played that inspire, thrill, and educate as well. Stop the ugliness!

TURNING BACK THE CLOCK

MGM has released dozens of classic oldies on videotape, and I just watched "Maytime", with Nelson Eddy, Jeanette MacDonald and John Barrymore. What a wonderful, wonderful film about an era that is dear to my heart! I would love to turn the clock back about 60 or 70 years to a gentler world, running at a slower pace. A world that whistled the tunes of Sigmund Romberg and Jerome Kern, rather than todays popular music with lyrics of sex, suicide, and sadism.

Try to imagine a life without television, plastic plates, disposable diapers, and rock music. A world free from racial tensions, freeways, acid rain, and atomic weapons.

Cities were filled with quality homes in all price ranges, built with pride, using fine woods, marble and slate. Row houses for the working classes, and luxurious, spacious mansions for the wealthy. Trolley cars gaily clanging down the streets, transporting people to work, magnificent downtown department stores, old fashioned amusement parks or band concerts at the gazebo in town square. No graffiti, inflation, or smog. Little crime or debt, low interest rates, and dollars backed by real silver and gold. Income tax and the dreaded IRS didn't exist.

Haunting steam locomotive whistles from trains transporting American made goods from one end of this country to the other. Automobiles well built, and easily repairable by shade tree mechanics. Movies larger than life, and projected on huge screens in sumptuous palaces, where stars and clouds floated above audiences enchanted by the sounds of magnificent

pipe organs, and colorful stage shows before each film showing. X-rated smut can't be found anywhere. Delinquency,
illegitimate births, and welfare are almost non-existent. Music
is beautiful and romantic, while dancers actually hold each
other.

When I was growing up, we lived in a fine row house with
high ceilings, rich woodwork, fireplaces, ceramic tubs, and
the warmth and friendship of neighbors who all knew each
other. We were at home evenings and the children roller
skated, played dodge ball, and hide and seek. On cold winter
nights, there was a fire in the fireplace, and we all gathered
around the radio. There were Monopoly games, Chinese
Checkers, Old Maid, Jack Straws, cards, electric trains, books,
and 78 RPM records.

It all seems so tawdry today. Casual sex, rampant VD,
drugs of every kind, hideous music, and ugly dancing. People
who make big money and have no talent are glorified.
Crackerbox houses and apartment buildings that are flimsy
and ugly are what is built today. Modern office buildings are
orange crates piled on one another with reflective windows.
Everyone is tense, in a hurry, and crime is so rampant that
citizens must have alarms installed in their homes and cars. It
isn't safe to walk the streets at night, and no one seems to know
their neighbors anymore. Quality of workmanship is a lost art.
I remember when things were worth fixing, now we just
discard them. When I was growing up, there was home milk
delivery, mother didn't have to work, and families could
afford to own their own home. Stores delivered things, and
you recycled the milk and soda pop bottles. Everyone had a
sewing machine and grandma made quilts. The Christmas
trees were real and the floors were oak.

After watching "Maytime", it just seems that life was
much more fun in those halcyon days gone by. Of course all
this sentimentality is perhaps a symptom of old age, but I have

always fought the passing of the things I mention as missing now. I was horrified when I heard the first rock and roll, and I wept witnessing the passing of the movie palaces, steam locomotives, and amusement parks. Sure, there is Disneyland, but there are exactly two of them in America, whereas there was an amusement park at each little town in those days I speak of so fondly. Today there are wonderful advances in materials with which to construct buildings, but those save money and do not give character, or individuality. Today there are computers that can solve complex problems in seconds, but 75 years ago those problems didn't exist. Today we have clogged freeways that are as smooth as glass, whereas 75 years ago, they weren't needed. Today we have TV, VCR's, C.D.'s, transistors, and dozens of wonderful technological advances that reproduce things in your home. Then, people went out to be entertained, talked, or visited. Even with these technologies, I still remember the time we didn't have them, and I liked those days best.

I know that we now have microwaves, dishwashers, automatic laundry machines, automatic transmissions, air conditioning, foam rubber, computers, and efficient furnaces. 50 years ago we got along fine without them, and we all were happier.

Maybe I was just born 50 years too late!

THE MINIMUM WAGE

The minimum wage gradually increases as the dollar becomes weaker, supposedly helping the poor, decreasing poverty, and giving a better standard of living to all. Exactly the reverse is true. The minimum wage is actually legislated unemployment. If the minimum wage is $4.50, the worker must produce $4.50 worth of value, or he won't be hired. Suppose a certain job isn't worth $4.50 per hour? As an example, a doorman at a theatre or hotel. They might add snob appeal, but if hard times come, they might be without a job.

In the early 60's, I had a large movie palace in Lansdowne, a suburb of Philadelphia. Harry Rendler was a retired man of 71 who needed a few extra dollars to help with his pension. He came by the theatre one day and asked me if I needed any help. I didn't, but at $1 an hour, I could afford a doorman to tear tickets in half as the patrons came by. He was a super guy, always had a smile on his face, was polite, and I felt good hiring him. The minimum wage was $1 per hour, and admission to the theatre was 75 cents. See what has happened in a few years? The theatre wasn't doing too well, and was below break even some weeks, and none too profitable other weeks. The minimum wage was raised to $1.25, and Harry had to go. I couldn't afford him any longer. If I could have continued with $1 an hour, I would have kept Harry.

The same story is repeated hundreds of times a day. The minimum wage keeps teens, and especially uneducated, negro, male, teens unemployed. They aren't worth the minimum wage, so they stay unemployed. If an uneducated, inexperienced, worker could be hired at their worth, everyone would be employed that wanted to be, and there would be no unemployment. Suppose, to teach how to work, a potential employer would be glad to hire a kid for $1.50 an hour to sweep the sidewalks, or some other inconsequential work. It is illegal to do so, thanks to the minimum wage.

The minimum wage has always prohibited people from working. The minimum wage has always legislated unemployment, no matter what level it has been. When the minimum wage was $1, there were plenty of people who were only worth 75 cents an hour that were prohibited from obtaining jobs, and were relegated to the dust bin of the unemployable. It is not only the unemployment that is bad, but the resulting psychological harm done to the person who is unable to work, and made to feel useless. In August of 1938, FDR set the minimum wage at 40 cents per hour. Those worth only 35 cents an hour were unemployed. Lots of people made 50 cents an hour, or 60 cents an hour, and lots of workers made $3 an hour. It all depended on their skills and desirability to the employer, which is ultimately fair.

If there were no minimum wages of any kind, unemployment would shrink to those who didn't want to work, were too old, sick, infirm, or unable to work. As a businessman, I can think of a lot of jobs I could create at say $2 an hour, but it is illegal for me to do so. Minimum wages radically increase the welfare cost, because those not employable at the minimum wage go onto welfare and get paid for NOT working.

It requires no skill to pump gas. 95% of gas stations are self service because owners are unable to hire workers for their actual value. So we are forced to pump it ourselves. The gas markup is maybe 15 cents per gallon, and a minimum wage worker earns 7 cents a minute!

In 1977, I restored an old house in Phoenix, turning it into a restaurant. It turned out beautifully, and did quite well. I hired waiters and paid them nothing. They lived on their tips. On each table was a small sign indicating that their total wages were the gratuities they received. The waiters were taking home over $400 a week, which in 1991 would be the equivalent of over $1000. The arrangement made them provide the best service to the customers, and the best waiters made the best tips. It worked out extremely well with me paying the waiters nothing! The chef and dishwashers were paid conventionally of course. One particularly irate customer became so obsessed with the signs that she called the IRS to complain. At that time, the rule read that a business grossing under $250,000 a year could do just what I was doing, and I barely escaped the bureaucrats. So who was harmed? No one! Were the waiters well paid? You bet! Were my costs lower enabling me to serve food at lower prices to my customers? Certainly. But good old bureaucracy has changed that now. Even waiters must receive a certain minimum wage.

I can think of no better way for a kid to grow up than to sweat long, hard hours doing something menial. Teaches them that hard work is good for you, and money is supposed to be earned and spent wisely. Minimum wage laws deny that important facet in a child's upbringing.

Wage and price controls rightfully upset most of us. Rent control always causes housing shortages. Price controls cause shortages of merchandise. Government interference in any field, especially setting prices, causes shortages. Minimum wages are "wage controls", and of course cause a shortage of jobs. It is all so logical! Minimum wages are price controls at their worst. Whenever there is a "control" over anything, the natural markets for that product are always upset, causing too much or too little.

Competition is wonderful, and thwarted by any controls. When labor is free to seek its own wage level by its skills, intelligence, experience, or location, there will never be any unemployment, assuming there is no welfare to pay people who refuse to work. Welfare, and the minimum wage are both disasters, sleeping in the same sorry bed with each other.

Since there are millions of potential workers who are not worth the minimum wage, why is it illegal to hire them at the wage they are worth? Beats me. Suppose government told you what you had to eat, where you had to live, when you had to sleep, and where you had to go? Is that much different than government telling you how much you have to earn? I get weary of pumping my own gas and having Uncle Sam running my life for me! Get government off our backs and let us prosper.

LIMITED TERMS

There has been a lot of talk about limited terms of office. America finally limited presidential terms to two, which is a beginning. But just suppose every Representative and Senator had a term limitation of say... one term! "Yup", as Gary Cooper used to mutter, one single term, and you're out. Think of the repercussions of that one. The length of term could easily be adjusted to match circumstances. I suggest one 6 year Presidential term, one 5 year Senatorial term, and one 4 year House of Representatives term. Elections to be staggered and held every year rather than every two years. In May of 1991, the Senate voted down a limited term bill. Naturally!

The most important thing to a Congressman is to get re-elected so he or she can hold that cushy job ad infinitum, ad continuum. The world's most exclusive club, the U.S. Senate, would have 100% turnover every 5 years, and the House of Representatives every 4 years. No more entrenched positions, seniority, snobbishness, and power trips. The continual "re-elect me", nonsense would stop once and for all time. No longer would re-election be even a slight concern, because it would be impossible. I am so tired of 97% of incumbents being re-elected. It is not only boring, but unfair, and provides us with the poorest of governments year after year, decade after decade. Anyone who thinks a long term office holder is an asset, is grossly mistaken.

Long term politicos learn the "ropes" O.K., but not to the benefit of anyone but themselves. Semi-permanently en-sconced in their office, they wield immense amounts of power, become crooked, unyielding, inapproachable, intransigent, and worthless to America.

Politics is the most crooked game around, and politicians are the most useless and worthless of creatures, forcing their party will on hundreds of millions of hapless, helpless citizens who pull levers at each election, thinking that Senator Blowhard is their friend in Washington. Nonsense. Old Senator Blowhard is his own friend, and no one else's except at election time. Politics is sleaze at its worst, comparable only to prostitution, only it pays more. Hookers deal with one customer at a time, giving something in return, whereas a politician steals continually, and gives absolutely nothing back for those votes. Democracy is actually ridiculous without single term limitations, because it ceases to be democratic. Incumbents can always get re-elected with their power and plums of office. Power corrupts absolutely.

If politicians could never be re-elected, the power trip would be greatly reduced. I can't think of a better way to reduce it than these three ways, and they are (1) Reduce their salaries to absolute zero, living expenses only, and let them live in apartments provided for them near the Capitol so they won't get in trouble. You say that only rich people could afford that? That's fine. What's wrong with rich people? They are smart enough to get wealthy, and their office would not allow a power trip, so they would do just fine. (2) Never allow them to vote any expenditures that would allocate any federal money for any welfare, never leave any budget unbalanced, never pass any law to protect citizens from themselves, (victimless crimes), and for each term in office, the federal land holdings must decrease by 2% until all public lands were sold, with the money from such sales used to eliminate the national debt. And (3) Reduce Congressional sessions to about 2 months per year, so they couldn't get into much mischief. Will Rogers said America was in its greatest danger when

Congress was in session, and he was right.

If they only had one term, they wouldn't continually bankrupt us with their vote buying by means of more and more spending to garner constituent approval.

Of course a Constitutional term limitation would have to be passed with a vote of guess who? Of course! The very ones that would have their power trip eliminated. Will it ever happen? Only if individual States do it to them.... which they should.

THE STOCK MARKET

This is being written from experience, logic, and knowledge of the subject, as well as knowing quite a few losers in that old American tradition known as the stock market. Experience? I have owned thousands of shares of stock, and over a period of many years, I am about even. Maybe a few bucks in the hole. A good friend of mine inherited quite a large sum of money some years ago upon the death of his parents. John had always been fascinated with the stock market and the inheritance gave him his chance. Within a couple of years he had lost it all. Anyone that has ever read on the subject will tell you more than 65% of investors in the stock market lose their money.

The stock market isn't investing, so much as it is gambling. Just as there are addicted gamblers, so there are addicted stock market players, or as they like to call themselves, "investors". They are gambling, only going by a slightly different phraseology. Personally, I hate gambling, but if I were going to do it, Las Vegas is a far more fun place to do it. The results are about the same: Losses.

Think about a basic fundamental of any stock or commodities trade, and that is for every buyer there has to be a seller. If you think a stock is a good buy, your stock is bought from a person who thinks it is a loser, and he wants to sell it. You want to buy pork bellies futures? Fine, except your futures will be bought from someone who wants to sell theirs. Who is right? It almost has to be 50-50 doesn't it? Maybe, but probably not. If your new acquisition was bought from a seller that had some type of inside information, you are the loser. About the only people who make any money in markets are those with inside information, and that type of trading is illegal if it is blatant.

A bit of history if you please. Prior to Oct. of 1987, the stock market had been steadily rising, and had even topped 3000. The higher it got, the more people invested. That in itself was a bad sign, because historically, whenever "everyone" is doing something, it is usually the worst possible thing to do. As more people bought stocks, they went higher and higher. I watched the situation with horror, knowing what was going to happen. It did on Oct. 19th. A few got edgy and began selling. The computer traders got into the game, and it became a torrent. The Dow lost 500 points in one day. A catastrophe for millions of investors who lost, in many cases, their life's savings. The exact same thing happened in 1929 when the market went berserk, and millions of people lost everything. They were doing what they thought was smart, namely buying stocks. But remember everyone else was doing the same thing.

Foolish bankers were lending depositor's money to borrowers who used the money to buy more stocks, and when the whole thing came tumbling down, everyone lost, including bank depositors who never bought a single share. If the term "contrarian" was in existence then, I wasn't born so I don't know, but that is what I am. I always do the exact opposite of what everyone else is doing, and usually come out smelling like a rose. Stocks? Humbug! If you want to really see what a "value" a stock is, look at the value of the total number of outstanding stocks in any corporation and then look at its "book" value. Generally the stocks are priced at many times the book value of the corporation they represent. Now how about those traders who are "in the know", or inside traders?

As an example, a man works for the Acme Corp, and has been accumulating company stock for a long time. As an employee, he doesn't like what he sees. A strike is coming, raw materials are becoming difficult to obtain, or a competing product is about to be marketed. He sells of course. The buyer might be you, who likes Acme products, thinks it has a rosy future, has gone up fantastically in recent months, and so on. You buy, and the person with information sells. Who wins? The seller with a bit of inside dope. If you are the president of Acme, and you unload your bundle, you might go to jail for so called "inside trading", which in reality is about the only way to make money in the stock market.

Buying stock is the same as allowing your money to be used by the president and board of a large corporation, trusting that they will do an excellent job with it. Officers and presidents of large corporations have so much power and so much money that they rarely understand economics, marketing, or efficiency. The corner mom and pop store is far more efficiently run than a large corporation with its ivory towers, executive suites and rest rooms. How can the isolated president of a large corporation possibly understand the life and tastes of John Q. Public? Most large corporations vie with the federal government to see just who can waste the most money, squander the most assets, and be the most inefficient. Some corporate blunders boggle the mind, and the Edsel is only one example out of thousands.

Billions of stockholder dollars have been lost over the years by actions such as merging the Pennsylvania and New York Central Railroads, which couldn't possibly work. The two roads had different computers, different locomotives, different signals, and competing routes. The stock went from $80 to less than a dollar in a pretty short time. Guess who lost? Chrysler went from good to bad and from bad to good and then bad again. Who lost? The president and C.E.O.? Of course not! It was the "investor" who bought when he should have sold, and sold when he should have bought.

Then there are the newsletter writers, hundreds of them, who write expensive monthly letters full of great stock market tips, graphs, moving averages, and succinct predictions. They are about as accurate as Jeanne Dixon's annual New Year's predictions. Millions of suckers put their trust in both. Stock market charts tell you what has happened, not what will happen, and they are not related. All the moving averages, charts, and newsletters in the universe will not account for natural phenomenon, war, political upheavals, and natural resource discoveries. No chart will predict death, drought, and inventions. If the writers of such letters and other like trash are so smart, why aren't they devoting their time and knowledge towards getting filthy rich themselves? They say they "like to help people", but they are only helping themselves.

Taking hard earned money and throwing it into the stock market is about like flushing it down the toilet, only it takes a bit longer. Fortunes have been made in the stock market, but they are few and far between, and usually were made by insiders who had advance knowledge of certain facts, which leaves out 95% of the public. Stock brokers don't care whether you make or lose, as their profits come from the trade. If they can convince you to endlessly move out of one, into another, and then to switch again, they win and you loose. Many lawsuits have resulted from such shenanigans. Popular singer Willie Nelson took a famous financial institution's advice, and is now totally bankrupt.

There is no end of people willing to take your hard earned money for their advice and counsel. There is also no end of people who stupidly go through life wasting money on every hair brained scheme that comes down the pike, including the stock and commodities markets. If you like to gamble, there is always Gamblers Anonymous to help you, but your local stock broker is in it to help himself, not you. That fancy Dan corporate president who makes a few million a year probably could take a few lessons from any small businessman.

Forbes Magazine for years has traded stocks with play money in two different ways. One way is for an office steno to throw darts at the list of traded stocks, and buy them. The other is to take all the learned advice from experts and buy what they recommend. In 1990 the dart throwers did better than the experts, and that is a fact. Tell you anything?

Want some advice? Since you bought this book, you are entitled to some. Here's mine. Pay every dime you owe to everyone. Pay off the house, all credit cards, buy a new car and pay cash for it, put a nest egg in the bank, write your will, and do a bit of traveling. Buy the best electronic equipment to entertain yourself at home in a royal style, have the best, most comfortable furniture, and owe no one. What is left after all of that is done, you can feel free to invest in whatever you please. What to invest in? My advice is, never in the stock market. Here are a few ideas.

Antiques always go higher in dollars over the long run. Antiques of every kind. If you are a male, perhaps antique toys, trains, or autos. Guns do well. If you are a woman, antique furniture, kitchen gadgets, wall hangings, dolls, and the like. The less of anything there is, the more dollars they will be worth, and that's an ironclad truism. There are no shortages of old Lionel Trains or Model A Fords, because as they become scarce, the price goes up. I have lots of old things which give me great pleasure, but only one share of one stock. At least I think I do. Somewhere. Manufacturers' Hanover Trust, (Manny Hanny), has one share of mine in one corporation, and they can't find it or I would have sold it years ago. I have written over and over, and decided it is hopeless. Another glitch in corporate America. They can't lose your collectibles because you have them.

Another idea is what has been actual money throughout history, and that is gold or silver. As this is written, silver is the best, because no one wants it, and it is priced less than its production cost. I own a silver coin that is almost 2,000 years old. Silver and gold have always been money. Pieces of paper with ink on them are no better than the producer or backer of that paper. Paper money is backed by absolutely nothing, and in actuality is worth exactly that. Nothing. We use it because the law requires us to use it. "Legal tender" laws put the force of government behind worthless paper money. Stock certificates represent a small ownership of a corporation. Bonds represent debt owed to owners of such pieces of paper, but none are actual investments.

Beware of tax free bonds, and for that matter any bonds. You can just as easily lose your shirt on those as any other piece of paper with ink on it. What you need to save your assets in is anything but a piece of paper. Tangibles are the thing. Things that are not denominated in dollars, yen, or pesos. Governments devalue those pieces of paper money at will, and this is known as inflation. By dictionary definition, inflation is "an increase in the money supply". It has nothing to do with prices going up. In reality, inflation is the value of money going down, due to its proliferation by governments who issue it.

In 1920 there was about $55 in circulation for every American. Today it is almost $3,000! Have prices gone up? No. The value of the money has gone down. Is a suit of clothes or loaf of bread worth more? No, the value of the money used to buy it is worth less, so it takes more money to buy the same things. This is government at work for you. Government prints money to pay its bills, and the money progressively becomes worth less. Historically, you can eventually put those two words together and they become "worthless". If there were millions of diamonds around, and they were easily mined and produced, they would have little value. It is easy to print money, but difficult to mine gold, silver, or diamonds. They have a tangible value that is caused by the capital and effort needed to produce or mine them. It costs virtually nothing to print money. Remember: THE MORE OF ANYTHING THERE IS, THE LESS THEY ARE WORTH. That explains why antiques are growing in dollar value, and actual paper dollars are shrinking in their power to purchase things. Your assets should not be stored in a denomination that has value controlled by a government, which means every government on earth. Store your surplus assets in tangible things like old records, your home, first edition books, or gold and silver.

The most brilliant economist that ever lived was probably Adam Smith who wrote his *"Wealth of nations"*, hundreds of years ago. Read it. In fairly recent times, there was Ludwig Von Mises who defined economics in two simple words. "PEOPLE ACT". That describes it all in a nutshell, and as far as I am concerned, you could put all the "economists" in barrels, send them over Niagra Falls, with survivors being sent to Alcatraz to scrape rust off of old prison cells, and the world would have a better future. Keep away from the stock, bond, and commodities markets, do the opposite of what the common trend is, store your assets in tangibles, and think for yourself. Real money can't be burned. Only legal tender can be burned.

INSANITY AND PAROLE

Like the so called "insanity" plea, parole should go the way of the Dodo bird, and fast.

Everyone knows if you threaten a child with punishment for some transgression, you should follow through with it. Telling a child something, and not meaning it is an invitation to disaster if you want your kids to grow up to be decent, law abiding, productive citizens. So what is the point in telling criminals that they will get 5 years in the slammer if it doesn't mean that at all, but much less? Where is the sense in releasing a criminal before his sentence is up? If you want to put him away so he won't be a danger to society, and punish him for the damage he has inflicted on the innocents, lets say what we mean and mean what we say. If the law says ten years, then it should be just that. Ten years, not five years, and not even 9 years and fifty one weeks.

It's a game brilliantly played by judges and lawyers. A game telling the players a word doesn't really mean what it says. Yes means no, and long means short. Almost as if we don't speak the same language. The principle of parole is supposed to be "time off for good behavior". Criminals should have thought of good behavior before they committed the crime, not in jail. If a crime has been committed, it must be paid for by whatever means the law provides, but time off for good behavior is absurd when it means releasing thugs back to the streets to begin again where they left off. Very few experts believe in "rehabilitation" any longer.

If a first offender is severely punished, perhaps he won't

become a second offender. If he becomes a second offender, then throw the book at him, but when you do, you'd better mean what you say.

The result of the parole system is not only an ever escalating crime rate, but the political creation of parole boards, mountains of paper work, huge administrative costs, and expensive investigations. Parole officers don't come cheap, and you have to have enough of them to keep track of every single parolee to be certain they behave themselves. It's much easier and cheaper to monitor someone who is incarcerated. If a reward for good behavior is desired, there are lots of possible perks in prison. A better cell, more interesting jobs, educational opportunities, extended visiting hours, and even a raise in pay, so the released prisoner will have a better chance at reestablishment in society upon release. Billions of dollars would be saved each year if the parole system were abolished. Let judges sentence convicted criminals as they see fit and as the law requires, without taking into consideration an absurd parole system. The parole system has so many flaws, irregularities, and expenses, that it is unfair to victims and society as a whole.

Perhaps the most unfair of all crimes committed upon society is the existence of the "insanity" plea. According to current legal practice, if a criminal was "insane" at the time he committed the crime, he can't be punished as he would if he were sane. I say, NUTS! Who cares whether he was insane or sane? Did the victim suffer less? Aren't criminals actually "insane", by accepted standards when they violated societal rules? Who is to judge "insanity" anyway? Psychiatrists? I have never known a normal psychiatrist. Why should such a plea even exist in the first place? It has nothing to do with a Constitutional guarantee of no unjust punishment. It is a total fraud that is continually exploited by clever lawyers. Should a murderer be any less reprehensible and pay a lower price if he is a mental midget, or supposedly has a screw loose? Even if he is insane, or was when he did it, so what? What possible difference can it make to society, or a victim, if a heinous crime is committed under less than desirable mental conditions? A fair trial is to prove what was done, not whether the criminal intended it or not.

Who cares? Other than allowing vicious criminals to go free or be under punished, what is served by an insanity plea? How about huge lawyer fees, letting scum out earlier, or incurring monstrous mental treatment costs? It is an absurdity that should be instantly erased from every state and federal statute book. Charles Manson, I am sure, is crazy. But why does he still live? Because he is insane. Because of pitiful, weeping, bleeding heart, liberal, do gooders who I would like to lock up because of their own insanity. Society steps on cockroaches, ants, and beetles. It kills mice, rats, and poisonous snakes. What is wrong with electrocuting a babbling murderer? Absolutely nothing!

BUSINESS

I know that this sounds like an extremely elementary chapter, but considering that a recent survey showed only 1% of American high school students had any respect at all for the businessman, and that most Americans think the businessman is greedy, selfish, and rich, perhaps this really is in order.

The word business can encompass many facets of enterprise. It can include manufacture, retail, wholesale, service, transport, or anything done for a profit and at risk. The words profit and risk are the key words to business. It is the potential profit possible from a business that causes us to take the risks to begin or buy one. In by far the majority of cases, those profits never materialize, and the risks taken are paid for with the entire life's savings of the would be entrepreneur. Allow me to illustrate the benefits and problems from personal experience.

In 1983, I decided to go into the video tape rental business in Philadelphia. I intensely dislike renting anything and want always to own something. A building on a busy corner in Philadelphia caught my eye, and was for sale. I made an offer on the building which was in an excellent location but was in poor condition. The video tape rental business was fairly new, and seemed to me to be a good opportunity. I had virtually no money, but owned my home free and clear. I took a risk which all business people take. I mortgaged my home to get the money to start the business. Out the window was the security of a free and clear home. The risk was starting a business I knew nothing about, borrowing money to do it, buying a building that needed repairs, and trusting in a hunch that it would work. Risk is ALWAYS part of business. If the business fails, as 85% of new ones do during the first year, the businessman loses his investment. It is a sizable risk, no matter what business it may be

Be it a hot dog stand, taxicab, rental property, service station, or any business, the person starting and operating that business takes immense risks with their credit, capital, energy, and time to start and operate that business. No one has ever begun a business without taking a grand gamble. The chances of it failing are overwhelming. My video store clicked, and we sold it 3 years later for a large reward after building it into a winner. The person who bought this successful business failed miserably because of a number of factors that cost her her capital, time, and effort. She didn't have what it took, and I did. Most businesses fail because the person starting or operating it doesn't have a feel for business, their customers, location, advertising, pricing, or numerous other things, all of which are important for success.

Advantages of a business are the fact that you can build equity in something that can be sold, can make far more money than you can at a job, and have the freedom of being your own boss. The risks are that you may lose what you invested, be liable for far more than you invested, work far more hours and suffer incredible mental and physical strain and anguish. Working for someone else may not pay a lot, but when the bell rings at 5 o'clock, you go home worry free. The businessman worries about his business 24 hours a day. The businessman can make so many mistakes that can cost him his life's savings, security, and even sanity.

He can buy too much merchandise or equipment. He can pay too much for his business, its building or more rent than the business can support. He can buy the wrong merchandise, place the business in the wrong location, advertise too much or too little. He can have too few or too many employees or pay them too much or too little. He can start a business for which there is no need. He can decorate it or name it wrong. He can price his merchandise or service so high no one will buy it. There are thousands of pitfalls in operating a business, and a thousand ways for it to fail. The risks are so high, that few succeed in it.

In the above mentioned video tape rental shop, we succeeded but not before we almost went belly up because of unforeseen mistakes. First of all, we had all the wrong tapes when we opened. We had the movies we liked, not the ones our customers wanted, so we had to change our inventory and buying practices. We had to adjust hours to suit our customers, not ourselves. We had employee theft, robberies, burglaries, and bad checks. We had leaks in the roof, equipment failures, and government gobbledygook that was unbelievable. We solved each problem as it occurred with thought, experimentation, and trial and error. No business is ever free of problems, and the tape business wasn't either. Just as we made it relatively trouble free, the large chains invaded us, and cut our business gross $50,000 a year. Our personal service and individuality made us still profitable, however, proving that a smart, small businessman can outfox and outlast any large one, as history has proven for 100 years.

A person buying and operating a taxicab or running a popcorn wagon can just as easily make mistakes and lose their shirt as can any other businessman. That taxicab has insurance costs, fuel bills, repair bills, and other expenses that must be offset by fares gotten from people wanting a taxicab. Suppose no one wants to hire a taxicab? Suppose someone starts a taxicab with a better car, or advertises more effectively? Suppose someone starts another taxicab business with lower prices, or has lower payments to make because he had more cash with which to start. Business is tough indeed.

It is business that furnishes the jobs in America, whether it be pouring steel, building homes, selling furniture, or pruning trees. It is business that collects the taxes keeping the towns and cities alive and working. It is business that makes America what it is. Without business, you would have the Soviet Union, poverty, and a drab existence. Business gives Americans the lowest prices possible, and the largest variety of things available to purchase.

Business is also about to go out of business because government is making it impossible to operate a business, and that spells the end of freedom and prosperity as we have known it for 200 years. Government and Congress continually pass laws and make regulations that makes the businessman an endangered species. Laws allowing employees to sue over the most absurd imaginings or supposed slights. Courts regularly giving huge settlements for inane grievances. And regulations beyond all tally is making the cost of operating a business so complicated, risky, and expensive, that fewer and fewer try it. This is causing unemployment, lack of variety in the marketplace, less competition, and empty store fronts. One of America's major achievements, allowing her to prosper beyond the wildest dreams of anyone daring to predict the future 200 years ago, is the free marketplace, unhindered by controls, regulations, crippling taxation, frivolous lawsuits, and bureaucrats everywhere at all levels attempting to thwart every move of a once free people.

Business is tough, brutal, unforgiving, and full of horrendous risks which would scare the pants off of the 99% of high school students in that recent survey who think we are not deserving of appreciation. Businessmen taking huge risks, working long hours, and racking their brains to be more competitive is the reason America became great. America's sinking into the mud of mediocrity, poverty, and a $60 billion trade deficit with Japan is thanks to those would be do gooders who would regulate and legislate us out of business.

I have always been a businessman, and have never held a job. Until you have tried to operate a business, don't knock it. It is far more deserving of recognition than it receives. Perhaps that's because the writers for the media, broadcasters for the media, and teachers have never tried it!

POLITICS

"There are two subjects I will never argue about, and they are religion and politics". How many times have you heard that? Religion is a very personal thing, and has absolutely nothing to do with the survival of America, but politics certainly DOES have to do with America's continued existence. Especially in the last 60 years, politics has virtually destroyed America. An old definition of politics is that it is, "the art of compromise". Compromise may be a small part of it, but the main part of politics is POWER. Power gotten with your money, energy, prosperity, and even sanity. Most Americans equate money with power. This is only partially true. With power, you don't need money. If you have unlimited amounts of money, the craving is for power. Power over others in the main, but plain, raw, brutal power is what makes the heart of a politician beat the fastest. Money gives power of course, because with a wallet full of hundred dollar bills, you can command attention, buy your way into virtually any place, and indeed will have power. But politics gives immense amounts of power, prestige, and authority without money. Political power is heady stuff.

Politics is the single most deleterious force going in America today. Politics is a total fraud. Politics is the Trojan Horse, wolf in sheep's clothing, and rotten to the core. When a man gets elected to a political office at any level, he becomes enamored with the power that office gives him. From the tiniest town, to the federal government, political office conveys power that is destructive to the holder of that office, and of course to the subjects over which that power reigns.

Politicians ALWAYS run for office under the guise of "helping". "I will do my best to help the poor, get that bridge built, keep that base open, get that highway funded, fight AIDS, clean up the schools", or a million other promises. "Charlie Blowhard is such a kind man, He gives of his time and effort to help everyone, isn't that wonderful?" Nonsense! Charlie Blowhard loves the power and rush he gets from lording it over his fellow man. Congressmen always seem to have your best interest at heart, isn't that correct? It may seem so, but they always vote for more bureaucracy, more taxes, more controls, more wars, more spending, and more "help", except it isn't help at all.

The latest scam is National health coverage. This will be a natural to get more votes, destroy the medical and insurance professions and industries, and cost more billions in either deficits or taxes. All this under the guise of "help". The obvious result will be poor medical care, horrendous levies on every American, and more socialism. (See chapters on socialism, and health care) We haven't had decent, reasonable medical care since the sixties when the power mad Congress and Lyndon Johnson signed into law the first socialistic medical care program. It can only get worse the more that politicos mess with it.

If ever there was an evil, it is a politician at any level. If ever evil was incarnate, it is in the form of an elected politician. Every time Americans vote, they vote not for a good person who will rid us of this, but for the usual "lesser of two evils". George Bush was the lesser of two evils when he was running against Michael Dukakis, but George Bush got us into a horrendous, brief war that killed hundreds of thousands, and accomplished nothing. Admittedly, we lost very few, but 700 oil wells were burning out of control in Kuwait, Saddam Hussein is still in power, and in Kuwait it is back to business as usual under an absolute monarchy. Everyone still hates everyone else over there, so the Bush war was pointless. Bush is a numbskull on economics, and at best a wishy, washy, eastern, liberal republican, who hasn't the remotest idea of what the trouble is with America.

Each year our dollars become more worthless, our debts climb closer to the sky, and more poverty occurs. The banks are bankrupt, the savings and loans are bankrupt, the agency supposed to save them is full of corruption and fraud, and every single politician in Washington is responsible for it all. The $100,000 a year the politicos in D.C. get as a salary is peanuts compared to the rich plums and extras such as travel, free postage, huge staff, glory, honor, prestige, and lifetime retirement after leaving office, if they don't die there.

Yet it is all so worthless. Washington, D.C. should be blown off the face of the earth, and the federal government reduced by 95%. Politicians are absolutely the most worthless, lying, fraudulent bunch of con men ever assembled into one place. P.T. Barnum was a prince compared to the average U.S. Senator or Representative.

After all, what is politics anyway? It is merely taxing everyone and spending it to benefit the most voters so the politician can stay in office. Is that a fair definition? It is a far different definition than "the art of compromise". Politicians have destroyed America by taxing the rich, and giving it to the poor, which will always outnumber and outvote the rich. The rich provide the prosperity and jobs, while the poor destroy the rich and prosperity, thanks to politicians. The last thing a politician desires would be for anyone to care for themselves. The most hideous nightmare for a politician would be for their constituency to say, "We don't want any more handouts, jobs, plums, influence, or help. We want you to vote no on every spending bill, fire 90% of your staff, refuse to use the franking privilege, never travel anywhere at public expense, resign all your committees and try to eliminate them, cease all speaking engagements, book writing, and finally, leave office at the end of your term."

No one helps anyone by giving them something for nothing. But that is basically what politics is at every level. It is that, plus throttling the minority who create wealth till they can barely survive. Politics is squeezing the productive sector, knowing they have it in their makeup to keep trying, just as it is natural for a living thing to fight for its life. A productive, innovative, creative person simply cannot stop, even though politicians make it virtually impossible to succeed. The more wealth produced, the more handouts the politicians can promise to poor voters who will keep them in power.

In America today, we have basically two parties, the Democrats, and the Republicans. There isn't too much difference between them at this point. It's more like one party with two divisions. Both spend recklessly, both increase the size of the bureaucracy, both pass endless laws and brag about it, and both haven't the slightest idea of economics, honesty, and how to make America prosperous. Politicians have ruined America and continue to do so.

If you don't believe in astrology, religion, vitamins, jogging, or a host of other beliefs, so what? Your nation isn't threatened either way. Politicians are not only a threat, but continually destroy our once great, free, prosperous land. All in the name of "helping". Politicians have violated the Constitution thousands of times with their laws, rules, regulations, and millions of government employees. They say they are "conservative" or "liberal". They conserve their money, and are liberal with yours! Everyone should vote "none of the above", if possible, at the next election, or next best, vote for anyone but an incumbent.

CONSUMERISM

I suppose it all began when Ralph Nader began his attack on the Corvair automobile. "Unsafe at any speed", became an instant best seller, damn near ruined General Motors, and destroyed the Corvair, which was a totally new automobile with radical engineering that included rear engine, air cooling, compactness, independent suspension, and economy. By the time Nader's slur hit the shelves, initial problems with the Corvair suspension had already been corrected. Ernie Kovacs, the comedian, had been killed in a Corvair, and Nader built his flimsy arguments over that, plus lots of spying on executives and other specious arguments. I still have that book, and it is not a credit to investigative reporting. Yellow journalism at its best. Not only did that book kill a nice little, innovative car, but it thrust Nader into a spotlight that has never been turned off.

"Nader's Raiders" became self appointed guardians of the consumer, and gradually expanded their coverage from the Corvair to every other facet of the American automobile. Nader and his gang quickly decided that anything protruding on a car was a heinous danger to humanity in general. As a result of this absurd pressure, auto makers eliminated fins, anything pointed, and even had to redesign radio knobs. Car costs went up, of course, and the foam rubber manufacturers were exuberant. But that was only the beginning.

Consumerism now occupies large offices in Washington, has life and death powers over manufacturers, and accounts for higher prices on about any item found on any shelf, and billions in costs to administer all this protectionism. By now, most Americans think we need this nonsense, and are convinced that manufacturers and businessmen will just get away with murder if the government bureaucracies charged with protecting the consumer didn't exist.

I say consumer protection is about as necessary as sun glasses to look at a lunar eclipse. Consumerism has grown like Topsy, and now pervades every facet of manufacturing, causing merchandise to cost more than it should, and making it difficult to export. 35 years ago, we had no "consumer protection", and everyone did quite well. America had been in business for close to 200 years, and had become the world leader in production, wealth, and consumer satisfaction, with a standard of living unmatched anywhere. We are now about bankrupt, and so much in debt that we may never recover. Consumer protection is partly responsible for this.

The cost of consumer protection schemes and departments are paid for with taxes and increased prices. Both are a blow to prosperity. "Caveat Emptor" is the old Latin phrase we learned in high school, and it merely means, "Let the buyer beware". That kind of protectionism costs absolutely nothing. Manufacturers don't want unhappy customers, and they never have. Unhappy customers spread the word and don't repeat. A product's reputation is one of its most valuable possessions. No manufacturer is so stupid as to make shoddy merchandise and expect to succeed or not be discovered. The very concept that government "protectionism" is necessary is a blatant lie, and it has been repeated over and over so many times that it sounds logical. The truth is that manufacturers and producers of consumer goods want to please, not defraud. They want repeat customers and good word of mouth reputations. All this government "protectionism" protects only one thing, and those are the bureaucrats that would lose their jobs if Americans demanded that this expensive nonsense stop dead in its tracks.

If an error creeps into design or manufacture, the correction will be made as soon as it is uncovered, and if the consumer is not happy, the ultimate "consumer protection" happens to be a court of law, not pencil pushing, rule making. leeches on the public payroll.

RUN FOR YOUR LIFE

The king is dead, long live the king! Jim Fixx, the so called king of joggers was found dead of an apparent heart attack on a lonely New England road. He was 52, supposedly in superb health, with a low heart rate, and all those thousands of miles of physical exercise behind him. He wrote numerous books and pamphlets, and lectured on the wonders of abusing the human body by daily jogging.

I hold the opinion that jogging is an absurd practice. It's something like racing your car's engine at full speed to prolong it's life! Let's assume, for simplicity's sake, that an auto engine may make 500 million revolutions before it becomes worn out, and just stops running. With excellent care and regular oil changes it may even turn twice that many, say a billion revolutions. If this is a valid assumption, then how could racing an engine possibly prolong it's life? The same principle could be applied to the human heart. If the heart beats 50 million times a year, which is close, and the average lifetime is 75 years, that's about 375 billion beats, and then it is worn out. Pretty good record for a little pump, isn't it? But how in the name of common sense, can attempting to make it run those billions of beats, in half the years, make it last longer? It's obvious that mild exercise strengthens the heart. Good diet, no smoking, and normal weight are important too. But punishing it with endless running can't possibly make it last as long as it would if it were allowed to work less than full tilt for several hours a day, not to mention the further punishment the knees, feet, back and other parts of the body receive.

The slogan "Run for Your Life", has to be the most absurd slogan ever dreamed up by twisted, mindless doctors, and the manufacturers of running shoes, clothing and other assorted paraphernalia. It should be, "Run for a shorter life".

For years, I was a volunteer, working as an official at one of America's toughest running events, the Kendall Mountain Run, which begins in the town of Silverton, Colorado, elevation 9318, and follows a course to the top of a mountain peak almost 4000 feet higher, and then back again. The air is rarefied at best, although at least it isn't hot. My post was always within 500 feet of the top, and each year I admired and congratulated the runners as they passed. The top runners will complete the entire course in approximately an hour and a half, while the slowest will take as much as four hours. Many remarked as they passed me, "I must be crazy", or "This is ridiculous". I always wonder how long these runners will live, or if they will just drop dead of a heart attack in mid course.

The jogging craze has not been going on long enough for the final chapter to be written. The death, from heart attack at age 52, of the country's most famous jogger can only be the tip of the iceberg. I'm sure many less newsworthy runners have been known to suffer from heart failure. I lived in Phoenix, Arizona for five years, and I saw a constant parade of joggers running during the heat of the day with the temperature climbing to 115 and even higher. Sweat pouring from their bodies, reddened faces contorted with agony, lungs gasping for air, they drove themselves on, day after day, punishing their hearts, legs, joints and minds in order to "prolong their lives". It's all so ludicrous, that it's mind boggling.

We've all seen short tempered automobile owners and silly teenagers racing their engines, mistakenly thinking it will make them run better, or "clean out the carbon", while in reality they are shortening the life of the engine by tens of thousands of miles. These nuts, and the jogging nuts, are both laboring under the same false assumption. Abusing an object, one the engine, the other the heart, will somehow make it last longer or run better. Will a light bulb burn longer operating at a higher voltage? Nope. Will anything be likely to last longer if it is operated at more than normal tolerances and speeds? Nope. Then why do the joggers persist with this absurd behavior?

My opinion is not medical, but personal, although doctors do seem to be divided on this question. The joggers merely select a medical opinion that agrees with their practices. But if the whole thing is so unbearable, why do they do it? Ah! That's an answer that has nothing to do with living longer, except as a peripheral benefit. They actually keep it up because of their addiction to the "natural high" they receive from running. When the body is burned, starved or abused, such as by running, it produces a strange chemical that is actually a derivative of morphine. Endorphins they are called, and the brain secretes these fluids as a protection against the pain of serious bodily damage. The physical abusers actually are heavily addicted to the high from this naturally produced drug. It's that simple. It feels so good, the idiots think it must be beneficial to their health. I'm sure it must be just as difficult to free yourself from this addiction as to one involving the use of nicotine, heroin or cocaine.

In my opinion, and remember this book is 100% my opinion, the poor jogger you see sweating and panting his way down the road is to be pitied. He is hooked on a false assumption, bolstered by his body's natural defense mechanism, so he continues on a program that wears out his heart, and leads him to an early grave. Perhaps this is a less painful death than from cancer or being hit by a car, but it is still a premature death.

Heart disease is the nation's number one killer. It's obvious there are many other contributing factors to this statistic, such as high blood pressure, poor diet, obesity, and even genetic defects, but I wonder why no one has ever figured out how many runners drop dead each year, and subtracted that from the other heart related deaths. Maybe if that were done, it would no longer rank as number one.

I have just never known a person who was normal weight, with no genetic problem, who is not under extreme stress, and who likes to walk, dying of heart failure. Moderation in all things is a good rule to live by, and it's not difficult to maintain good health by eating correctly, walking a lot, sleeping well, and in general enjoying life.

Jogging is like smoking. It is never enjoyable at first. It only becomes so after the body gets hooked on the chemical.

SOME ADVICE TO BLACKS

In this chapter, I have no intention of mincing words or beating around the bush. That's not my style. This advice is sorely needed!

It is no mark of achievement to work for government, no matter what race you may be. Washington, D.C. is close to 80% negro, because government jobs are a common goal of most Negroes. When I was growing up in D.C., the negro population might possibly have been 10%. Government offers job security, minority hiring quotas, and no challenges; but is a totally non productive form of work. No government has ever produced anything, but is a destroyer of liberty, freedom, and wealth. If you really want to achieve, do it in the private sector through productive work. There are those in life that live off of others, (government employees), and those that live off of themselves, (private sector employment).

The civil rights laws only benefit you in certain ways. You have every right not to be discriminated against, and Rosa Parks was a hero. Such legislation was long overdue. However, laws that allow you to usurp the rights of others BECAUSE you are negro is an insult to you. It is impossible to ever attain equality, even with two snow flakes. Equal opportunity is what you need, not equality, and any law attempting to establish "equality" between males and females, Negroes and Caucasians, fatties and skinnies, tall and short, strong and weak, or what have you, is doomed to fail. There never was, and never will be, any such thing as "equality".

In order to be recognized and appreciated by your fellow

humans, you need to be an achiever, not just "black". Being negro is no reason for anything! Acceptance has to be achieved without force, because force is a negative thing, whereas voluntaryism is a positive reaction to excellence. That means studying, learning, and working hard; not marching, threatening, and voting for politicians who promise you nothing more than ever increasing amounts of welfare and "rights".

When a law is partial to any portion of society, it is a clear indication of that sector's inferiority. Think of it! If a law requires special treatment of the handicapped, isn't that indicative of inferiority? They are, aren't they. They need such laws don't they? The same is true of any law legislating special things for special groups. Laws favoring negroes as opposed to "whites", Koreans, or Japanese, are obviously an indication that negroes are inferior. If I were negro, I would work very hard to eliminate any laws favoring my race. If negroes make it on their own, rather than on laws of force, there will never be race problems. Laws forcing integration actually legislate inferiority. The race being forced has to be superior, or force wouldn't be necessary. That is logic and common sense. You must work for the elimination of such laws because they make you out to be inferior, and you aren't.

The very word "black" is always contrasted to "white". In every civilization, black is always regarded as bad, and white is regarded as good. It is a fact, and whoever started calling you "black" should be shot. Now it is "African American", which is equally incorrect. Thank Jesse Jackson for that one. You are not "African Americans", but Americans. You were born here, grew up here and are citizens of America. You are not "black", any more than I am "white". You are not "African Americans", any more than I am a "Dutch American". It is demeaning and an insult.

You MUST get off the welfare rolls!!! It kills all ambition and pride, and foments hatred among the taxpayers. You are not inferior, just betrayed by your supposed friends, the altruists, and would be helpers. Altruism is a nasty word to me. The American Negro, and the American Indian have had all dignity, ambition, and incentive killed by the handouts from a misguided government, mistakenly trying to help.

Your children are your hope for the future. Begin to nurture, discipline, and educate them so they can become productive adults.

You MUST stem the destructive tide of teenage pregnancies, illegitimate births, and single parent households.

Stop destroying things and begin caring for them, be they homes, neighborhoods, automobiles, mates, offspring, or personal belongings. Your males ages 15 through 30 have given you an undeserved black eye, (note the word "black"), and you must rein in this terrorism. When a group is 2% of the population, and commits 50% of the crime, as is true with young, negro males, you must not blame others for being afraid of you and wanting to be away from you.

Limit the size of your families, which will enable you to provide better emotionally and financially for the children you have.

Learn from Caucasians, rather than victimizing them, creating an atmosphere of fear and hatred. Civil rights laws have in no way lessened the gap between the races, merely polarized feelings that were there all along.

Strive for education, honor, and independence, not life on the dole, which includes being a welfare recipient, living in public housing, or accepting wages from a counter productive government. Expect honesty and integrity from yourselves and your children, and see to it that they learn to read, write and speak correctly. There is no reason to ever be able to distinguish one race from the other because of slurred words, poor pronunciation, or bad grammar. Stop taking the easy road, and begin to realize that the greater the effort, the greater the reward.

Never take anything from anyone without giving something for it. Learn to despise welfare, or any handout from anyone at any time. Learn to work for everything you get, and spend it wisely, not on drugs, alcohol, or instant gratification.

Become cultured, not taking the easy way. This means reading good books, listening to good music, appreciating good art, and watching good films. Action, violence, and obscenity are out, as is any art form requiring little or no talent.

Government housing and welfare programs have stripped you of your dignity, and kept you from becoming responsible, independent, respected members of society. We do not mindlessly despise you as you might think. What we despise is having to support you! We despise your filthy neighborhoods, indisciplined kids, crime, and destruction. We despise living in fear of you, and knowing that our hard earned money is spent on you for welfare, extra police, public housing, free medical care, and even cleaning up your graffiti. We resent having our money spent on people who rape, murder and rob us. We hate our neighborhoods being destroyed, cars stolen, and not being safe on the streets.

The Eastern Liberal Establishment has ruined you with their useless government jobs, altruism, endless welfare programs, and public housing. Unlike the Irish, Germans, Polish, Jews, Italians, and Orientals who made it in America with horrendous language barriers and no welfare, you have not made it BECAUSE of the welfare and handouts which have destroyed you. The Civil War has been over for 125 years, so that excuse will no longer play. You have no language problems, and no citizenship problems. You are your own problem, along with the ruination of you by government.

The "white" man with his welfare, and even your own race with their votes for welfare, are not your friends, but your enemy. We are tired of your slums, lack of self esteem, and illegitimacy. We are tired of watching our cities turn into no man's lands, and gang killings for the fun of it over some mythical "turf". Get yourself in gear, and do something for yourself. We would be ever so grateful!

SMOKING

Is there anything more pitiful than the nicotine addict? Or anything more irritating? According to most reports, nicotine is the most addictive drug known to man, and I feel truly sorry for anyone caught in its grasp.

Most smokers begin by trying to be "cool" or "sophisticated", when but a mere teenager. By the time they realize how ridiculous it is, it's too late, and they are hooked. The rest of their lives are spent puffing away, smelling up every place they go, burning holes in furniture, offending non smokers, and in general making a nuisance of themselves, wasting thousands of dollars, and dying prematurely from lung cancer.

Cigarette smoke is highly offensive to non smokers who, according to current figures, account for 74% of the population, versus the 26% who smoke. Not only is it offensive, but inhaling another's second hand smoke can be just as irritating and cancer causing as actually smoking.

Several years ago, the chief of the Scottsdale, Arizona fire department told me 90% of his non arson fires were caused by smokers. The arsonists are a sick breed that cannot be counted here, but the billions of dollars worth of damage caused by smokers is just as sick.

The whole thing, as viewed by a non smoker, is ludicrous. Here are these fools spending $2 for a little pack of paper covered tobacco. They take one out, strike a match, and suck the putrid smoke into their lungs, then blow it out into the air, stinking up everything, and offending everyone. Smoke that dulls the taste buds, stains the fingers and teeth, and covers windows with brown film. Smoking that dulls the sexual appetite, makes breathing difficult, causes cancer, burned garments, auto upholstery, rugs, sofas, chairs, desk tops, and kitchen counters. A habit causing untold damage each year to restaurants, hotels, motels, homes, and offices. A habit responsible for thousands of deaths each year from raging fires in homes and apartments. An addiction accountable for people walking around with oxygen bottles and breathing apparatus due to incurable, terminal emphysema. It's smoke filled rooms, overflowing ashtrays, and ghastly smells day after day, week after week, and year after year. All because of a habit, usually acquired as a teenager, that is so addictive it requires herculean efforts to shake.

If you own a restaurant, don't hire a chef that smokes because his taste buds are so dulled that he will overseason everything. Don't rent a hotel room that has been inhabited by a smoker, as it will smell stale and reek of old exhalations. Isn't it fun to ride in a closed car with a smoker who blows the poison out and clouds up the windows, yellowing the upholstery? Ever kiss a smoker if you are a non smoker? Absolutely nauseating!

Even when they aren't sucking their coffin nails, they still stink. Smoker's clothes, and living quarters are so foul it is unbearable to visit them or have them visit us. When they stop, everything suddenly tastes so wonderful they invariably gain weight. Their sex drive escalates and everything smells so clean and fresh. Then they become extremists like me, except I have never smoked.

I never smoked because I never felt so insecure as to want to imitate the rest. Even as a kid, I never much admired the local heroes on campus. If parents would encourage their kids to think for themselves and do what they think is right, smoking generally wouldn't be tried. Smokers are indeed on the descent and laws are being passed that many smokers believe to be unfair. It is illegal to smoke on airplanes and busses, and may soon be on trains. Restaurants are discovering the wonders of catering to non smokers, as are hotels and motels. Smokers are becoming enraged at the rising anti-smoking tide making them unwanted guests at many places both public and private.

Is smoking a right? Maybe it is if no one else suffers, but that is virtually impossible. Since smoking cannot be practiced without impinging on others' freedom, you just have to favor laws prohibiting smoking in public places.

I once owned a non smoking restaurant, and currently own two non smoking hotels. People came in and ask if there is a smoking area in the restaurant. The answer was always "yes", with the plastic trash bag being pulled out and shown as the "smoking area". This is hilarious to the non smoker, but not funny to the addict. Then there was the guy who said a restaurant was a public place and he had fought two wars for the right to smoke in public. My answer was that it was not a public restaurant but my restaurant, and I could dictate any conditions I wanted. As a lifetime rabid anti smoker, I feel good that more and more smokers are taking the cure and saving their lives by stopping. They used to be militant, but now are apologetic about their filthy practice.

Humphrey Bogart and other stars of the 30's and 40's helped to foster the habit. Bogey was never in a movie when he wasn't sucking a cigarette. He died an early death from lung cancer. Movies seem to have stopped pushing the smoking habit as the ultimate sign of sophistication and glamour, and it is common to see an entire movie without a single smoking actor shown. Children are being educated about the dangers of smoking, and the decline continues.

Advertising is prohibited in certain media, and I must admit to having a problem with that. Advertising is a form of speech, and should not be impinged upon, no matter how deleterious it is to your health. Unless the argument of government protecting its citizens by prohibiting advertising of poisonous substances is valid, which it may be. While that might be a moot point, government subsidization of tobacco farmers is not, and should be stopped immediately.

The freedom to choose in America is gradually lowering our addiction to tobacco. Education is working, and America now has a lower percentage of population smoking than does practically any other place on earth. Ain't it grand?

THE 5th AMENDMENT

I have had my go rounds with the IRS. I'll never forget when I had a camera stolen from my car in the 60's, and deducted it from my taxes. The IRS auditor asked me for a receipt. No kidding, a receipt from the thief! As I slammed my fist down on the desk and screamed at the stupid bureaucrat, she trembled a bit, and decided that thieves do not give receipts. That was the first time, but not to be the last.

In the early 70's I attended a seminar in Phoenix given by a man named Marvin Cooley. Cooley's line was that since the 5th amendment states you don't have to testify against yourself or incriminate yourself, filing and even signing to the truthfulness of a tax return is a violation of your 5th amendment rights. It is a Constitutional right, and no one disagrees with that fact. The seminar said basically that you don't have to file an income tax form because if you did, and you signed it, you would be testifying against yourself. Cooley said that if you signed it and there was a mistake in it, you could be prosecuted for lying under oath. Sounded reasonable enough to me, so I did it for 5 years!

One day in 1984 a man walked up to my door and knocked. He presented me with a summons to appear in court for "failure to file an income tax return", for those years. In actual fact I had indeed filed my taxes, deliberately leaving off my signature, and a few items of information, but paying the IRS each time. So I wasn't guilty of "not filing". I quickly hired the best criminal tax lawyer I could find. We talked for a long time and I queried him about the 5th amendment theory. He said he was sure it was a legitimate defense, that signing and filing a tax return was the only way government had of finding out about your liabilities and determining your tax bill. Indeed it was a clear cut violation of the 5th amendment, and was literally testifying against your self, because there was no one else that could testify against you. He further bore out my previous knowledge that under the United States Constitution you are innocent until proven guilty, but that the reverse is true with the IRS, who finds you guilty until you prove yourself innocent, a further violation of the Constitution. I then asked him why it had never been found in favor of those violating IRS rules, but in reality following their Constitutional rights.

He said it was because no one had ever spent the big bucks it would take to carry it to the Supreme Court, and take a chance that the court might find for a Constitutional principle rather than doing their usual job of deciding if a good judgment might upset the government's apple cart, right or wrong. It is a lot of expense, and the chances are it might fail in the highest court, not because it was a wrong pleading, but because the court often cares not a whit about the Constitution. It has become a legislating body.

Robert Bork, a brilliant, but defeated Supreme Court candidate in his book, "*The Tempting of America*", (Macmillan,

1990), on page 158, argues in favor of not rocking the boat. "The decision may be clearly incorrect but nevertheless have become so embedded in the life of the nation, so accepted by the society, so fundamental to the private and public expectations of individuals and institutions that the result should not be changed now...To overturn these would be to overturn most of modern government and plunge us into chaos". Never have I disagreed more. "We may be wrong, but we have always done it this way, so don't try to change us now", in other words I beg to differ Judge Bork!

The very concept of not changing something, even though it is wrong, leaves me absolutely outraged. This is not logic, reason, or justice. Maybe we are lucky Judge Bork didn't make it, although he seems more logical than at least half of the current justices.

Suppose someone paid the bill and carried it all the way to the Supreme Court? Suppose the Court decided that it was indeed a violation of the Constitution to force people to testify against themselves by filing income tax forms and signing them. So what? Is freedom less important than slavery? Is force more important than free will righteousness? Wouldn't it be far better for government to slash its hundreds of billions of yearly waste and allow the citizens to file freely, and not be guilty until they prove themselves innocent? Haven't we had enough of the gestapo like IRS seizing anything they want under the most specious of reasons?

I think the IRS is the closest thing America has to utter slavery, which the Constitution also bans. The IRS tactics violate every principle upon which our country was founded.

I was found guilty by the judge of "not filing"; which I did. I was fined $5,000, and made to accurately file all my returns for those years, which I did. I also paid a hefty fee to my lawyer. Was I guilty? No, but I couldn't afford to appeal. Was, and am I still outraged? You bet! I lost that one, but won all the rest of my confrontations with the IRS, most of which were so outrageous as to be unbelievable.

In August of 1986, I received a call from Barbara Peterson of the Denver IRS office. She wanted to know when I was going to pay my 1977 income taxes! Flabbergasted, I reminded her that was 9 years previous, that I filed timely, and paid what I owed. Must be a mix-up, and she promised me to look into it, re-audit, if necessary, and solve the problem. I heard nothing more till I read in the local newspaper that my hotel had been seized by the IRS! I was in a distant city for the winter. Lovely, huh? This time I knew exactly what to do. I hired another lawyer, this time an ex-IRS attorney in Boulder, Colorado named Dawson Joyner who took one look at the mess and filed suit. I cashed a nice check after that one, and was paid interest as well. I have won all but that damned 5th amendment one and I am here to say that if I ever get rich, I intend to take the big bucks necessary and fight that one all the way to the highest court in the land, hoping that they might just stop legislating for once, and decide Constitutional vs Unconstitutional. Signing your name and giving information on that tax return is nothing more than testifying against yourself.

What Marvin Cooley didn't say was that although the 5th amendment might seem to give you the right not to sign and fill in those tax forms, it had never been adjudicated as such. For that I wish I could wring his neck, as he caused me a lot of expense, besides actually lying in his seminar.

ARE THEY EVER THE SAME AGAIN?

As a man well into his fifties, I have never been drunk, never smoked cigarettes, and never experimented with drugs of any kind. No pot, no cocaine, nothing. Basically, I am clean as a whistle. Perhaps this background has instilled in me a certain intolerance for those who do participate in such self destructive behavior. The consequences of smoking and alcohol abuse are well documented, but there is a certain danger in drug usage that no one seems to have noted. Once a person has "done" drugs, it has been my observation that their minds are permanently altered.

I have been told over and over again that under the influence of drugs, one can hear music as one has never heard it before, think deeper thoughts than ever before, see colors of an incredible brilliance, and have a heightened sense of taste, touch and smell. Sex is supposed to be better too! Perhaps this is true, but what I see of people who tell of such experiences makes me doubtful. If they wish to alter their natural perception of reality, that's up to them. The point of this is that I feel they have undergone a permanent change.

The story, not apocryphal, is told of the woman who was obsessed with her dizzyingly supreme thoughts while under the influence of marijuana. In order to capture her exalted mental state, she installed a note pad and pencil by her bed so she could record such magnificences upon experiencing them while under the drug. She "turned on", and wrote down all the heavenly callings and sublime solutions to problems so she could act on them at a later, more sober time. Next morning she awoke to discover that her scribblings were utter gibberish and totally unintelligible.

The freaky looks, oddball lifestyles, and weird tastes in music, clothing, furnishings, and art make drug users or ex-drug users easily identifiable. They are always to the left of center politically, seem to have affinities for long hair, beards, granny glasses, and psychedelic music, even though the so called "hippie" movement has been dead for 20 years. They still love those Volkswagens, often still practice poor hygiene, or at least look like it, and are always skinny it seems. It is difficult to describe the aura around these people, indicating to me anyway, that they either still do, or at one time "did" drugs. It leaves a jumbled set of reasonings or blurred sensibilities that are obvious. Does any reader agree?

If you have trouble understanding acid rock, Zen Buddhism, goat's milk, and laser shows, you have probably never used drugs. I honestly feel those who have experienced the effects of drugs have irreversibly altered their minds. I have asked various people if they feel they are different than before they ever tried drugs, and the honest ones admit they do. Those who deny any change are either still using drugs, and are therefore protective, or are simply incapable of remembering their mental states or attitudes prior to experimentation. The telltale signs of permanent mind warp are evident everywhere about them and their lives. They are usually still useful citizens, only slightly "different", and the difference is obvious.

Years ago I had an employee named Beverly who had done a lot of LSD years before. She was pretty far out anyway, but even though she hadn't done any drugs for many years, she could be walking down a sidewalk, and sometimes automatically "go on a trip", which sounds pretty scary. Since I have never taken "a trip", I can't really understand what she meant, other than I am glad it never happened to me.

Without experiencing something for yourself, you can't

possibly know what it is really like, be it an orgasm or a lobster tail. One of the reasons I never tried drugs is because I might like them! As it is, I don't know what I missed, and I never intend to find out. I am happy and at peace knowing that my mind and ability to reason is intact. I can get high on the reality of the sun setting behind snow capped mountain peaks, a symphony of Beethoven, an opera by Puccini, real French vanilla ice cream, a roaring fireplace, or any of hundreds of wonderful experiences easily brought to mind. I don't need drugs! There is great reward in having protected logic and intelligence from mind altering drugs that leave a certain amount of crippling, be it ever so small. An ability to rise above the harsher realities of life, rather than taking the totally non productive route of escaping into a drug induced euphoria has a lot to say for itself.

Just as all our experiences in life change us in some way, so does experimentation with drugs. The permanent mind alteration brought about by drug use is not a positive change, but a negative one. As a matter of fact, the illogical behavior, avoidance of responsibility, and political stances of an entire generation of ex and current drug users is having a disastrous effect on this country and the world.

PUBLIC

The so called "common man" has been negated and ignored without question. The common man however, is the one that has turned the wheels of civilization, run the machinery, dug the ditches, plowed the fields, laid the bricks, fixed the roofs, and "done the work". Without the common man, America might never have been what it was, and sadly isn't any longer, namely the richest, happiest, most prosperous land on earth. We have lost that distinction and have crashed.

Outrageously, the common man has been relegated to the dust bin of American achievement. Now it is the elite, college educated, "middle classes" that are the prime focus of the media and bureaucracy. As I write this, it is December 1991, and America is in deep recession, with the economy totally stagnant. As the politicians hold hearings, wrangle, and argue over what to do, they have overlooked us. I have no college degree and am proud of it. I am not a lawyer, and even more proud of that fact. I have never inherited a dime, and am proud of that also. I am a common man. The type for which Aaron Copeland wrote his wonderful "Fanfare For The Common Man".

No matter where you go, what job you apply for, or who may interview you, one of the first questions asked is "Where did you go to college?" I see a continual stream of lame brains that have P.H.D.'s (piled higher and deeper) plus every other degree known to man. They usually couldn't hammer a nail, change a tire, cook an egg, or do anything really worthwhile. Their complicated state of mind is worthless. As I watch the

House Ways and Means Committee struggle with the recession they have created with endless spending, laws and regulations that have strangled America, it is laughable to see them try to decide what additional legislation they must pass to help the economy. The expensively suited, well educated people appearing before this committee haven't the foggiest idea of anything.

But the common man does. He inwardly knows the problems are in Washington, with its rules, regulations, bureaucracy, and gobbledygook. Us common people know it is difficult to live now without infringing on some bureaucracy's territory and coming under scrutiny. Life has become difficult and unprofitable with mighty government hovering over our every move. A government we are paying about 95% of our income to maintain, and since that isn't enough it prints money to pay for the rest. How frightening!

I lived in Philadelphia for many years. Philadelphia was basically a working class town. West Philly, Kensington, South Philly, Frankfort, plus lots of other places are and were working class neighborhoods with row houses, corner bars, wonderful churches, and neighborhood schools. If you like movies, "Rocky" came from a working class Philly neighborhood. The empty, rusting, and burned out factories were manned by working class, common men. Marvelous, common, working classes who raised families, worshiped their God, scrubbed the steps, saved, struggled, and toiled their entire lifetime and were eminently successful. The backbone of America. Wonderful people.

I watched the common man sabotaged by government. I saw government regulations destroy his working place and put him out of a job. I saw the welfare system destroy his neighborhoods, forcing him to move at great expense, just to survive. I saw neighborhoods and jobs that had been secure for a hundred years destroyed in less than a decade. In Philly, once great corporations that provided security and jobs for hundreds of thousands of working class families are now non existent.

This all began to happen when Franklin Roosevelt took office. Unfortunately, FDR has become an icon for the working classes. In reality he should be the opposite. Before FDR there was no welfare in America. Yet no one starved, and everyone lived to about the same age as they do now. Before the FDR welfare, people bought homes, women didn't have to work, and the dollar was supreme. All of the urban destruction, recessions, manufacturing loss, foreign invasion, out of sight prices, and of course lowering standards of living, are the logical result of a bit of yeast fermenting the whole batch.

The first time you give something away, everyone else wants some. It becomes like a spreading disease. Give something to any group, class, strata, and everyone else wants in on it. Government, under orders from FDR, made the mistake of robbing from one group and giving it to another, and the yeast had been activated. It has never stopped.

The result of this corrupting of American society has had its greatest effect on the common man. As the corporations, wealthy, and entrepreneurs have been robbed, their ability to create jobs and security has been crippled virtually 100%. If a corporation is taxed to extinction, it cannot furnish jobs. If politicians can convince the masses they are their benefactor rather than their ruination, the chain will continue till everyone is destitute.

All I hear from the Ways and Means hearings is, "tax the rich", with variations. Not a single suggestion that Washington's Party be disbanded. America is ruined to the degree we are taxed at any income level. At 95% or better, America is out of business. The common man is always the first on the hit list because he is the most vulnerable. He is virtually extinct, as are his former neighborhoods, stores, and churches. They have become ghettos, slums, and no man's lands. America's cities have been trashed by the common man's replacements which do not possess the work ethic and all that goes with it.

Philly's former pristine, neat, cared for, working class neighborhoods are gone. It's all over for the most part. There are enclaves in South and East Philly where you can walk the streets and not be afraid, but it is a struggle to maintain these still wonderful places. The typical row house neighborhood in West Philly I lived in, went the way of the dodo bird 20 years ago. I used to sit outside on warm summer nights, sprinkling the grass and talk to Foster Bixler next door. Forget it now. Burned out hulks of buildings, abandoned cars, and desolation is what remains of West Philly.

The common, working class man has been decapitalized. Where did the money go? It went to Washington in the form of outrageous and mostly hidden taxes to support worthless Congressmen and bureaucrats. For every dollar in direct taxes you pay, there is another dollar plus you never see, but pay anyway. No wonder there are no American manufacturing jobs any more. Who can afford to furnish them? The massive wealth transfer went first to Washington, and then to Japan, not directly to Japan. The common man was dispossessed first, and then after the politicians used it, the Japs came in and milked us further.

As the epilogue of this book says, we need to stop the god damned party in Washington, and do it pronto. It doesn't matter whether you are a democrat, republican, or independent, it is the attitude of "STP" (stop the party) that matters. Who cares which party is the worst? They both are a disgrace and can only think of more government, not less, and shifting the deck chairs on the Titanic. The Titanic, like America, was the most wonderful boat afloat. The American Titanic is sinking because the politicians are not commoners like us. They think in the stratosphere, and cannot see the forest for the trees.

Commoners like us can think and hopefully act. It doesn't take huge brainpower to realize if you tax people to death they will fail, be unhappy, and hopefully get really angry.

One of the partners of the publishing house that has done this book thinks we will have to go totally down before we can rise. Warren might be right. The other partner as well as myself think there is a chance America might be saved and the party stopped. Jim and I hope America will throw the bastards out, throw welfare out, throw millions of laws out, and restart our engines before we crash.

If this book does nothing else, hopefully it will make the common man rise up and stop the Washington Party that has destroyed America, cost us our prosperity, wealth, morality, security, and happiness. I am ashamed I was born and raised in Washington D.C. No, my family never worked for government. When I was a kid, government wasn't 1% of the size it is now. Washington D.C. is virtually unrecognizable to me now. The grotesque buildings, crime, filth, drugs, smog, and shallowness amazes me. Washington's suburbs have the highest incomes in America. All stolen from us commoners over the years. A big syphon, money hoses coming from common people all over America. A huge drain of our resources and wealth. All going to a literal cesspool of corruption, greed, avarice, and cowardice called our Nation's Capital. Cowardice because they take our money not with ability, hard work, sweat, or competition, but with laws, regulations, and taxes. Taxes on everything we buy, not just on what we make. Taxes on every phone call, head of lettuce, light bulb, automobile, television, or book we purchase with their worthless paper money. Hidden taxes that have destroyed the common man, his neighborhoods and security. I hope you get the point of this!

KEEP 'EM ALIVE

Society insists on keeping people alive who would rather die. Several examples of this are readily brought to mind. Suicide is illegal in many states. Of all the insane laws ever to be put on any books, that one is it. It is actually illegal to commit suicide. Think of it. If you attempt to commit suicide and don't make it, you can be prosecuted and punished. As if a person wouldn't be in bad enough shape at failure, he is now taken to court. Suicide is common when there is deep depression over a loved one's death or terminal illness. It is the government's job to protect you from your enemies, not to protect you from yourself. Suicide prevention costs a bundle, and is not government's job.

If a person has terminal cancer and they want to end it all, why not? If a man has lost his wife, is elderly, has no one to care for him, and he wants to do what he thinks will place him next to his wife, why not? If a person is mentally ill, depressed, or otherwise, and chooses to end their life, why not? Whose business is it anyway but the one who owns that life?

Hooray for the elderly Florida couple whose kids were grown, they had a lovely life, and no problems of any kind, except they were getting old and feeble. They kissed, wrote a note explaining everything, left a will, went to the garage, started their late model Lincoln, and died in each other's arms-painlessly, from carbon monoxide. No terminal illness, nursing homes, loneliness, or poverty was going to get them. Wasn't that a wonderful thing to do? I think so.

I don't want to live if I can't enjoy life. I don't want to

spend years fighting cancer, old age, imbecility. or loneliness. I have had a good life, enjoyed it, raised my kids well, and would consider it a great thing to end it if I thought the remainder would break me, cause me much pain, require intense care, or make me live it by myself if I were old. Phooey! I'll go into the garage and start the engine, leaving a note wishing everyone well. I'd rather leave the dough to my kids than give it to hospitals, nursing homes, and doctors. And I don't want to be kept alive if I am in some coma, or other helpless, hopeless state. Consider this my "living will". Don't keep me alive! It has been said that 90% of tire troubles occur during the last 10% of tire life. It is also true with the human body.

Those that get rid of themselves avoid enriching the medical community and leave it to whom they please. Those believing in euthanasia, (mercy killing), also help their surviving mate if he or she is in good health. Far too many husbands or wives have extinguished their life's savings in a futile attempt to prolong the life of the other, leaving the surviving one penniless after the fight has been lost. Stupid! Death happens to everyone eventually, why fight it?

Look at a drunken bum on a street, sitting wrapped in a filthy blanket on a sub freezing night. Am I supposed to feel sorry for him? If he decided to commit suicide, or froze to death, would I interfere? Nope! Do I feel sorry for those lazy creeps any more than I would if I stepped on a cockroach? They are human cockroaches. Further, should my tax dollars go to keeping him alive? Absolutely no, except of course they do. Should tax dollars be spent to maintain the rubbish of humanity who don't care for themselves? Why should tax dollars go to "suicide prevention" programs? If they don't care for their own life, why should anyone else, other than a loved one or relative?

If a terminally ill patient wants to be injected with a drug that will put them out of their misery painlessly, who should object? There are too many cases of living vegetables being maintained on life support systems at taxpayer expense, even though parents, mates, or children of the comatose person begs for them to be allowed to die in peace and dignity. For such not to be allowed, is sheer folly, and those idiots picketing outside of hospitals when such finally happens, should be locked up for getting in the way.

If a woman, single or married, gets pregnant and doesn't want a child, why should I care if she aborts it? Whether "life" begins at conception, at 3 weeks, 3 months, 6 months, or at birth is not the point. The woman's body is hers just like my property is mine. If I want to take an ax to my furniture, or run my car without oil, it is mine and I can do with it what I want. My possessions do not belong to "society", any more than the baby in that mother's womb belongs to society. It is just as futile to legislate what a mother may do with an unborn baby in her body, as it is to legislate any other form of so called "morality".

Lots of times people are at the end of the line as far as life's desirability is concerned. It may be the death of a loved one, the breakup of a marriage, bankruptcy, being uncovered doing something very embarrassing or illegal. Death might very well be better than living the rest of a life in pain, misery, or in jail.

When tax monies are used to keep alive the inept, retarded, foolish, insane, sick, or dangerous, it is wasted. Preserving people that cannot, or will not preserve themselves destroys a race, not just the pocketbook. Why not kill the healthy animals and save the sick? Nature doesn't operate that way. Nature sees to it that the weak, old, sick, and deformed are eaten or killed quickly so they don't breed and debase the species. Strong animals fight for life and survive. Weak animals die. Only humans seem to love the weak, helpless, sick, aged, infirm, insane, and criminal. At least some humans do. Not me. Humans stomp the strong by taxing them to death, and uphold the sick, weak, and stupid with taxes. Fine way to reach Utopia!

AMTRAK & RAILROADS

In 1969, with the enactment of the law creating AMTRAK, America lost over 50% of its passenger trains. Not only did we lose over 50% of our passenger trains, but the trains lost their individuality, charm, competitiveness, and romance, which had described them for over 100 years. They became just another bureaucracy, wasting money by the hundreds of millions of dollars each year. Even the employees who run the trains are no longer uniformed like railroad men, but airline pilots.

Over two decades later, each railroad ticket is subsidized about 38% by us taxpayers, who just pay and pay for endless government waste. America now has passenger trains that all look alike, go very few places, have an extremely poor on time record, serve sterile food, an "800" number that often isn't answered for long periods of time, and operated with little of the old loyalty, romance, and pride that railroaders used to possess, especially in passenger service. Gone are the days when an engineer could be identified by his distinctive whistle technique, and would always do his utmost to keep the schedule, or "advertised".

I LOVE trains! I have been a railroad fan since early childhood, and probably have a ton of books and magazines on the subject, not to mention thousands of slides and photos of my favorite lines and operations. Trains are one of my life's addictions, so I really know whereof I speak.

For many years railroads were not allowed to abandon their unprofitable passenger trains, made so by heavy subsidy of the competition on highways, in the water, and especially in the sky. Railroads have always paid property taxes on their rights of way, just like we pay property taxes on our homes and businesses. They also pay personal property taxes on equipment. Railroads have always built and maintained their own roadbeds, tracks, stations, police and safety systems, as opposed to government built, owned, and operated airports, highways, and waterways.

If airlines paid the cost of airports and safety systems, tickets would probably have to be priced double to break even. If truckers paid the actual cost of the highways they use and destroy, rather than low user fees, their rates would be so high as to be of no competition whatsoever with railroads. If water haulers paid the cost of the Coast Guard, and waterway maintenance, even their price structure would not compete with railroads.

Steel wheels running on steel rails are the most frictionless form of movement yet discovered by man. The friction of rubber tires on pavement, overcoming the resistance of water on boat hulls, and the high energy cost of flying, are many times the mechanical effort and energy consumption used by railroad trains running on easy curves and gradual grades as is railroad building practice. As a further indication of efficiency, a two man railroad crew can easily move over 10,000 tons of freight from one place to the next with no highway congestion or interference. It takes one man to move far less than one hundred tons over highways. Airplanes require such immense horsepower and consume so much fuel, that only the most valuable, time sensitive, and lightweight freight is hauled.

Passenger trains haul passengers on a "per passenger, per mile, per gallon of fuel" ratio so far and away lower than any other form of transport that comparisons are actually bizarre. Amtrak manages to do it much more expensively than did the individual railroads Amtrak replaced. Amtrak's cost becomes lower each year as equipment becomes uniform, more modern, and certain work rules are gradually changed, but it will never be a subsidy free system.

Amtrak is so bad that for ten years Santa Fe refused to allow the use of its former crack passenger train's name, the "Chief", and "Super Chief". Santa Fe wanted to keep the memories and reputation of these trains cherished, not tarnished by bureaucracy. We have now joined every other nation in the world by socializing rail transport, to the detriment of everyone. Kids think Amtrak has always run the passenger trains. They don't know of the glory days before Amtrak, when 100 mile per hour trains scorched the tracks between major cities and vied with each other to give the most deluxe, fastest service. They don't know of the wonderful foods served on china plates, and eaten with the finest silver plated flatware on linen tablecloths in the glorious dining cars. They can't imagine a railroad providing a luxurious red carpet for passengers to walk on from station to the cars, or splendidly liveried attendants beaming genuine smiles to their charges. Gone are the on time running, wide, roomy berths, and gut wrenching, tear provoking, lonely, locomotive whistles piercing the night's stillness. The passenger trains of old are dead. Long live memories of the passenger trains of old.

When diesel locomotives came on the scene, their advantage was multiple engines being operated by one engine crew, and going far longer distances without servicing than steam engines required. Lots of potential savings, but savings which still have not been realized due to chicken hearted management being afraid to lay down the law to labor. Changes that would say in effect, "a day's work for a day's pay". Steam locomotive crews didn't work by the hour, but by the distance traveled, called a "division", which was usually about a hundred miles. At each division, a crew change took place and the locomotive was either replaced or serviced.

Those division points are as archaic and ridiculous as horse whips in the automobile age, yet they still exist. Amtrak has managed to allow conductors to go through two or three divisions, meaning they only get perhaps $100 per hour for riding a train, but many engine crews still change at each division point, making their work day as little as 2 hours, for which they receive a full day's pay.

I can name countless absurdities of Amtrak and the current railroads that violate every possible sense of logic, common sense, customer relations, and first grade economics, but this isn't a book on railroads. Where is the advantage of diesels if the built in labor economies are not utilized? Diesel locomotive costs are many times that of steam engines, and they don't last as long. Maintenance costs and fuel costs are higher as well. Their advantage is in labor savings, which still has not been realized by Amtrak, and for that matter, railroads in general.

Over the years, some work rule reform has taken place on the railroads, but it has been so gradual they show little profit based on money invested, and are considered a poor stock investment. Railroads used to say if they could only get rid of those damned passenger trains they could put their house in order, but that wasn't the problem and their house is still not in order. It will never be in order until their labor situation is corrected. Far more competitive prices could be offered by railroads if management would only stand up to unions at once, rather than at last. For every year antiquated work rules continue, railroad capital is dissipated, plant degenerates, and needed modernization and maintenance is postponed due to valuable money being wasted on unneeded labor. This has been going on for 50 years now!

Railroads now haul less than HALF of the freight they used to haul. Jobs have been lost that wouldn't have been lost if management had long ago insisted on work rule reform that would have saved business now lost forever.

An interesting study was done a few years ago by a railroad magazine, comparing the cost of operating current state of the art diesel locomotives with 1945 state of the art steam locomotives, including labor, fuel, repairs, capitaliza-tion, and replacement. Current labor and fuel costs were used. Believe it or not, the steam locomotive won hands down! When diesel locomotives replaced steam, diesel fuel cost about a nickel a gallon. It is now about a dollar a gallon. Coal has gone up in price far less. Steam locomotives are utterly simple mechanically, and initial per horsepower cost is far lower than diesel. Diesel overhaul and maintenance is much higher than simple steam maintenance and overhaul.

It is interesting to think that if locomotives had been saved rather than cut up and sold for scrap, they might be once again running over the roads, thrilling onlookers and making wide eyed kids dream of a career in a locomotive cab rather than in an airline cockpit.

None of man's inventions and achievements has quite equaled the sound, smell, and sight of a steam locomotive. Whether it be pulling a mile of freight cars, a string of sleek passenger cars, or standing still, the steam locomotive is the most human of all mechanical devices. It has always evoked the strongest emotions from admirers of machinery. This is why restored steam locomotives pulling special trains full of happy passengers cause traffic jams and tears of loving remembrance everywhere they run. Old men hold up tykes to see the engine, hoping they will assimilate the ambience, beauty, charm, enchantment, fascination, and even sex appeal of the steam locomotive all at once, that a lifetime of association has given the seniors. It can't be absorbed that fast, but they must attempt it. It is left to old men like myself to remember, and to pitifully scribble endless words on paper, attempting to convey the indescribable aura and sound of the almost extinct iron horse. Sic transit gloria mundi.

THE CONCEPT OF GOVERNMENT

When America was founded, a government was conceived that was to be controlled by the people, and operate with their permission. The concept was for government to protect its citizens and administer justice. You can search the Constitution from beginning to end, analyze it with a microscope, and you will find not much else as a prerogative of government. The "United States" was to be made up of individual states, each competing with the other, and having their own governments which would not pass laws in conflict with the U.S. Constitution. Most of the Constitution speaks of the various intricacies of the U.S. Government, saying who shall be elected, how long they shall serve, and details of the every day operation of such government. The "Bill of Rights", unfortunately, does not have a provision giving us freedom FROM government, other than as listed in the 10th amendment, which has been largely ignored by Washington.

This book has much to say about the inefficiency, selfishness, greed, and usurped power of government. The Constitution doesn't speak much about limiting government's power, because in their wildest dreams, the Founders never thought it would get so out of control. They neglected to put into the Constitution the words saying, "Government shall do NOTHING not herein contained"! So it has become like an out of control forest fire. A gigantic octopus with tentacles reaching into every crevice of our lives, sucking our blood.

As a casual example of the misunderstanding of people in elected positions, consider the N.B.C. Sunday morning TV show, "Meet the Press", on May 5th, 1991. On the show was Governor Bill Clinton, of Arkansas. He made a statement that didn't seem too important, but which is certainly indicative of the general mind set we now witness in 100% of government employees, the Congress, and most of the world's population for that matter. He said, "Government is to solve problems and make progress". Get the point? The Constitution said no such thing.

Around the world people look to various governments to "solve problems" as the Governor said, and this is a grievous error. It is looking to the fox to protect the henhouse. It is asking the thief to guard your home. The problem of misunderstanding governmental ability to do anything, except at a huge cost, is fooling everyone. A Bill Moyers special on P.B.S. May 28th, 1991 was a slick piece of yellow journalism if there ever was one. The piece showed many out of work, poor, and sick people, and every couple of minutes a cut was made to news clips on the Iraq war. The inference was that if America hadn't spent so much on that war, these people would have gotten more handouts. The lie is that government has a lot of money automatically, and according to Moyers' philosophy, government should be spending it on the poor, schools, the sick, unemployed and other cases of need. This is wrong.

Government doesn't have money to spend unless it first steals it from its subjects in several ways, charges perhaps 50% for handling, and then administers it abysmally. Government doesn't have any money at all without confiscating twice as much as it doles out.

When George Bush had what everyone thought was a heart problem and was rushed to the hospital, everyone was screaming "WHO IS RUNNING THE COUNTRY?" Dan Quayle? The plain fact is that NO ONE SHOULD BE RUNNING THE COUNTRY. The country, under the founding fathers' directives in the Constitution, said basically that the country should run itself, with government doing a bit of protecting and administering justice. The concept of government, as put forth in the Constitution, is called "limited statism" by some, but no matter how you express it, the fact is perhaps 90% of federal, 50% of state, and 25% of local government needs to be abolished.

When Thomas Jefferson was Secretary of State, the entire department had but 7 employees, and the world hasn't grown any larger. It is said that each Congressman uses over $400,000 worth of franking each year!

So much of our money is being confiscated by government, and it is being done in such an insipid way, that citizens really do not know what has hit them. They just think prices have gone up over the years, which isn't true at all. The value of the money has gone down. As is indicated in another place in this book, we Americans are being taxed at a rate of 95% or better, and getting virtually nothing for it. These taxes make our product cost to be extremely high and non competitive.

For far too many years, management and labor have quarreled with each other over wages in a shrinking market. The market is shrinking because our merchandise costs too much to produce, and its cost makes it non-saleable in the world. Jobs by the hundreds of thousands have been lost and hardships multiplied thousands of percentage points because of intrusive government taxation making it impossible to trade or compete. It is neither management nor labor's fault that the problem exists. It is the fault of government for making our money so worthless, and corresponding prices so high in this money. The problem exists around the world in greater or lesser degrees. America does not have a monopoly on confiscatory government filled with useless bureaucrats. It is my fervid hope that the emerging former communist lands do not copy us or any other bureaucracy in the world, but should copy our Constitution with changes as I mention in the chapter called "Rewrite". Then they may have a chance!

Businesses, families, farms, and factories all operate extremely well without government interfering. People go to work, hotels rent rooms, mothers mother, restaurants serve meals, and in general we all do very well without government, other than its protective side, such as the police. But when we have to operate with increasingly worthless money and interference in every facet of our lives, we simply cannot compete with other nations in trade. With the concept of government as it now exists, we will fail in a very short time unless drastic cuts are made to once again free us and allow us to compete.

The media and political scientists continually harp about "democracy" as being the hope of the world. Rubbish! Democracy got us where we are now! It is voting yourself a representative who will dole out largess from the public treasury that has bankrupted us, and this was done with "democracy".

Freedom is the magic word, not democracy. Freedom to do what you please as long as you harm no one else. Freedom didn't create poverty. We grew to greatness with freedom, and the more we lost, the less we prospered.

The initial and successful concept of government made government our servant, and now we are enslaved by it. When a system, or concept of government ceases to serve its governed, and instead oppresses them, it is time to change or remove that offensive government.

I hope it isn't too late, and I hope I stir some feelings with this compilation of thoughts. If it is, and I can't, it was nice for about 150 years.

WELFARE

It is difficult to realize just how much welfare there is in America today. By welfare, I mean government transfers of assets to non governmental individuals, businesses, schools, corporations, families, students, the sick and aged, transportation agencies, and hundreds of other places. Welfare of the private sector must be rightly called "charity", examples of which are church support, family support, or the like. Welfare is handouts from governments at all levels, from town, up through county, state, and federal. The money for welfare is obtained from taxes and debt incurred by the disbursing governments and their agencies. Most regard it as necessary, desirable, and impossible to delete from society. I must disagree.

Welfare is basically "something for nothing", except there is no such thing as "something for nothing". All things have a price. Welfare given to one takes from another in some form or other. Something for nothing is a total non sequitur. Welfare is theft from the haves, and a gift to the have nots, with perhaps a 50% handling charge.

Welfare is issued for two basic reasons; humanitarian and political. There are no other reasons for welfare.

As far as humanitarian reasons, poverty about sums it up. However, the word "poverty" means totally different things to different people. Donald Trump has been limited to spending several hundred thousand dollars a year by the courts. To Trump, this is possibly the "poverty level", whereas to me, 1% of that would be riches. To a person who has always lived poorly, poverty may be $200 per month. Government figures as to what constitutes "poverty" are meaningless .

Welfare has been doled out to admittedly middle class persons to aid them with their heating bills. Welfare has been given in the form of student loans at cheap interest rates, even though parents are affluent. Welfare is given to the elderly regardless of their economic condition in the form of medicare, medicaid, property tax relief, cut rate rides on government owned transport systems, and recreation programs, to mention a few.

Yesterday in the super market, the fellow checking out in front of me was about 6' 4", 45 years old, husky, extremely well built, and was driving a fairly new pickup truck. He was the picture of health and robust manliness. He also had checked out three video tapes, so he had a TV set and VCR, besides his pickup. He paid his bills with food stamps. Was he able to work? Damned right! Was he a "poverty case"? Many recipients of welfare have no "poverty" problems.

Next is political. Politics has a great deal to do with welfare, because politicians get elected by handing out government money to constituents. They can stay elected by the same means. It is desirable to obtain and hold on to political office, as it pays well, has prestige, and huge amounts of intoxicating power. Power seldom available to a non politician. Power is a heady thing, and once having tasted the thrill of power in politics, few ever want to return to a normal life.

It is all simple then, right? Welfare is issued because the recipients don't have enough money, and because it buys votes for the politician handing out the money. Elementary my dear Watson.

Getting rid of all welfare would be the best thing that ever happened to America or any other nation. The most obvious advantage is that you would either get rid of all the weak, sick, and lazy, or they would learn to care for themselves with their own hands, brains, and devices. "But what about the poor"? What about them? Welfare has never made a poor person rich, but it has made us all poor.

Welfare has destroyed two major races for all practical purposes. Too many American Negroes and Indians are unproductive, under educated and underachieving. Their numbers are rife with crime, illegitimacy, and disease. The problem is welfare, provided by well meaning, liberal sob sisters, who think handing out money to the poor will help them, and of course by politicians who relish the votes at election time.

The results of this welfare to Negroes and American Indians are tragic but obvious, as a trip through North Philly, Harlem, or a reservation will demonstrate. If these two races had never received a dime, but allowed to provide for themselves, all would be much different in America today. All of the whining and crying about slavery makes not a whit of sense as far as the Negro is concerned, nor do the Indian's claims about the white man's abuse. Slavery ended over 125 years ago. Indians abused and murdered whites as often as whites did it to Indians. Many other races came here, couldn't speak the language, and were also persecuted by those already here, and made it nicely. The name "Paddy Wagon" came into use when so many Irish being hauled away by the police gave their name as "Paddy". The term "WOP", began when so many Italians, "With Out Papers" were picked up that the three letters, W.O.P. came to be synonymous with Italians. Jews were crammed into hideous lower east side tenements, but decided they would make it, raise their kids right, keep clean, and be honest. They did, and in a grand manner, even though they were hated by just about everyone. So language, color, or harsh treatment are no excuse for a race not "making it". The two races that never "made it", the Negro and American Indian, are literally the victims of welfare. No one has ever been permanently helped by welfare, and what brief relief has been afforded, has had an extremely deleterious effect on character.

Chapter 75 277

There have been poor people in all civilizations since time began, and no one has yet figured out how to get rid of them. The poor are universal, and always will be. In a society with no poor, there will be no rich. A wise man once said if you took all the money and equally divided it, within ten years the same people would have it again. Probably true. Welfare can't possibly give a stupid worker brains needed to make him a manager. Welfare can't possibly help a poor person nearly as much as he or she can help themselves. In every society as in every building, there are the top, middle and bottom. If a society were filthy rich, a rich man may have an income of a billion dollars a year, and a poor man may only make a hundred thousand. The hundred thousand man would be classed as "poverty". It is impossible to ever eliminate the bottom sector of a society, because the very act of classifying results in "levels", no matter how meaningless they may be.

Older citizens whose kids are raised and houses paid for can get by easily on "poverty" levels of income. Young families with house payments, kids, car payments, and insurance premiums to pay, required a lot more money, but still live poorly in spite of their high incomes. The term "poverty" is meaningless.

"How about the poor that are unable to work?" If I must have an answer for everything, I would say that humans are wonderfully kind and generous people, and throughout history there have been people who could not work, but were cared for by church, friends, relatives, or even passers by. There are certain sad situations existing in the world that just cannot be fixed by anyone at any time, be it drought, flood, earthquake, or poverty. You just do the best you can but there is no reason why government should be responsible .

No matter which example you use, welfare is not government's job. Government has no money, except that which it takes from its subjects. A church, on the other hand, has voluntary members and voluntary contributions, which can, and are distributed by the church to the needy. Other service organizations exist, such as the Lions, Kiwanis, Rotary, Salvation Army, United Way, American Cancer Society, and the list is endless. Contributions to these organizations is voluntary, their work is marvelous, and no political results are involved, nor is government. This process is known as "voluntaryism".

The Founders never intended for the government they created to "help". The intention was to "protect". If Thomas Jefferson, or any of the Constitution's writers, and our nation's Founders came back from the grave and took a look at what our politicos have done to this land, they would be absolutely appalled.

Welfare is perhaps the greatest problem in America today. It has destroyed us under the guise of "kindness", "help the needy", and other like phrases which make us all poor in the long run. Now for some examples.

The way to avoid poverty is to work. Various jobs pay various amounts of money, and command various intelligence levels, aptitudes, and abilities. Everyone has to do the best they can with what they have, and that's as simple as it can get. Under a free system, there can be no equality. Our Constitution doesn't promise equality, nor make any provisions for it, just like it doesn't make any provisions for welfare. Free men are not equal, and equal men are not free. Welfare exacerbates prejudice, whereas hard work and achievement eliminates prejudice.

Working for low wages might not be what one wants to do, but if there were no welfare, one would do what one had to do to survive. It's that simple again. Those unable to work will have to be fed by those who do work, but not by compulsion, as welfare is, but by charity.

Welfare is evil, and it isn't hard to see what welfare has

fostered. Welfare is extremely addictive! America has third and fourth generations of welfare recipients that haven't the foggiest idea of how to work and hold a job! They live in welfare housing, receive welfare checks and food stamps, and never do an honest day's worth of work in their life. The neighborhoods in which these people live are cesspools of crime, filth, and degradation. Welfare has done this. If no handouts from any government were ever given to anyone at any time, there would probably be no slums. Working class neighborhoods? Yes, and poor neighborhoods, but not slums. Slums are the result of no work ethic, no care, and no effort. Working people care for what they own, no matter how humble. With no welfare, the weak would just learn to work or die. Die? Yes, die.

What is the purpose in keeping a person alive who hasn't the desire to keep themselves alive? Why feed a person who will not work to feed themselves? At best we are, "strengthening the weak and weakening the strong", which is a direct quote from Abraham Lincoln, and he thought this was a bad idea. Welfare has paid for millions of illegitimate births. Many women have children to support themselves with welfare checks. The more kids, the bigger the checks, filling America with millions of unwanted, uncared for kids who grow up to be like their parent or parents is not the correct road to Shang-Ri-La.

Welfare has ruined the medical industry. The last time the hospitals and doctors were reasonable, efficient and even kind, was before medicare and medicaid which were installed in the mid 60's. Welfare encourages fraudulent treatments, and fraudulent medicine, all to get that welfare check. Welfare encourages and fosters cheating, quackery, and deception wherever it is, with no exceptions.

Welfare in the form of government subsidized mortgages with no money down, has ruined the cities of America.

Handouts which destroyed us. Welfare of any kind, at any level cannot be justified. Social security is not welfare, but a government sponsored retirement plan. Certain sections of the social security system are welfare, however, and this is what has bankrupted the system. Being paid for the rest of your life for a real or faked injury or disability is what has broken the social security system, and that is plain welfare. I feel sorry for someone injured and debilitated for life, but it is not government's job to care for them. If it happened on a job, let the former employer's insurance care for the victim, and if not, charity will have to do.

No one wants to work at a low paying job, even though there are plenty of them. With no welfare of any kind, people would do what they had to do to eat, so low paying jobs might be taken after all.

Farm subsidies are welfare. The food system has not benefited from agriculture subsidy. America has paid much higher prices for its food, thanks to farm welfare.

Freeways are welfare too. When government built freeways, not only were neighborhoods destroyed, but so were the privately operated, for profit, bus, trolley, subway, and ferry systems. They were taken over by government and, of course, operated at horrendous losses, not to mention the destruction of the cities. The cities are America's greatest loss, and it is thanks to welfare.

The Constitution no where gives the federal government permission to redistribute wealth, which is what welfare does.

Most major cities are now extremely troubled by gang warfare and gang violence. Is it not a fact that most gang members live in public housing or are subsidized in some way by welfare? If you don't have to work, might as well keep busy, establish a "turf", kill, fight maim, steal, and make yourself into a local hero among your peers, not by how hard you can work and advance, but how bad you can be. Suppose

these toughs had to work or starve? Suppose welfare recipients had to produce or die? Would we have gangs if we didn't
have welfare? Quite possibly we would not.

The media loves to find some welfare recipient who wants
to get off the dole. They spotlight them, probably pay well for
the interview, and hold them as typical examples, which is a
blatant lie. For every one trying to get off the welfare rolls,
there are a thousand that will stay there forever, increasing the
bill by endless procreation, which offspring will probably also
not work, live off the dole, have more illegitimate kids, and
extend the chain ad infinitum.

If you get a welfare check, why work? If you work and it
is taken from you to give to the poor, why continue to work?
We are rapidly reaching that point in America. I have yet to
hear a single good reason for welfare, other than for a situation
that should and could be taken care of by voluntaryism. If we
weren't taxed to death, we might just be far more concerned
about the poor and be able to give to them. As it is, we have
nothing left after paying taxes on our income, interest, home,
car, food, telephone, gasoline, wages, retirement, and yes,
even our social security. No wonder church attendance has
gone down, with the resultant inability of churches to care for
the poor. Welfare is a pox on our nation that not a single
politician would vote to eliminate. So we are stuck with our
downhill race into bankruptcy of the purse and spirit.

INFLATION

Recently, while researching for a book in a local newspaper morgue for 1920, I came across an interesting fact. There was $55 in circulation for every person in the U.S. in 1920. As of 1991, there is almost $3000 in circulation for everyone living in the U.S. That's a whopping 60 times the amount of dollars PER PERSON in circulation now than there was in 1920, 70 years ago.

The dictionary defines inflation as, "an increase in the supply of money", and that definition is surely correct, although modern economists and bureaucrats will disagree, saying that inflation is price increases. They are not the same, although they produce the same phenomenon. 75 years ago, the federal government couldn't increase the money supply by making a bookkeeping entry and starting the presses. Our money was backed by gold and silver in 1920. Unless the fed could come up with an equal amount of gold and silver to put away in its vaults, it couldn't print more money. No slimy tricks then. The expression, "sound as a dollar" was accurate.

Today, the dollar, pound, franc, mark, yen, and for that matter all currencies are mere pieces of paper with ink on them. There is no currency in the entire world backed by anything other than government laws that state their money must be used for trade. These currencies are manipulated daily by these governments to suit their whims, and basically none of these currencies are worth any more than the actual paper on which they are printed. It is one gigantic fraud. Other pieces of paper such as deeds, promissory notes, or titles have value, but currencies are absolutely worthless, as they give title to nothing, promise nothing, and have no stability of any kind.

The more of anything there is, the less they will be worth. It is certainly true with currency. If there were still only $55 per person in circulation, each dollar would have to buy more, correct? If each dollar had to buy more, prices would be lower, workers would earn less, and the dollar would be worth far more. But the result would be the same, right? Wrong! It might seem to have the same result because as the supply of currency increases, it becomes less valuable, and prices and wages go up. But the difference is that anyone whose savings are denominated in that currency is decapitalized, and savings becomes pointless. As the currency loses value, the saver is wiped out, so no one with any sense saves! Savings is necessary to make an economy and banking system work.

As government increases the currency supply, prices and wages rise at the same time, and this is called "inflation". Who is harmed? The elderly, people with surplus assets who save them in banks, and, of course, the reputation and stability of America. If there are no savings, banks can loan no money to start businesses and factories to create jobs. If a person puts a hundred dollars in a bank and earns 7% interest, pays taxes at the rate of 30% on the interest earned, and there is a 7% inflation rate, it is a net loss.

Who creates inflation? Since we now know it is accurately defined as an increase in the supply of currency, why and how is it done? Government would like to blame industry for inflation, but that is ridiculous as no one can increase the supply of currency except the federal government. Why does it do it? Because it always spends far more than it takes in, and the increase in currency supply pays the bills. Why does it spend more than it takes in? Because politicians use this device almost 100% of the time to get votes to stay in office. In actuality, inflation and re-election are coupled together like two box cars.

How does the government inflate the currency supply? By a slick little device known as debt. When it can't pay its bills it borrows, selling treasury bills and bonds to investors, who are promised certain amounts of interest for lending government the money. These sales of debt increase the supply of currency by that amount. Every time a government sale of bonds, notes, or certificates occurs, the currency supply is increased by that amount, less the debt that is redeemed. Of course, the redeemed debt is always microscopic compared to the new debt acquired. The U.S. Government is said to have a debt of well over 5 TRILLION dollars as of early 1991, and some say it is as much as 10 trillion, counting social security obligations and the hundreds of billions in interest due over the years.

The sad fact is that anyone who buys these government debt instruments helps to decrease the value of the very dollars they are investing! The more sold, the more dollars that are in circulation, and the less they are worth. The chances of a government debt investment showing a profit over the years is remote. Not in actual dollars, but in purchasing power. The fact that dollars looked the same in 1930 when they were backed by gold as they do today is the great trickery. Today they buy about one fifteenth as much as they bought in 1920, but look the same. Today prices and wages are 15 times what they were in 1920, but the dollar looks the same. Savers have lost their shirts and have been decapitalized. Inflation is perhaps the greatest crime ever perpetrated against a citizenry by a government.

OUT FOR A JOY RIDE

PUBLIC SCHOOLS

Of all the examples of just how bad "public" things can be, schools are exemplary. America's public schools are graduating kids who can't read road signs, find their own country on a map, add, subtract, or use correct grammar. A bumper crop of dummies who know nothing of history, art, or music, and are unfit for just about anything other than perhaps slinging hash at a greasy spoon. There the cash register tells them how much change to give, and they only have to push picture buttons, rather than real numbers on a cash register. America's public schools are an utter disgrace, and make a mockery of the word "education".

What to do? Enough money has already been thrown at them for anyone with a modicum of intelligence to realize money won't work. Government "programs" such as head start, feeding the kids, sending them to schools in better neighborhoods, bussing, coddling, begging, pleading, threatening, setting standards, and the entire nine yards worth of government gobbledygook won't, hasn't, isn't, and can't work. Government is incapable of doing anything well, efficiently, or logically..

Want examples? From the June 10, 1991, Forbes. "The public school system of New York City (population 7 million) has more bureaucrats and administrators than does the educational bureaucracy for the entire nation of France (population 56 million). From a Sept 16, 1991 Rocky Mountain News story, (AP), paragraph two says, "More than two thirds of elementary school science teachers lack adequate preparation in science and more than 80% of math instructors are deficient in mathematics, according to a report issued by the Carnegie Commission on Science, Technology and Government". My files are full of such stories. In tiny Silverton, Colorado, population 500, all records for spending have been broken by budgeting the incredible amount of $16,000 per student! A tiny town with a school board gone amok.

What to do? I have another of my radical ideas.

First of all, realize that every child doesn't have the same mental capacity. All kids shouldn't go to college, and as a matter of fact, very few should go to college. There is nothing wrong with doing manual labor, fixing things, building things, or operating things for a living. Any work is good, no matter how lowly it may be. In other words, abandon the false idea that all kids are capable of, or need college. Forget it!

Second, teach kids their future trade while they are in school, no matter what the trade may be. High school is not too early to inculcate the beginnings of a trade such as carpentry, mechanics, plumbing, building, accounting, writing, design-ing, or computing. Trades should be part of an education. There are many classes of kids from many and varied back-grounds, and they all require different types of schooling. The son of a chef may want to be a chef, so algebra, trig, or calculus is absurd. This means there should be lots of different types of education in schools, and for that matter, lots of different types of schools that cater to different classes and types of students. This is all leading to the third point.

Third, get government out of education. America's edu-cation system must be made private. All schools must even-tually be private schools, and operated for profit. Without profit there is no incentive for excellence, an ironclad rule. Disabuse your mind of what we all have been raised to believe, that education is a "right" of everyone, and it is government's job. If it is a right, damned few are getting that "right" in the decaying public school systems.

Suppose parents were responsible for their own children's education, rather than government? Isn't that a radical idea now? Parents bring their kids into the world, raise them, support, clothe, house, and toilet train them. They teach them to speak, dress themselves, walk, go to bed, and eat, so why can't they be responsible for the rest of it? Why is that such a radical idea? Only because the world has been brainwashed by the socialists into thinking education is a "right", not a parental duty, which it is.

Education is as much the duty of parents as clothing, feeding, and housing a child till it is grown. Government has taken that responsibility away from parents and performed it miserably. It is time parents resumed it themselves. This means property taxes must be cut by perhaps 75%, which is the part schools take. The money parents save can be used to educate their kids as is their rightful duty. Parents would provide the type of education they want for their children, and certainly not the same for all. With all schools private, and government having nothing to do with them, schools can be as varied as weather, music, architecture, or food. Schools for apprentices whose parents want them to adopt a trade, and schools whose parents want their kids to be educators, scientists, mathematicians, or the entire range of human endeavor.

No longer would childless couples have to pay for other children's education, and homes would be available for a far larger portion of Americans because the insipid property taxes would be cut to the bone, or even eliminated all together. No amount of money thrown at the current system will make parents more responsible, as responsibility has been removed from their lives, and it shouldn't have been. The less responsibility placed on members of a civilization, the poorer they will perform, and that's what ails us now.

I know you will say some parents may not be smart enough to see to it that their children get an education. Well, that's what is happening now WITH the public school system. Look people, parents directly guide their kids in their formative years, and experts say that by age 6 a child has already absorbed 50% of all they will ever learn, and that's why various "programs" can't, and won't work. If the parent is a bum, they will probably raise bums, whether the school is public or not. If the parent is a working class parent, they will usually raise working class kids. It is a basic truism. Government schools haven't changed one iota.

I went to an excellent private school from grades 5 to 10. I finished in the public schools. I will never forget the absolute trauma I suffered when I was thrust into that huge public high school with its poor teaching, and masses of kids wandering around aimlessly with not a chance of getting a good education. This was in 1950. I graduated in 1952 from a public high school, and was 12th in a class of 174. I was offered a scholarship, and believe it or not, the school was so bad that

I took off every Wednesday, never once took a book home, and never even came close to being taught the things I was taught in the 9th grade of that private school. In 1950 it was a joke, so nothing has changed in the last 40 years. The funny thing is that the public school had fantastic facilities, as most public schools do. Wonderful gyms, shops, and buildings, but no one was learning a damned thing. Public school teachers are hired by government, paid by government, and perform about as well as government employees, which is pretty bad!

How can this miserable system be transformed into a private system? I think I have a way. It can't be done all at once, that's for sure. It has to be done gradually, and here is my idea. It can happen in a big city or a small town. Take a school that is either unused or has a low enrollment. Advertise it for sale by the school district, with the understanding that it is to be sold for use as a private school, without qualification as to what grades or curriculum it will teach. After it is sold, it will forever be off the property tax rolls, and will always be a school. Every child attending that school and removed from a public school, will have their parent's home relieved of property taxes as long as that child or children are in that school. If the parents are living in an apartment, that apartment will have that portion of the building's property taxes removed from the tax rolls, and the landlord will lower the apartment's rent by that much. No government chits. The idea is to work with the property tax alone.

As that school succeeds, another public school will be sold and turned into a private school with the same property tax benefits to the school and the homes of the attendees. Gradually, the entire public school system will become private, using existing buildings. No government interference into courses, school calendar year, achievements or whatever. Keep government out of it entirely. As this phenomenon occurs, schools will gain a reputation, adjust their tuitions to the market, and teach what is desired by their customers. It will be the market at work with no interference by government.

Free people always do what they want to do, and succeed as they are able or choose. They rise to the limit of their abilities and guide their offspring as they see fit. This is as it should be. Government has no more business being in education than it does telling you when to eat, sleep or drink.

Now look at government supported colleges and universities. There should be no government support for any college or university. Millions of kids use college as a postponement to actual work, dawdling the semesters away, skiing, taking absurd courses, drinking themselves into insensibility, drugs by the bushel, and all sorts of nonsense that has absolutely nothing to do with education. It is so cheap they might as well go, that's all. With all government funding removed from all education, college would be for those who want an education and will work to pay for it.

Government funding of colleges has ruined them. Largess from various government treasuries has made them the same as the public schools, which is zilch. Government funding of colleges has filled them with loafers, keeping them from starting out in life with a job, and further wasting everyone's time and money.

Can you imagine how much money would be saved if the federal government stopped all funding and control of education? Suppose the states did as I propose and stopped also. There would be no property taxes pretty quickly, and America would have its children educated as they should be, namely as their parents chose, not by any government "standards", or through "programs", all of which are worthless.

"Public schools are bad because teachers are so poorly paid", is another lie. Public school teachers work less than a thousand hours a year, which is less than half of a normal worker's time put in on a job. For this they get an extremely high rate of pay. Based on an hourly rate, far more than most any other occupation.

It's time we threw out the public school system on a gradual basis, and got government out of education. Just because we have done it this way for over a hundred years does not make it sensible, correct, or logical. Jesus said, "If thy eye offend thee, pluck it out". Public schools offend me.

THE GNP (Gross National Product)

The term G.N.P. was changed to "G.D.P." (gross domestic product) in December of 1991, supposedly to eliminate foreign activities from domestic corporations or some such bureaucratese, but the analysis remains unchanged.

Newscasters and network "economists" rarely speak of the plight of America without mentioning the GNP, or Gross National Product. This figure goes up or down, and is supposed to tell us how we are doing. A sort of national thermometer. If the GNP is up, we are producing a lot, and if the GNP is down, we are in trouble. The GNP is defined as the total goods and services produced in America. Except for one thing. The GNP figure INCLUDES government spending!

Get the point? Let me explain. When a figure on our economic health includes government spending, it is a totally specious figure. Health of America depends on our manufacturing, selling, producing, growing, exporting, and all of these happy kinds of things. If the GNP were a compilation of goods and services WITHOUT government spending, it might mean something. The federal government "spends about $190 billion a year on goods and services", according to Senator Carl Levin, D-Michigan. This makes it the largest spender, not of its money, but our money, so it isn't "product" or profits, but money confiscated. The power to tax is the power to destroy, and taxes plus printing press money is used to describe our economic health!

Since government has no money to spend unless it takes yours or prints more, government spending is actually reverse gross national product. The bigger government gets, the higher the GNP will go, even if we take out national bankruptcy. How prosperous are we with this immense GNP? Well, we are the largest debtor nation in the world, have a $60 billion yearly trade deficit with the Japs alone, and owe everyone. Our banks and S&L's are broke, insurance companies are none too healthy, pension funds questionable, a million out of work, consumer debt is stratospheric, and the GNP looks great!

How many government figures are accurate anyway? Since government is destroying us on a gradual basis, why should it tell the truth about anything? It rarely does, but the citizen has no way of knowing how wrong the figures are, or how much the bureaucrats lie. Take inflation as an example. We read the newspapers and they say we had .04% inflation last month. Figures fresh from the bureaucracy, of course. Yet with that small amount of inflation, cars went up a few hundred, gas went up a quarter, Wheaties up to $3.15 a box, and I can't afford health insurance. All this with 4% inflation a year? You must be kidding!

Saddam Hussein told his subjects outright lies about the war situation and governments have lied to their subjects since time began. Japanese believe the war was America's fault thanks to government and school brainwashing of the populace. Government has a monopoly on statistics in America. We are all supposed to believe the computer read outs from Washington? Not me! I'll bet all government issued figures are wildly exaggerated in favor of government. Why not? If everything is terrible and government made it that way, which is a fairly accurate statement, why should that same government tell the awful, accurate truth? If a mistake can possibly be covered up in any way, we all will do it. "Me? I didn't forget to wash the dishes, I was too busy, and I had a couple of important phone calls".

The biggest liars in any situation in history, in all nations, in all time periods, have been governments. In war or bad times, the populace is lied to in grand fashion in order to boost morale, conceal blame, and get re-elected. Hitler told the Germans all was well, and Tojo told the Japs the same. Stalin murdered millions and advised the Soviets everything was going just fine. Everyone lies and exaggerates statistics to make them look good. You think government doesn't do that? I have a bridge for sale in Brooklyn which I will let go at a rock bottom price. Call 1-800-I TRUST U.

The G.N.P. (G.D.P.), which includes government spending is about as meaningful as another repentance by Jimmy Swaggart.

I LOVE MY COUNTRY, BUT.....

It's a bumper strip I have seen, and it says, "I love my country, it's my government I worry about". Often the cutsie bumper strips have much truth in them! I refer to many facets of our government in this book, but one of the most insipid is the so called "forfeiture laws", and they aren't limited to the federal government . States have lost their minds as well.

In a suburb of Denver, forfeiture laws took the entire net worth of a pawn shop owner . Local police suspected the shop keeper of being a fencing operation for stolen goods. So they moved in, seized his entire shop and everything in it ! There was no evidence of the pawnbroker being a "fence", and the police admitted it. After careful scrutiny of all his books and records, the police had made a horrendous mistake. Rather than give everything back with a long letter of apology, with local politicians seeing to it that such forfeiture laws were changed, the police demanded $50,000 to return what was rightly the pawnbrokers' business property. He said, "Hell no", and the arguing began. Finally the bills began to pile up and the man gave in to the $50,000 ransom. In lieu of the $50,000, the businessman was given a list of merchandise the cops wanted to keep in return for his business. The list included all guns, power and hand tools, and other goodies, many of which still belonged to the man's customers . It was all documented in the Rocky Mountain News and was shocking, to put it mildly. Neither police or the local government denied it took place and that the Constitution had been raped. I have yet to see any note of apology or amends being made by that small local government. It sent shivers down my back and up my arms.

The "right of the people to be secure in their persons, houses, papers, and effects against unreasonable searches and seizures", happens to be the backbone of the Fourth Amendment of our Constitution! In another section of that hallowed bill of rights, "cruel and unusual punishment" is prohibited .

In late 1991, Andrew Schneider and Mary Pat Flaherty of the Pittsburgh Press did an outstanding series of 6 pieces on the forfeiture laws, giving examples and even photos of innocents who have had their property, businesses, and even personal possessions stolen from them by government. If these two courageous journalists don't get Pulitzers for this, something has gone awry in Pulitzer land.

In the series, innocents have been stopped for no reason, lost their homes and businesses with police conduct that would make even the KGB blush. From part 5: "In Washington State, where the maximum criminal penalty could have been a $10,000 fine, an elderly couple served 60 days for growing 35 marijuana plants and lost their $100,000 house. On March 6, 1990, the state of Washington seized the couple's three bedroom home and the five acres it's on. The man was 69 and his wife 61. Neither had ever had a single brush with the police. The man admitted to the police he was growing the stuff for his own use and even took them to the shed and showed it to them. He was attempting to control pain from severe cluster headaches. The $100,000 property, 130 miles south of Seattle, was their entire life savings."

In another part, the story is told of a couple who had worked long and hard to establish an air charter business out of Las Vegas. One day, the man took a 74 year old passenger and 4 locked boxes to a small airport outside of Los Angeles. Unknown to the pilot, the boxes contained over $2 million in cash. He was held on drug trafficking charges and his plane was seized by the government. He had to file for bankruptcy and now drives a truck for 22 cents a mile. The couple lost everything they had spent their life working to accumulate. How was the pilot to know who his passenger was? Suppose you picked up a hitch hiker who was being tailed by the Drug Enforcement Administration, and your passenger was carrying drugs or other stuff that is deemed illegal? You could be arrested and have your car taken by the DEA!

Under the forfeiture laws, if you have company visiting you in your home, and the visitors possessed drugs and were arrested in your home, your home could be seized! There is virtually no safety anywhere for innocent people if just the right set of circumstances happen to occur. Why hasn't this been stopped dead in its tracks by the Supreme Court? Is America so far down the road to total enslavement by government that no one has the guts or ability to stand up and say NO?

Slavery cannot endure forever without the masses rising up and freeing themselves. But slavery can be installed so gradually that you hardly even notice it. Just like a frog in water under a low flame. He will never protest because it happens so slowly that he is cooked before he knows what is happening. The water temperature rises slightly each day.

Forfeiture laws are so unconscionable and unconstitutional as to be straight out of science fiction. Does this really happen in America? You bet it does, and it happens every day.

If you sell your house and carry back a mortgage as millions have done, it is possible you could lose it all. Over and over again government drug agents have seized houses in which they have found drug law violators. Not only seized the property, but the mortgage holders have lost their life's savings through being unable to collect further payments legitimately due them. Cars, boats, homes, airplanes, clothing, and anything that can be imagined is seized by government under forfeiture laws and never returned to the rightful owners, but usually sold at various auctions for pittances. This is America?

Like I said in the beginning, "I love my country. It's my government I worry about". Could Hitler's SS have been worse?

INSURANCE

We all need insurance to protect ourselves from losses, lawsuits, fire, accidents, and other hazards of life. It would be foolish to drive a car, own a home, or operate a business without insurance. But insurance rates keep going up, up, up. Especially in big cities, insurance rates are almost prohibitive. Why do rates keep escalating? Simple. Because insurance companies have for so many years been paying most claims without question. No questions asked, just file a claim and presto! A check magically arrives. Companies claim it is cheaper to pay than to litigate. I must disagree with that because the insurance company isn't paying anyway, but passing the high cost of settlements on to the insured. I guess it is cheaper to pay than to litigate if your customers are paying!

That philosophy has resulted in insurance rates so high that in many cases, businesses fail, doctors stop practicing, and an incredible imbalance has occurred in our society. That imbalance has caused an unearned wealth transfer every bit as gigantic as OPEC caused in 1973 when crude oil went from $2 a barrel to $40 a barrel. Wealth transfers are fine as long as they are earned or deserved, but what the insurance industry has done is not deserved. This type of wealth transfer usually occurs in the private sector, with a few exceptions.

One exception is SEPTA, the Philadelphia transit system, and for that matter most transit systems in America, because they are all owned and operated by government, and "self insured", meaning the taxpayer pays. In a typical case in 1986, a SEPTA bus was waiting for a red light in North Philadelphia with about 15 passengers on it. It was standing still and weighed in at about 20 tons. A car ran into it from the rear at a speed so slow that no damage was done to the bus, and only slight damage to the car. Guess what? Every passenger as well as the driver went to the hospital! Cases of bus accidents with 15 people on the bus and 20 being injured are common. Bystanders simply get on the bus to take part in the settlement. That wealth transfer is going from government to undeserving recipients, rather than from an insurance company to undeserving recipients.

SEPTA, for the year 1987, budgeted $32 million for claim settlements. I have a friend who works in that department. He says they pay virtually all claims, no matter how absurd, and it makes him sick. That little deal at the stop light in North Philly probably cost taxpayers a quarter million dollars, all of it undeserving and unearned. But back to the private sector.

Accidents do happen. Doctors do make mistakes, and fires do happen. But the settlements and insurance costs absolutely boggle the mind. Lawyers are one of the main problems. Shakespeare was right, of course, we should kill all the lawyers first . (See chapter on whether lawyers should defend the guilty.) Should lawyers be in business to cause huge wealth transfers from the insurance companies to the undeserving? I think not. Shouldn't insurance companies defend themselves against false claims? Perhaps they don't have enough staff, or possibly they give in too easily. I am certain that a good lawyer working for SEPTA would have a salary far less than the hundreds of thousands of dollars that little bump in the night is going to cost. Right is right and wrong is wrong, and no insurance company, or anyone else for that matter, should ever compromise with wrong or evil. Fake insurance claims are both evil and wrong.

Thousands of doctors in America have gotten out of the

baby delivering business because their insurance rates are so high they can't afford coverage, and wouldn't dare practice without it . Rates wouldn't be so high if insurance companies fought fraudulent claims more vigorously and a limit was placed on possible awards by juries and courts. Reform is long overdue . These things aren't new.

When I was a tyke growing up in Washington, D.C., my Dad was a corner druggist . A woman filed a claim on him because she bought a Baby Ruth candy bar and she claimed she broke her tooth on it. The insurance company laughed her out of their office. Today they would probably have paid. When I was 16, I was carefully getting out of a parking place, looking everywhere, and suddenly heard a scream from behind. I got out of the car and a woman was laying on the ground. I was horrified, called the police, and the woman was taken to the hospital. I was scared to death. I told a porter at my Dad's store about it . Horace Proctor asked me her name and I told him. He broke up laughing, saying that the woman had made a career of falling down in back of cars and getting huge insurance payments from innocent people. I passed that information on to Liberty Mutual, and they never gave her a dime. I lucked out.

This isn't meant to say there is no such thing as an injury. There are so many false ones. In our video shop in Philly in 1985, we had a customer named "H". H always wore a neck brace and was employed by one of Philly's bigger industries. He had hurt himself in a faked accident he confided one day, and he was receiving huge settlements, full pay, and would probably buy a fancy house as soon as the final settlement came. He wasn't injured. One time he came into the shop without his neck brace on and I said "I guess you got your settlement because you left your neck brace off today". He had simply forgotten it and frantically went home before anyone saw him. Easy to forget if there isn't any pain anyway!

Another customer was an electrician and had been burned by a short circuit. A minor burn, that's all. He was in no way disabled, by his own admission. His settlement enabled him to buy a huge, fancy house in a neighborhood totally out of his class, and pay cash for it. Unearned wealth transfers from a non protesting insurance company to a claimant who had a clever lawyer. Whose insurance rates went up? Every businessman's. Who eventually paid? Customers who had a nickel added to each item purchased perhaps, or every citizen who had their taxes raised. Who suffered? Everyone.

Insurance settlements are out of control in America because of shyster lawyers, weak insurance company administration, no limits on settlments, and pure greed for undeserved wealth, no matter who has to pay or suffer as a result. My auto insurance in Philly was $1275 and in a small Colorado town it is $195. Tell you anything about what is going on in the big cities with their big ambulance chasing lawyers and lower class scum doing a fine job of receiving undeserved wealth transfers? It should.

A PROPERTY TAX PROPOSAL

Note: This chapter appeared in a major Colorado Newspaper, and a series of letters were exchanged between this author and Colorado's Governor Roy Romer, (democrat). He never could understand the beauty and logic of this proposal.

It should be obvious to all levels of government that the citizenry is angry about our high property taxation. Preservationists know all too well that buildings are lost, not because of a lack of interest or appreciation, but because the taxes are so oppressive. A derelict masterpiece needs to have many times its purchase price spent on it to make it usable. Taxes pile on taxes, and it simply becomes impossible. I have a proposal that will not only equalize property taxes, but strongly contribute to the revitalization of cities, reduce air pollution, and eliminate virtually all race problems. It has wonderful potential and simplicity, and at the same time eliminates several layers of bureaucracy.

"ALL PROPERTY TAXES WILL BE 1% OF THE LAST SALE PRICE, OR 1% OF THE COMBINED COST OF LAND PLUS CONSTRUCTION COST, AND WILL NEVER GO UP OTHER THAN IN DIRECT RATIO TO INFLATION. LAND NEVER HAVING BEEN SOLD, SHALL PAY $25 PER ACRE PER YEAR. FALSIFYING FIGURES WILL BE A FELONY. NO PROPERTY WILL BE EXEMPT".

That's it! It is so simple. Think of the ramifications. Older citizens will never be taxed out of their homes unless they sell. Retirees who bought their home 40 years ago for $10,000 will have a $100 per year tax to pay. When they die and the property is sold for perhaps $100,000, the new owners will have a thousand dollar a year tax to pay. Taxes will never go up unless the property owner sells. Immediately, bad neighborhoods will become desirable. Homes can be bought cheaply there. No taxes can be added for restoration or fixup. An affluent person can buy a wreck of a building for $10,000, spend $100,000 on its restoration, and the taxes will remain $100 as long as he owns it. When or if it is sold, the taxes will go up to 1% of the sale price.

Restoration will be in vogue. People will move back to the cities, and the millions of miles driven each day will diminish, alleviating air pollution. People will once again patronize downtown businesses, walk to work, and neighborhoods will be stable forever. Integration will be accomplished as many in those neighborhoods will remain, while others will take their profits and go. Those "bad" neighborhoods have the most desirable buildings for restoration and can provide a splendid life style that America hasn't seen for 50 years. The suburbs won't suffer, as most residents will remain. But the inner cities will blossom and be restored for both residences as well as business and manufacturing. Rents will stabilize, and wonderful old apartments, hotels, and office buildings will be saved, restored, and have reasonable rents. Fuel consumption will be drastically reduced, and trolleys may once again be fashionable with their silence and cleanliness. Magnificent buildings will never again be demolished, but restored, not because of law but because it will be economical to do so.

With the obvious integration, the crime rate will plummet, and police activity radically decrease. Major cities will become livable and stable forever. It will virtually stop "white flight", school problems, decay, and all of the problems most cities have suffered for 50 years. America will once again be proud. No government force will be required, and no subsidies. The

F.H.A. and all the multi layered bureaucracies concerning themselves with integration and civil rights can just as well fold their tents and disappear. There will never be another HUD sale because all neighborhoods will become viable permanently. No one ever need worry again about "changing neighborhoods" when buying a home.

It has always been wonderful to restore buildings and preserve America's heritage. Unfortunately it doesn't work out on paper because after purchasing a derelict architectural masterpiece, there is no remaining incentive with exorbitant taxes added for restoration costs. While this plan may cut property tax revenues slightly and make the whole thing too simple for most bureaucrats, think of the savings for America. No more assessors, no more tax court fights, less fire, police and other government employees, less crime, less pollution, and far lower budgets everywhere. The lower collections will be far offset by lower expenses.

America's major cities have wrung their hands for over 5 decades as their tax bases withered, magnificent buildings were destroyed, crime escalated, and major population shifts occurred to the benefit of the suburbs. Everything has been tried except the simplest thing of all, and that is to tax people for what they paid for something, and leave it alone.

The building trades will not suffer, but be assisted. Rather than new buildings, fine old ones will be saved, perhaps at even a higher cost, but to everyone's advantage. Consumer prices may go down as manufacturers see the savings in using extant buildings rather than constructing new ones. The art of retrofit and restoration will become respected. Depreciation for taxes will not change, but continue to include total costs. The cities will be saved, the pollution, crime, and decay eliminated, as will much bureaucracy. It will no longer be desirable to move constantly, but put down roots and stay put. Europeans have been doing this for centuries.

The section allowing no exemptions is a key point. State and local governments and agencies will be paying to themselves, of course. Most churches have been in existence for many, many decades, and their taxes would be microscopic, but no one would be exempt. The federal government would begin paying taxes on all those millions of acres they own, abuse, and sit on at taxpayer expense. Maybe they would begin selling it! One of the main taxation problems in America has always been inequality. It would be totally eliminated. Everyone would pay on an equal basis, and no single acre or building would be exempt, no matter who owned it.

Could there possibly be any greater goal than to stop America's decay and turmoil in the cities? Wouldn't it be nice not to have to ever see another tax assessor again, and look with dread for the latest property tax increase? Wouldn't it be great to eliminate all property tax inequality forever? Could there possibly be a more simple way to accomplish all of this with no coercion, no government force, no bureaucracy, no new laws, and court tests? Is there a simpler way to save our precious buildings that daily are destroyed with dynamite and the steel ball? The only business I can think of that would be harmed is the business of demolishing things! A 1% property tax based on the purchase price alone can save America's cities. Which state will do it first?

THEY DON'T MAKE LAND ANY MORE

That is the oldest of land sales gimmicks, especially used by those hustlers of some arid patch of desert in the west like the late Malcolm Forbes' "development" near Alamosa, Colorado. Forbes magazine has had ads in it for years pushing that barren pile of tumbleweed and sage.

Anyone who has ever traveled, and especially in the west, has to realize that there are hundreds of millions of acres everywhere to be had. About the only place the land has run out is near the major cities, and especially in the east. There is enough land in America to last for thousands of years, even if we don't reach "ZPG", or zero population growth. Everywhere you go there are wide open spaces, be it north, south, east or west. Thousands of square miles of uninhabited land obtainable for a song. Land that has water, percolation and even fertile soil. Land, land, land. Drive from New York to Florida and you can go for miles without one visible inhabitant. This land may not be near a major city, near entertainment, or other civilized endeavors, but there is plenty of land. Some of the "for sale" signs are so old that you know they have been there for many years. In Kansas, New Mexico, or California there is land for sale everywhere.

The hackneyed slogan "They don't make land any more, so you'd better buy some", is such a shallow, transparent sham. It is a shame so many people fall for it every year. I did! 30 years ago, I fell for it in a place called Toltec City, Arizona. It was midway between Phoenix and Tucson so the sales pitch said. "Just think, you can go north to Phoenix or south to

Tucson". All true, but still rubbish. 30 years later it is still a patch of sand and not worth the few thousand dollars I paid for it, and never will be. But I bought and made payments for years till it was paid off. Sucker me! Now I warn you.

First of all, you should never buy land or a building without seeing it first. Go there. Never think the current deal is the best deal, or even a good deal for that matter. Be assured that your sales person works 100% for a commission, and if they don't sell they might starve quickly. They'll say anything to make a sale. That Forbes plot in Colorado shows mountains and greenery, and it all looks so great to a big city person longing for a place to "retire". You wouldn't want to retire there if you were Jesse James and wanted for murder in all 50 states!

Some guy buys land for $50 an acre, subdivides it and sells lots for $10,000 an acre. He grades a few roads, draws pictures of the "soon to be built clubhouse and golf course", has an artist glorify the whole thing, makes up a color brochure with a map exaggerating distances, and everything else, builds a fancy entrance, and hires some salesmen. Sales people that are preferably far, far away from the site, because the closer you live to the place, the less likely you will be to buy.

Anyone living in the west wouldn't buy that Forbes place, but they might be interested in lush Florida. Easterners are always thrilled with the west, so they are prime targets for Forbes and like frauds. People in the north want to live in the warm south, and hot Southerners want a cool place in Maine. Work the Johns, offer them what they don't have and are too lazy to go see, is the principle. Get a few bucks as a down payment and you are off! The ones holding the bag for yearly property taxes are the foolish buyers, which I was once. Take my advice and hang up!

The further away you are from this wonderful investment, the worse it will be. Even if they want to fly you there for free just to show you the place, forget it. There are always catches, and the easy ones will feel "obligated" when the pressure begins. As I said before, hang up!

In the twenties, thousands fell for land promotions in Florida, most of which was under water, and would never be of any value. They should have hung up! There's plenty of land, and if you want some, go there and see for yourself.

BANKS

Banks were started long before there was paper money. When gold and silver were the medium of exchange, it got kind of tiresome carrying around all that weight. Security was desired, so a safe keeping place was devised. You could put your gold and silver in a "bank", and it would be free from theft. You paid for the service, and received a receipt for your "deposit". You could get it out anytime by presenting your receipt, or "passbook", as we now call it. Money sitting in a vault doesn't earn any interest because it isn't working, so banks began lending out the depositors' gold and silver to responsible borrowers as a service. The interest received was split with the owner of the gold and silver. The bank's share covered their costs plus a profit, and the depositors' share was for letting them use their gold and silver. If the loan went bad, the banker was responsible.

Eventually it was discovered that when people wanted their gold or silver, it was inconvenient to have to go to a bank to get it out. It was heavy, so a system of bank "notes" was devised, which we now call paper money. Paper dollars used to be issued by various banks which had their names on the money. The dollars represented actual gold and silver in those banks that issued it. Then "checks" were issued by banks, and you could write a check for so many dollars worth of gold and silver which you had in your "account" at the bank with which you dealt. Gold and silver coin was mixed with paper money representing gold and silver in storage. The paper could be converted anytime into the real thing. It was convenient.

Of course the federal government's paper money also was backed by gold and silver, and could be redeemed for the actual metals on demand. The paper money was called "silver certificates" and "gold certificates".

The word "dollar" has an obscure German derivation, but it originally meant one forty second of an ounce of gold. Obviously that meaning has changed! A person would have on deposit in a bank ten thousand dollars as an example, and the bank might pay the depositor 5% interest for the use of that money. The bank would lend the money at a rate of 8%, the 3% difference being their profit to cover the building, employees, insurance, advertising, printing and other expenses. Banking was a good business and profitable. The best bankers were those who made loans to responsible local borrowers who they knew would pay back the money. Generally, a reserve of cash or money was kept in the bank's vault in case someone wanted to draw out their money or a large quantity of it at one time.

Banks often required loans to be "secured" with property or other valuables in case the borrower might default. The bank would then take the security and sell it to pay off the loan. If the banker knew his customer well and had many dealings with him, he might loan money without security, based on the borrower's reputation or net worth. These were "unsecured" loans. If a banker paid too little interest, depositors would withdraw their money, and if he paid too much, he might go bankrupt with depositors losing their money. He could make bad unsecured loans, or secured loans with insufficient security, both of which might put the bank in danger. There are lots of ways to do a bad job in a business, and the same is true with banks.

Banks still make secured and unsecured loans as they used to, but also make government backed loans which require little responsibility on a loan officer's part. Loans to bad risks.

If the loans go bad Uncle Sam will make them good. A banker can now loan many times the amount he has on deposit by borrowing from the government. The interest rate paid by the banker to the government for such loans is called the "fed funds rate", and is lower than prime by a couple of points.

Bankers have loaned billions to bad risks such as third world countries, nearly bankrupt corporations, and millions of loans to bad risks. The strange part is that when a banker doled his money out to bad risks, they usually did it with a bang. A small guy with a sterling record would be denied, and the banker would loan a half million to some terrible risk. The whole house of cards has fallen on stupid bankers who seem to hate the little guy, but love to go bust in a big way. Payoffs? Maybe, but it can't be proven. The S&L's went broke through political skullduggery in part, plus overpriced real estate that fell in value. Banks seem to have been just plain stupid.

The old friendly banker has become a thing of the past. The federal government requires that the bank get your social security number and report all dealings with you to the federal government, including all interest you may receive, and any large transactions.

In 1912, J.P. Morgan appeared before the House of Representatives to testify. His interrogator was Samuel Untermyer, a slick lawyer who didn't like bankers. He asked Morgan if money and property wasn't the most important thing for a banker to look at when making a loan. Morgan testily replied, "No, sir, the first thing is character". Too bad it no longer is that way.

Bank advertising is so patently false, as to be ludicrous. Banks are said to be "A tower of strength" because they "have assets of $43 billion", or advertising of that type. Look at a banks financial statement to see what a "tower of strength" they really are! Their assets always are close to their liabilities! If they have $43 billion in deposits, they invariably have

$42.5 billion in loans of their deposit or fed money. Where is the "strength" in loaning out someone else's money or government's money? About the only "assets" a bank has are their buildings and machinery, plus a infinitesimal amount of "reserves" which reserves are mere bookkeeping entries anyway. No more gold or silver. Nothing but paper, ledger entries, and huge amounts of loans. The old banker who was so conservative as to really be a strong community personage has disappeared.

Banks used to be built to look like fortresses, with huge safes and bars to give the appearance of safety. Maybe they are built differently now because they are different. If you have a home worth $200,000 but owe $175,000 on it, your net worth is $25,000, not $200,000. The same is true with banks, only their advertising indicates otherwise. Since a bank's assets are close to its liabilities, there is no strength.

Then there is the FDIC, or Federal Deposit Insurance Corporation, perhaps a penny in assets for every dollar it insures. The FDIC insures banks. The FSLIC insures savings and loans and went broke first. It will cost taxpayers an estimated half trillion dollars to bail out the failed savings and loans. FDIC will follow the FSLIC into bankruptcy, but we have no firm costs on the bailout yet. If you had your insurance policy with a company that had no assets, would you feel safe? How can you feel safe with your money in a bank? I don't, but it is safe, because the federal government will make it good when it all goes bad, except it will make it good with more paper money that has no backing.

60 years ago, the world's banks had gold and silver to back their money used in transactions. Now all the world's money is mere bookkeeping entries, pieces of paper with ink on them, and are absolutely worthless. Where did the actual wealth go? Probably in private hands, at least I hope so. Everyone should have some. Gold and silver ARE money, and are valuable. A

piece of paper with ink on it has no real value, only purchasing power because government says we must use it.

Next time you walk by a bank and think to yourself, "Ah, there's a tower of strength that I can always depend on", think again. It is just a building with a business in it that has assets close to or possibly even less than liabilities, may be in serious trouble, probably will not be friendly, loves government backed deadbeats, and isn't concerned about you at all.

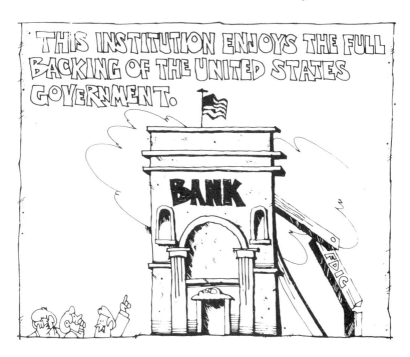

OPERA

It is Saturday, and the Metropolitan Opera is on the radio. Thank you Texaco for providing over 50 years of this enjoyment! Today's Opera is Der Rosenkavalier, by Richard Strauss, and it is wonderful! The second act of this semicomedic opera is on, along with the, unique Strauss harmonies, Baron Ochs, making a fool of himself and being made a fool of by the clever Octavian. Even though you know Sophie will get him in the end, it is still so wonderful to hear it over and over again.

When you listen to or see opera, you are witnessing man's highest achievement in the arts. I have thought about that statement for years and still believe it to be true. Opera combines totally different art forms in one performance. Singing that taxes the capacity of the singer, music that does the same with the orchestra, and staging that often is far superior to any Broadway production. Lighting, sets, beautiful theatre, wonderful stories, and lush productions make opera the greatest art form. The Metropolitan far outshines any other opera company or house in the world. But it requires a hell of a lot of effort and determination to appreciate, and even understand. Nothing in life comes without work, unless it is pure dumb luck, which happens to very few.

Early in life I realized anything worthwhile requires work, and what is worthless comes easy. Another truism I have never found to be false. Kids like junk "music" because it is easy, requires no talent to perform or write, is mere loud noise, and it will be lucky to survive a year before it is all forgotten. Few kids can think deeply enough to appreciate classical music, and few parents insist on its inculcation into their brains at an early age. Hopefully, as life progresses, deeper things will begin to attract.

Opera is the last thing to be appreciated. Classical music is far easier to absorb than opera. Many classical music fans dislike opera as I did for many years. I hated opera! "It puts me to sleep", I said. "It's boring". "Yuk", and a host of other rationalizations as to why I was too lazy to investigate. Then I sat back one day about 30 years ago and said to myself, "There must be something to this, I will look at it in depth and see what it is really about". I did, and it is wonderful. But not easy.

I will freely admit that opera plots are often silly, can be told in a few paragraphs at most, and take 3 or 4 hours to tell in an opera. I admit that if opera were as simple as the basic plots of the story, no one would be interested. Yet opera requires the finest voices in the world, trained endlessly to adequately sing opera. Opera music can be terribly difficult to play and conduct. Conductors have to not only see that the orchestra is playing well, but that sets, lights, voices, timing, costumes, and special effects are equally coordinated.

When I decided to look at opera other than with expletives and shallow remarks, I tried Madam Butterfly first. It took only a couple of times to be completely involved with the haunting Puccini melodies, tears streaming down my face over the sheer tragedy of it. Then came Aida, La Boheme, and Wagner's music that is so wondrous as to be indescribable. On it went till I was hooked. After 30 years, my knowledge is still woefully small, but my appreciation grows with each performance I see or hear.

Now I get opera on video tape, and never miss a Texaco broadcast. We all have our favorites, and I dislike dissonance in any music, especially opera. My loves are Puccini, Verdi, Wagner and Mozart, but others aren't far behind. If you want to try to learn it, Rigoletto is excellent for a beginner, as is Carmen, or Butterfly. Opera is nothing you can "master" in a lifetime. It is one of life's pleasurable efforts which are often never conquered totally.

Opera is nothing you can use at a cocktail party to show yourself brilliant, as most attendees will know nothing about it anyway. Opera is a personal experience I guess, and one that is as difficult to describe as this is difficult to write. Trying to write about and describe a sneeze or orgasm is about like trying to write about a love of opera. Damned near impossible, as it is something to be experienced and felt, not described. How can I describe the "humming chorus", or the sextet from Lucia? How can I describe the unabashed tears that always come in La Boheme when Mimi dies? You can't, but to experience these is to be carried away to heaven!

Is a hamburger comparable to a finely prepared meal with superb sauces, dressings, and wine? Is 3 chords and "baayybeee" comparable to the Beethoven 9th symphony? Popular music, with its gutter like words and "music", is so despicable as to be revolting to a mind that has even a smattering of education and culture. But that education and culture was difficult to obtain, just as is a love for beautiful opera. Can New York's Chrysler building be compared to a Phoenix tract house?

It just takes work. But it is worth it. If you read this and are curious, go buy an album of Rigoletto, read the synopsis, and listen to it 5 times over and over. You'll be on your way.

THE CRITICS

Everything in life is a matter of opinion. Be it religion, politics, art, music, film, food, or beauty, it is mostly opinion. This book is about my opinions, and you will hate part of it because it disagrees with your opinions. Opinions aren't usually a commodity that can be sold. The exception is the critic. Be it of film, food, art, or music, critics are highly paid, and in my opinion, usually dead wrong! I am a film nut. Movies are literally a spice of life for me, and I watch them continually, mostly on video tape. In the small town in which we live, we have a wonderful theatre that is spotless, comfortable, reasonable and individually owned. It gets our attention quite often!

If critics rave about a film, we will usually pass it up, we are so much in disagreement with their opinions. At Christmas, 1990, a film titled "Home Alone" was released. All box office records were broken, and the public loved it. A little boy accidentally gets left home in this wonderful 75 year old home while his parents go off to Europe. Burglars attempt to rob the house, and this kid stops them time after time in the most hilarious ways. The crooks are portrayed as bumbling fools with sinister looks, and the kid is the most inventive boy since Thomas Edison. It is hilarious, impossible, silly, and great. The house is so warm and wonderful. The Christmas decorations are splendid, and the kid is super. Add it to your tape collection! Guess what? The critics roundly denounced it. Naturally!

The critics swooned over two of the most god awful films

ever made, namely, "My Dinner With Andre", and, "The Gods Must Be Crazy". The first is 2 hours of crashing boredom, with two male critic types talking about inane things over dinner. That's it! The second was shot in 16 millimeter with no sound. An amateur home movie complete with grain and added sound effects. It concerns a Coke bottle dropped from a plane passing over Africa, and the adventures of that bottle. Every silent film gag is reused with terrible photography, plot, and direction. Utterly inane, but the critics howled over it, giving it loud acclaim. Critics love avant-garde films requiring little talent or expertise to write, film, or produce. Beware if they like it!

Then there are the music critics who love newish, dissonant, abstract sounds thrown together and called "music". They regularly pooh pooh the likes of composers such as Saint Saens, Beethoven, or Bach. The French have never yet duplicated the likes of Camille Saint Saens who wrote such wonderful, brilliant, harmonious, exciting music. His 3rd symphony, the "Organ Symphony", just makes goose bumps run up and down my back. When he completed it he said, "I have given my all in this composition". It is wonderful, yet critics say Saint Saens was "shallow". The critics are shallow.

Art critics dote over the modern painters who throw paint at a canvas, and produce obtuse, mysterious, ugly works with no rhyme or logic to them, yet roundly condemn any artist who paints with superb realism and expertise. Which requires the most talent? Which do the critics love the most? You know.

Architectural critics love "modern" buildings that look like a child's blocks piled upon each other, or glass cubes endlessly stacked in boring ways. Perhaps the most beautiful office building ever built is the Chrysler Building in New York, or the Wrigley in Chicago. They have never been equaled in the almost 70 years since they were built. The newer office buildings in New York and Chicago, which cities

I think have the best commercial buildings, are the likes of the World Trade Centers; two tall rectangles sitting next to each other. Ugh!

Philadelphia and its suburbs probably have the pre-eminent residential architecture in the world, what of it hasn't been torn down or wrecked, but architects and their critics never express admiration of these buildings, praising instead all that is new and "sophisticated", usually meaning, "requiring no talent". As I write this, Philadelphia is getting ready to build a new concert hall on South Broad Street to supplement the wonderful Academy of Music, from whose stage Abe Lincoln spoke, and Tchaikovsky and Mahler conducted. Too old hat for the critics. The plans for the new hall are so sterile and ordinary they can only be compared to New York's Lincoln Center, which is talentless. North on Broad Street in Philly is the gone to seed Metropolitan Opera House, now used as a church. The "Met", as it is now called, is one of the grandest concert halls on earth, needing only a careful restoration to bring it into world wide acclaim as the virtual "perfect" concert hall. Will it ever be restored and used again? Probably not, as the critics are against it.

I do not want to ruin anyone's chances of gainful work, but the critics are so off base in my way of thinking as to be ludicrous. I truly believe my way of thinking reflects the America that knows what work, achievement, love, beauty, and patriotism is. And to you I aim these pages. A pox on the critics.

THE MEDIA

Didn't you ever wonder why the newspapers, radio, television, and magazines have such a left wing slant? I know it sounds like paranoia, but I believe it. Admittedly the media gave Ronnie Reagan a pretty good ride for his 8 years, but aside from that, I can think of only a few major communications outlets that aren't terribly slanted.

CBS is the worst of the networks. Dan Rather, "60 minutes", and even Harry Smith on the morning show are almost anti-American at times. Major newspapers such as the New York Times, Washington Post, and rags in other major cities never give real America an even break as far as coverage or bias is concerned. PBS is notorious as is NPR, (National Public Radio). Few doubt the liberal, left wing bias of the media. The question is, how did it happen?

All the stars, reporters, broadcasters, and personalities must have college degrees to be hired. That might explain a lot. Elementary and high school are the basics, and little political thought is inserted into courses there. However, in college, kids are taken over completely by their professors, and that instruction will most probably influence their opinions for life.

The liberal slant is a mere carry over from college days. When communism and socialism spread here in the 1920's and 30's, it was all the rage among the intellectuals. Russia was starving, but that didn't matter. Roosevelt's diplomatic recognition of Russia in 1933 gave communism legitimacy, and American money saved them in the nick of time.

It was chic to believe in communism and socialism 60 or 70 years ago, and especially by the teachers, professors, and academicians who have carried that infection along over the decades like a virus. Each succeeding generation is infected, and passes it along. Karl Marx fervently believed the way to overthrow capitalism was to get the teachers first. They have. Even though communism has failed totally, the mind set of teachers and professors remains left, and their students still become infected. It shows in their writing, teaching, and broadcasting. How does one stop the infectious chain reaction? I don't know.

Socialism is twisted logic, but the eggheads take to it like a duck to water. Of course it won't work, can't work, hasn't worked, and totally ignores the basic human instinct to better ones self. Who wants to give away the fruits of their labor? In socialist Sweden's last election, the left took a savage beating. Even in Sweden, people are tired of paying, paying, paying, and getting virtually nothing for their effort. There is no difference between socialism and communism. Communism is merely advanced socialism.

We are fed left wing propaganda by our media, professors, and teachers on a daily basis, and no one has yet discovered a drug to kill that virus. Anyone want to buy shares of CBS?

EQUALITY?

For over 200 years, America has lived, legislated, and preached equality. Equal rights, equal treatment, and equality under the law. Court dockets are filled with equality cases, usually going under the term "civil rights". Everyone is supposed to stand for equality. Except that the American federal government does not practice nor stand for it.

The Congress has passed, and the President signed, a new series of tax laws removing many income tax deductions for the wealthy. Ever since the Income Tax Amendment was made part of our Constitution over 75 years ago, equality has never been part of it. In the beginning, income taxes were levied only on the very richest. It deteriorated until the wealthiest paid as much as 90% of their income in taxes. Even the tax reform act of 1986 still had two categories. One for the rich and the other for the not so rich. Never in the history of the income tax in America has there ever been true equality for everyone.

I wonder why the inequality of the taxing system has never been tested in court. How is everyone being treated equally under the law when some are taxed at higher rates than others? I would think this gross inequality would make a dandy civil rights case. "All men are created equal", but all men aren't treated equally under tax law.

All drivers have to obey the same rules of the road, whether they drive a Mercedes or a Ford. All violators of laws are supposed to be treated equally in the courts and by law enforcement officials. If you aren't treated equally with other violators, you have a civil case. All persons pay the same prices in stores. There isn't one price for the rich and another price for the poor. All classes get one vote. Rich students are graded the same as poor students. Women want equal treatment in the job market. Everyone desiring equality or equal treatment can usually get it with a lawsuit. But taxation has always been unequal, and in this supposed land of the free, there is no reason why a court shouldn't uphold the theory that unequal treatment is unfair and probably unconstitutional.

From each according to his ability to pay is not fair. That theory was espoused by Karl Marx a hundred years ago, and his movement is all but dead as this is being written. Discarded as so much rubbish in a can. But this Marxian principal of inequality remains in America. Does Congress really have the Constitutional right to levy taxes unequally, and at the same time force equality in everything else? The fact that it has been going on for many decades does not make it right. Even in property taxes there is equality, and if the assessor makes a mistake, the victim has recourse in the courts to make the system equal for all. Sales taxes are the same for all people regardless of their wealth. Everyone pays the same gasoline taxes, excise taxes, lodging taxes, and driver's license fees, regardless of wealth or station. Everyone pays the same rates for electricity, phones, stamps, and fares on public conveyances.

Truly the most unfair thing in America is the government's practice of taxing citizens unequally. This needs to be straightened out promptly, with Congress and the I.R.S. forever being prohibited from taxing anyone unequally ever again. The federal tax system has to be the most outrageous abuse of the principle of equality. Why has this not been noticed before? If it has, I have never heard of it.

WHATEVER HAPPENED TO CONEY ISLAND?

This was written July 11, 1986, after a revisit to the place, and what was written then still applies.

I went to Coney Island in the early 50's when I was in my teens. It was a really neat place, in spite of the fact that even in the 50's, the majority of its turn of the century glitter had been destroyed by two catastrophic fires. In the heyday of Coney Island, there was nothing in the entire world quite like it. Hundreds of millions of light bulbs and attractions that have never since been duplicated blew the mental fuses of all who went. It was so absolutely splendiferous as to be impossible to describe, and the remaining old black and white film records of it must only vaguely portray it as it was. A very scarce book is out there somewhere on the subject of Coney island, and I hope eventually to find it to add to my collection. But I remember it in the early 50's with its still vibrant attractiveness, and excitement. In the fifties, the great old rides were still there, including Steeplechase, with its wonderful carousels, and rides. The parachute jump, the Cyclone, the huge ferris wheels, and wonderful wooden roller coasters were still there. Nathan's hot dogs, theatres, and crowds were there in the early 50's, and all having a great time.

Amusement parks as a rule have bitten the dust, to be replaced by so called "theme parks", but Coney Island is still there. It is still there because it is literally an island off the southern edge of Brooklyn, and is handily adjacent to over 10 million people, so there is no shortage of surrounding population looking for amusement. The interesting fact is that amusement parks with less than a tenth of the surrounding population still thrive in America. In Florida hundreds of millions of dollars has been and is still being spent on parks, so the concept is not dead. But Coney island is a skeleton. A recent visit to Coney Island has left dreadful feelings of utter remorse in my soul. Coney island is a skeleton, with most of its bones missing.

Coney Island no longer sings with happy people having a good time. It is a barren beach with a small boardwalk. The great rides are missing or rusting away. Graffiti everywhere, and hundreds of empty lots that used to house the world's greatest play place for the working and other classes. The theatres are gone and I wouldn't go there at night for any amount of money. It is a sort of "no mans land" I suppose. There are plans to "revitalize" it, and a few entrepreneurs are going to try to get it going again, but I wouldn't invest in it. A desolation pure and simple. What happened? Easy!

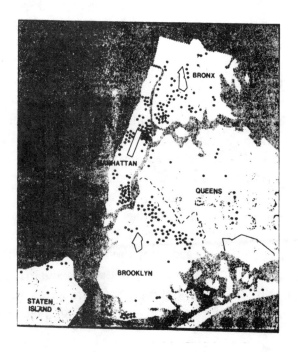

The map shown tells the tale. Note that on Coney Island there are ten public housing projects. Count them. Nothing will kill an area faster than a housing project. Look at the map again to see other areas of New York. Queens has virtually none, thanks to continual political pressure over the years, and it is still the safest place to live in New York with little crime and stable property values. The South Bronx is a no man's land totally, and the reason is those little dots indicating housing projects. In the early 50's, when Coney Island was still alive, so was the South Bronx. The South Bronx was a wonderful place to live! Beautiful, statuesque, well maintained apartment buildings, stores, and theatres. Fine homes and schools. I remember it well. Now it looks like Berlin after World War II. Public housing projects totally destroy every neighborhood in which they are placed. That is so obvious and indisputable that I wonder that anyone ever argues the point.

Look at the map again. See the bad and good parts of Brooklyn? They absolutely correspond with the housing projects, as do the neighborhoods in the upper east side of Manhattan, and the lower east side. Public housing is an atomic bomb with a delayed fuse placed in any neighborhood, and New York is classic illustration.

What happened to that most wonderful of all places of amusement in the entire world? What happened to Coney Island? What the major fires didn't get, the public housing projects destroyed. Is there still a desire by the 10 million inhabitants of the New York area to amuse themselves? Certainly! But would they go to a crime infested, dangerous, filthy, graffiti loaded, smelly place like Coney Island? Of course not.

The horror of public housing is that it accomplishes absolutely nothing. The residents destroy what has been built for them on a regular basis, and after only a couple of decades or so, most public housing projects are so trashed by their occupants that they must be replaced. By then the entire area has been abandoned by everyone except these denizens of the slums. Former businessmen and home owners have had their life's savings destroyed by politicians who placed these hideous government subsidized dwellings in their midst. No one has won and everyone has lost.

The examples of public housing demolition of former fine neighborhoods is 100% provable and demonstrable. There have never been any exceptions to it. Where public housing is put, there goes the neighborhood. In the case of Coney Island, it is all the more tragic because a world reknown amusement area has been destroyed by the politicians with their vote getting public housing. There are a lot more votes to be gotten from thousands of public housing dwellers than there are from perhaps a hundred citizens living in homes that used to be on the same site. All glories eventually fade they say, but Coney Island was bombed by the politicians with their votes a plenty, neighborhood destroying, public housing projects.

WHAT WOULD YOU DO?

That is a common question, and one I am always prepared to answer. I would do a lot of things differently! Here's a few questions that might be asked of me, and my answer.

Question: What would you do if you were a U.S. Senator or Representative?

Answer: I would work extremely hard to remove laws, stop all wealth transfers, balance the budget by reducing taxes, and above all get rid of bureaucrats and bureaucracies with all possible speed. An immediate federal hiring freeze and federal wage freeze would be a primary goal. Gradually eliminate all federal assistance, food stamps, controls, and courts. I would work night and day to sell all federal lands, businesses, and enterprises to the highest bidders, and use the money to pay off the national debt. I would eliminate the IRS and income tax, as well as every single federal tax of any kind, raising money exclusively through a national sales tax. I would work hard to wake everyone up to the absolute evil of government, except as an extremely limited necessity.

I would campaign to eliminate every penny of foreign aid, and attempt to force a Constitutional rewrite as the chapter in this book mentions, and try to make everyone see the absolute beauty of strict neutrality. I would eliminate Congressional franking privileges and do everything in my power to limit everyone to one term as is also in a chapter in this tome. I would vote to eliminate all cabinet posts and related bureaucracy, except for Treasury, State, Defense, and Interior. I would probably ruin my health!

Question: What would you do if you were President?

Answer. Same as above except I would be able to veto just about everything, which I would do if it involved more government and more spending. I would probably be assassinated.

Question: What would you do if you were rich?

Answer. I would pay every dime I owe to anyone and use all my wealth to attempt a peaceful voter overthrow of the rascals that have destroyed us in Washington. I believe people can be made to think and act for their country's best interest if it is logically pointed out to them that what is going on now is certain national death. I would use all available monies for advertising, speakers bureau, TV commercials, and any way possible to inform America that we might save ourselves if we would just let people be responsible for themselves, no matter how much it might hurt.

Question: What would you do if you could control anything you wanted?

Answer. I don't want to control anything and wouldn't want to control anything. I just don't want to BE controlled, and I don't want anyone else to be controlled, other than normal things such as speed limits, hurting anyone else, murder, and common sense laws against fraud, theft, and violence. Control, other than of one's kids, employees, and ones self generally is sick in my opinion.

Question: If you had your way, the poor and sick would starve or die wouldn't they?

Answer. Maybe, but preserving one's life is that person's job, not government's. Keeping healthy, fed, housed, educated, and alive is no responsibility of anyone but yourself, or your parents, if you are a child. Since government has taken on the job of robbing the producers to feed and care for the lazy, inept, sick, and poor, we have all gone down the tubes. Nothing has been accomplished except a tidal wave of poverty, laziness, joblessness, illegitimacy, and crime. Cruel as it may sound, nature's way is to let the weak die and the strong survive. That way the race is strengthened. As it is, the race is weakening at breakneck speed.

Question: What would you do for all those people who now work for the federal government when you eliminated those jobs?

Answer. I would give them notice, severance pay, and eliminate jobs by attrition first, which is about all any employer can do when an industry fails or is closed. Those people you are so worried about have been sucking the very life blood out of America for 6 decades now, so I don't feel too sorry for them. With the burden of the federal government and its hidden and exposed taxes, plus millions of laws and regulations removed, prosperity, production, and productive jobs will return so fast that it will make everyone's head swim. Those former federal buildings will be snapped up by businesses and corporations as headquarters, and they may hire the ex-government workers after they learn to work, be polite, and efficient.

Question: Who will regulate all the things that are regulated now? Won't everything fall apart?

Answer. Hardly! Things will come back together is more like it. Regulate education, transportation, agriculture, commerce, housing, ad infinitum at the federal level? What a terrible ideal. Let each state do as it sees fit, but federal regulations have had a stranglehold on America for far too long. As good old Moses said at the Red Sea, "Let my people go".

Question: Isn't it kindness to help people?

Answer. Yes! But federal programs that have destroyed the economic and moral fabric of America is not kindness. It has been, and is, theft. To borrow an L.B.J. ideal, "taking from the haves and giving to the have nots", is of no benefit to either, but destroys both. The haves decide not to work so hard because it is all taken from them by taxes, and the have nots realize they don't have to do much either because all the taxes are given to them. Frustration and laziness is the logical result, and it is all too obvious today. Help on a voluntary basis is wonderful, but I want to pick who I give to, not be robbed by government and have it distributed to those who vote "right", after a 50% handling charge is subtracted by the bureaucracy.

Question: Are you serious about all you say in this book?

Answer. I have never been more serious in my life. Some chapters are humorous, but all are true. As far as the more serious matters, such as government proliferation and decay of lifestyle, it's time someone said it the way it is. Pussyfooting about, trying to please publishers, dealers, races, classes, ethnic groups, and economic sectors, is a waste of time. I have ideas, knowledge, and have an excellent objective brain that has been needing to say what is written here for decades. Now it may be too late, even if this does get read. Far too many people can barely read, and of course couldn't possibly understand logic. If they could, they might be too chicken to vote for their country if it might cost them a check, or some mythical "benefit". The idea that government can give you nothing until it takes twice that much from you in a hundred different ways is not an easily understood truism.

Question: Aren't you afraid something might happen to you if this ever gets printed and widely read, and especially if it takes root?

Answer. Yes, but what could happen to my country makes it worth it!

WHY DON'T AMERICANS VOTE?

Don't ever underestimate the basic justice and "gut" knowledge Americans possess. The preceding expresses much of what they have been aware of for decades, but perhaps have never thought of in just the way I have put it. It is this undeniable gut feeling that keeps Americans away from the voting booths on election day. This intuition says politicians are selfish, stupid, interested only in themselves, and as Mark Twain once said, "It could probably be shown by facts and figures that there is no distinctly native American criminal class except Congress".

Americans feel inwardly it makes no difference who they vote for, prices will still go up, education will get worse, crime will increase, and taxes will become more unbearable. They may not know WHY these things happen, but they come about when Congress is in session. Americans know politicians are a lying, thieving bunch of rapscallions, and always will be as far as they can see, so why vote for any of them? In actuality, by not voting, Americans indeed ARE voting. That lack of voting says, "a pox on both your houses, I won't dignify you by voting. I'll stay home to show you how little I respect you". Politicians are a proud bunch. They puff up like a blowfish when they get on the floor of Congress and give speeches, sometimes to an empty house, if you ever watch C-Span.

Politicians think they are smart, but they aren't. Like bureaucrats, they are drunk with power, overpaid, underworked, undeserving, and beneath most Americans who work for a living. The old saying goes that, "the trouble with politics is that you end up being governed by your inferiors".

The way to get Americans to go back to the voting booths is for politicians to vote themselves a one term limit, vote to whittle the federal government down to about 10% of its current size, state government to about 50% of its current size, and make similar reductions at all other levels. When America sees the budget balanced, gobeldygook eliminated, and Washington, D.C. have a 75% housing vacancy rate, they will vote till their hands get blisters from pulling those handles in favor of the party that does it. If any party can do it, it is the Republicans, because they are an established party. I have often wanted to rename the Republicans the "LOTS" party, which means "less of the same". They never seem to want to stop this nonsense, but to slow it down. That's not enough.

In order for the Republicans to pull it off, they are going to have to admit partial fault, and vow to do better.

Republicans tell us that the Democrats have controlled Congress for lo these many years, but they fail to note that Republican Presidents have signed those bills! The blame is with both. Americans will not return to the polls till the candidates learn basic economics, reduce their salaries, balance the budget, pay off the debt, and back the dollar with something other than the "full faith and credit of the U.S. government", which has to be the funniest phrase ever coined. The federal government has no credit, and anyone who puts faith in that bunch had better consult a psychiatrist pronto!

P.S. This book is important. It needs to be circulated and read by all intelligent, open minded Americans. It needs to be given away as gifts for birthdays and Christmas. It needs to be donated to libraries and loaned to friends. Do it!

THE WASHINGTON PARTY

Next week I'll be 90 years old, and since I am so damned ancient but still lucid, I have been under considerable pressure to write down my recollections of the "Great Washington Party", which ran for 60 years in Washington D.C., ending rather abruptly over 30 years ago. I'll try. While it was up and running, the world had never seen anything quite like it. There was money, money, and more money spent on that enormous bash. Seemingly an inexhaustible supply of broads, booze, favors, publicity, power, glory, and luxuries that would have blown your mind. Honestly, there had never been anything in history like it.

The Party attracted millions of celebrants to the Washington D.C. area, and it was a no holds barred gasser! Republicans and Democrats were the two parties in power then, and both were having the time of their lives.

I was born in Washington D.C. in 1934, and grew up there. I delivered the Washington Post as a kid, and went to school and college in D.C. My ancestors came to Washington in the late 1700's and have lived there ever since. It was a great place to grow up. When I was born the party had already been going on for a couple of years, but it really hadn't gotten into full swing as it did when I was in my forties and fifties.

President Franklin Delano Roosevelt (F.D.R.) started it with a fantastic government expansion and building program to get us over the famous depression. The stock market crash of 1929 wasn't the depression, but helped to precipitate it. The depression really got going after F.D.R. took office. He was elected 2 years before I was born, died when I was 10. I can remember his death pretty well, just as I can still remember where I was on Sunday, Dec. 7th, 1941, when the Japs bombed Pearl Harbor. My Uncle Ernie said when F.D.R. died, the first radio reports indicated his body had turned black, which he said was symptomatic of arsenic poisoning. No one ever saw his body, so maybe Ernie was right.

Roosevelt's party invitations were mailed almost immediately after he took office. He had run on a "conservative" platform, but partying was on his mind. By the end of his first term, new cabinet positions and federal agencies were running full tilt. Guests were continually arriving to imbibe at the federal table of goodies, but it was still a rather sedate affair. I graduated from high school in 1952. We had survived W.W. II, and Truman had marched us off to Korea. I was 18, and wasn't really aware of the Washington Party even though it had become a pretty wild orgy by then according to my Dad, who died in 1963 still cursing Franklin Roosevelt to his death bed. Dad died of lung cancer, virtually unheard of today since few smoke anymore.

By the fifties, festivities had begun to outgrow Washington, expanding to the suburbs of Maryland and Virginia. After Korea, we had relatively peaceful years under President Dwight Eisenhower. All he seemed to want to do was play golf, a real party pooper. Other than the outrage of appointing a man as Chief Justice of the Supreme Court who had absolutely no judicial experience, and showed it, the Eisenhower Washington Party years didn't show much expansion. Eisenhower almost cut the party off when he unexpectedly balanced the budget once. No one went home, but not many celebrants arrived either. Even so, it was still a lovely affair, with many corporations, unions, and lobbyists headquartering themselves in D.C. They never missed an event, and bought splendid homes in the northwest section usually, so they could be close to the action.

When I was a teenager, my parents bought a lovely 40 acre farm 40 miles south of D.C. for $9500. It was a couple of miles from the Chesapeake Bay, and had a large house and 2 barns. The party was so small then that no one lived as far from D.C. as 40 miles, and the roads weren't that great. The Party crowd didn't live far outside of D.C. during the Eisenhower years. As the 60's came, and Korea was over except for the 40,000 troops which stayed there, believe it or not, until 1993, we saw a gradual increase in the size of the Washington Party. Kennedy, Viet Nam, and Lyndon Johnson came with all the promises of a "Great Society", and the civil rights movement of the mid sixties. Then the revelry began to expand in a big way. John Kennedy's wife, Jackie, loved the Washington social scene, and they gave huge bashes at the White House, inviting people from all over the world to come. It was grand! Musicians, artists, poets, and authors were continually making the White House scene, even though they weren't really good artists, musicians, poets, and authors. Still, the lights were never turned off in D.C. and it had become a 24 hour affair, with limos and Mercedes cruising the D.C. streets night and day, full of happy celebrants having a wonderful time at the glittering Washington affair. It was just splendid! There were actual shortages of tuxedos, caviar, whiskey, and cut flowers. The purveyors of party favors such as booze, food, influence, limousines, and expensive clothing got rich and were always in attendance at the daily events. The banks were more prosperous than ever with huge deposits from the D.C. attendees. Everyone was drinking, eating, and living high off the hog.

By the end of the 60's and into the 70's, bureaucracies were every-where, joyously making rules and regulations for just about everything and everyone all over America. Happiness reigned supreme. Restaurants, office suppliers, communications networks, hotels, influence peddlers, lobbyists, hacks, computer salesmen, builders, decorators, limousine leasers, guides, writers and editors all were partaking of the favors provided at the great festivity. The salaries were high and going higher. The food was excellent and drinks were everywhere. All were acting as if they were the saviors of humanity, promulgating rules, regulations, laws, and printing huge amounts of money to spend. By then the military was having a fine time as were the regulators who seemed to be more and more numerous. The regulators were having so much fun telling everyone what to do and making millions of rules that I honestly believe they had more fun than the others for a brief period. When the party began to end, the regulators were still high as kites, writing new rules as though there might be no tomorrow, and relishing every minute of it.

By the end of the seventies, the Washington Party had become an opulent, unrestrained, blast. Partyers were writing checks for billions and billions of dollars for all sorts of favors and fun projects. Nothing was too good. Nothing too expensive. The best of everything. Welfare for those not lucky enough to be there, weapons past all imaging, ships, planes, bombs, programs, subsidies for everyone, more and more laws and rules to make the party goers a prosperous lot. It was so much fun to enforce those little rules that saved us from our enemies, ourselves, pollution, drug dealers, and a host of other evils conjured up by the happy helpers. My people who sold office supplies and furniture, made out like bandits I am sure, although I wasn't around to witness it in person. By then I had left D.C. and was looking back with fond memories of my childhood, but disgust over the rapidly growing wild frolic in my hometown. By the 70's our old 40 acre farm in Southern Maryland was worth hundreds of thousands of dollars just because it was so close to the party going on in D.C. Too bad they sold it for $17,000 in 1956. That's how big the affair had become.

Jimmy Carter was elected in 1976. He was kind of quiet and not real bright, but the party didn't let up. It required a lot of revelers to perform all those joyous tasks of governing, taxing, and helping everyone. What a wonderful time everyone was having at the big banquet table in D.C. During Carter's time he opened more doors for party people by controlling lots more things like prices and wages. More and more people came to D.C. to live, prosper, and get rich at the party. Could heaven offer more?

A lot of people thought the party might not be as much fun when

Ronnie Reagan was elected because he promised during his campaign to shut the party down. The neighbors around the country were tired of the noise, influence, and cost. Ronnie promised to stop the world's greatest party dead in its tracks. It wasn't long after he took office that everyone knew it would all be O.K., and more were invited. Boy were they invited! Under Ronnie Reagan the Washington Party really turned into a good time for everyone. The military and weapons makers became the honored guests. Nothing was too good for them during the Reagan years, and they were treated as absolute royalty, no party favor being denied. By then we were borrowing heavily from others to pay the party's bills. The Japanese were happy to advance the money for it. World War II was forgiven and it was as if Pearl Harbor, Bataan, and Corregidor never happened. "Just give us the money and join the party", were the exhortations. They were only too happy to oblige, and they brought cars with them too, as well as TV sets, VCR's, cameras, and computers. Everyone bought their stuff, as American merchandise had been going through a period of bad quality and under capitalization due to the high taxes levied to support the Party. The Japanese had no defense worries, and their nation didn't have an expensive party to support, so they could ignore patents, make stuff with cheap labor and sell it everywhere at low prices.

By the end of Ronnie Reagan's term, the Washington Party had gotten so big and was costing so much that everyone just lost track of it. Money for the party was no object, and no cost too high. The Party just printed more money and sold the debt to anyone that would buy it. By the late 80's the Washington party was the envy of the world. Everyone wanted to be invited to the world's biggest catered affair which hopefully would never end.

Things got even merrier when George Bush was elected. There was a little bit of worry when he promised no new taxes", but he was an old line Washington Party man from his early days and knew how to keep it all going. He did. A couple of years later he had to raise taxes to pay for the Party's continuance, and it did cost him a few popularity percentage points, but the bills had to be paid and no one wanted to spoil the Party! So taxes were raised, and besides, a new funding source to keep the party going presented itself, and that was a tiny invasion of one Arab Country by its neighbor. That was all that was needed to expand the Party to even greater, more joyous heights. The hundred million dollars a day spent "protecting Saudi Arabia" was off budget anyway, so no one need know about the actuality of it all. 'Eat, drink and be merry", was the rule. Never let anything slow or put a damper on the world's largest, happiest party, the Washington D.C. Party.

Only a few Americans lost their lives in that brief Kuwait war. Like Korea and Viet Nam, the purpose was "to protect others", and "spread democracy", so the cost didn't matter. Naturally the invoices for the little affair were paid by printing more money, plus other nations' contributions. After the little Kuwait thing, the party was going better than ever, but George Bush seemed to have lost favor because of the economy. In actuality Bush's decline began when he violated his "no new taxes" pledge, which caused Americans to distrust him. At any rate he lost the election.

The new President had run on a platform of stopping the party, (STP), because the national debt was out of control and the voters were sick and tired of the party which was bankrupting everyone. Promises of candidates never meant much, everyone knew that. It was the rhetoric that counted. By the late 80's and early 90's, even the would be party stoppers, budget balancers and columnists were making so much money, their condemning it only made them richer, and have even more fun.

The President elected in 1992 on a platform of "stopping the party" happened to mean what he said. He was a total unknown independent named John Scott whose "stop the party" slogan got him a 52% popular vote majority. At the same time a rather large number of congressional incumbents had been defeated by newcomers to politics with little money but who also used "Stop The Party", or "STP', as campaign promises. Western and Southern States had elected the most STP candidates, both Republican and Democrat. It was almost like a new party had come on the scene. Oregon's STP candidates lost as did New York, Illinois, Maryland, Virginia, Massachusetts, Delaware, and Vermont, but STP candidates did quite well everywhere else, and enough new Congressmen and Senators were elected to uphold the new President's vetoes, which were generally vetoes of any new spending, or expansion of the federal government.

Thurgood Marshall, a liberal Supreme Court Justice, retired in 1991 and was replaced by a strict constructionist, Constitutionalist judge name Clarence Thomas who voted and spoke eloquently against a federal government exceeding its Constitutional bounds. Other more conservative judges began voting with the new judge, and the highest court in the land itself suggested rewriting the Constitution to forbid unbalanced budgets. I'll bet you youngsters never realized there were budget deficits and inflation each year.

It was a real party pooper, I'll tell you. By 1993, Washington D.C. real estate prices had plummeted, and the federal budget had been balanced. Inflation had come to a screeching halt, and there was outrage everywhere in old Washington D.C. Party goers who had been joyous for years and years at the Washington Party's bountiful table were suffering from bizarre withdrawal symptoms, like an alcoholic or druggie stopping cold turkey. The suffering that went on in Washington D.C. was just pitiful. Most of D.C. was suddenly cut off from their source of excitement, sustenance, happiness, well being, and prestige. It was awful! Thousands of families had yard sales, selling their belongings, trying to sell their houses, and leaving the city with hope of getting employment back home. They were out of luck at home too, because no one would hire an ex-Washington D.C. party attendee. All they knew how to do was shuffle papers and party. Work was an unknown factor. Being a former Washington D.C. resident became a mark of shame for the ex-Party goers, and they suffered mightily. Unfortunately, these ex-patriates from the Party could get no government help in their hour of need.

President Scott and Congress had stopped all welfare for ex-Washington Party attendees, and gradually phased out all welfare. Welfare, for you who are not familiar with it, was getting a handout from government for doing nothing. The Supreme Court upheld the cut off. With the rewriting of the Constitution, the federal government was forever forbidden from giving any subsidies of any kind to anyone or any thing at any time, including foreign aid. There used to be a lot of funny things going on in Washington at the Party!

The exodus from Washington by the party goers was so great that entire sections of the city were empty and being vandalized. The party grew smaller and smaller, and every time they moved it to another location, the STPers would find them and abuse them terribly, taking their jobs, money, and security. It was an unceremonious end to the world's biggest, most lavish, longest running, most expensive party. Washington D.C. became a virtual ghost town with empty buildings everywhere. Gradually the buildings were bought at low prices by corporations and businesses needing office space, and a few actual workers began to filter into Washington. Those glossy office buildings at such low prices were a wonderful buy for producers of machinery, consumer goods, and even medical care. The new workers found incredible buys in homes abandoned by the party goers.

With the Party over, America began to reorganize itself. Some missed the rules, regulations and laws that gave them an advantage over their competitors. Some businesses and corporations failed totally without the Washington Party and the protection and subsidies it gave. But no one missed them anyway as their products and services weren't reasonably priced and were of poor quality. The Japanese suffered too, as the public had grown tired of seeing everything on the shelves and in the showrooms with Japanese names. It then came to light that the Japanese had been buying millions of acres of farmlands, businesses, casinos in Las Vegas, motels, restaurants, and large office buildings in major cities. The entire Japanese Nation had been attending the Washington party vicariously, with Japanese in America sending party favors back home where they were enjoyed very much. Americans discovered this through a clever series of exposes' in a Washington newspaper, which stories were syndicated in most other papers throughout America. TV stations did nightly coverage of the disgrace. Gradually, the popularity of Japanese products faded, and it became shameful to own anything Japanese. By the year 2000, the Japanese had suffered hideous financial reverses, and all their investments in America had soured. They sold their properties at give away prices and went back home.

President Scott vetoed every government spending, expansion, and regulation bill, and invariably Congress upheld the veto. At the same time, thousands of federal laws were being stricken from the books. By the year 1998, the STP party was a controlling force in all states, the economy was in fine shape, and the dollar had risen against all world currencies to its current place of strength. The unemployment rate was at an astonishing low of 3%, most of this being kids out of school for the summer and retirees. The cost of welfare was almost zero, food stamps had passed away in 1994, and the national debt was down to 2 trillion dollars, reduced from the 5 trillion it had risen to by 1992. The post office had simply disappeared after carrying the mails had been deregulated. American cars were of top quality and selling extremely well. American TV sets had begun to appear in 1993 and were rapidly replacing Japanese sets as they wore out. A small firm in Mississippi had begun making wonderful VCR's and camcorders which were all the rage, and selling everywhere. A competing company in Texas was gaining ground, and the Hamilton Watch Co. in Lancaster, Pennsylvania had begun making watches again.

By the year 2000 it was all over for the Washington Party, and memories were fading of its glory years. Washington D.C. was once again prospering, only with producers rather than partying bureaucrats. The Japanese had vanished from the scene, and as you know their old cars are collector's items today. All that hullabaloo about royalties on patents that the Japs hadn't been paying for 40 years bankrupted their major industries when the lawsuits were settled. Young kids today don't even remember the old Japanese names of Sanyo, Sony, Toshida, Honda, and all those other funny sounding names.

In 1996, the Social Security phase out began. Those over 40 had a choice of getting a full refund or staying on. Those under 40 were taken off, refunded all they had put in, and told to save for old age by investing in a private annuity, hundreds of which were available. The last payment should take place about 15 years from now.

In 1998, the entire interstate highway system was sold to the highest bidders. About half of it was bought by the various states, and the rest by private enterprise. But 100% of the old interstate highways became toll roads.

Truckers began shipping their trailers by rail between cities, and millions of gallons of oil was saved as well as highway congestion eliminated in many places. When the interstates became toll roads, people began to commute less, and use more public transport. Many owners of the interstate highways shut down whole lanes and laid tracks in them near cities and began running private rail systems for the commuters. You never knew the interstates weren't always toll roads? Kids don't know anything!

Oil consumption had reduced itself to only a third of what it had been ten years before in 1990. Our small fusion electric plants were built beginning in 1997. There used to be lots of ugly large towers with wires strung on them carrying electricity between generating stations and the cities. They were torn down a long time ago. There also were huge brown clouds over cities, and America used millions of barrels of oil every day to run their cars. Sounds strange, I know.

In 1994, the State of Colorado passed a remarkably sensible tax law making taxes on property exactly 1% of the property's purchase price. It took a lot of hard petitioning and campaigning to get it passed, and the entire State government was against it as it would throw all the assessors and tax bureaucrats out of office. Property taxes were no longer based on value, but the actual purchase price, no matter when it occurred. It narrowly passed the November election and became law. Then an amazing thing happened. All the slum properties were immediately bought by investors and restored! Wonderful old Victorian homes in bad neighborhoods were snapped up for a song, as the taxes would never rise and were based on the cheap purchase price, not what they would be worth after restoration. Families began moving back to Denver, commuting diminished, and auto use declined. People began walking to work and fine neighborhoods sprouted up in the Colorado cities. By 1996, 5 other States had passed similar laws. New Hampshire, Wyoming, Virginia, Maryland, and New York did it first. By 1998, all States had the 1% tax rates, and the American cities were reborn again. Now, as I write this in 2024, there isn't a slum left in America of course. When the 1% tax laws passed, the old racial problems just faded away. Everyone was living in the same neighborhoods. Lots of the former black slum dwellers decided not to move when the laws were passed. With the end of crime in the former bad neighborhoods, everyone fixed up and restored. Surely you have seen those horrible photos of the old "slums" of America. They really existed before taxes became 1% of the purchase price. Property taxes before were at the whim of what was known as an "assessor". It's no wonder there were slums, crime, race hatred, and the like. The 1% tax phenomenon had nothing to do with the Washington Party of course, but it happened when citizens realized how much better everything seemed with the huge load of government off their backs. It was a wonderful idea and spread almost instantly.

You who are under 50 have no memories of slums, huge electric plants, Japanese merchandise flooding the stores and highways, and of course inflation and a big Washington D.C. federal government getting in everyone's way and costing so much money that the country was on the way downhill and fast. I know it is difficult to imagine an America messing around the world in everyone's business but their own, sending troops everywhere, and having a huge army, navy and air force. You might not believe it, but the State Militias used to be called the "National Guard", and these men were taken away from their jobs and families by that little Kuwait affair in the Mid East. The year 1992 was perhaps the most important year in American history, being as important as 1776 when we went to war with the British. 1776 got us our independence and 1992 stopped the party!

Oh! I forgot to mention one thing about the Party. The Drug enforcers were having the most fun it seems, and when STP President Scott came into office in January of 1993 after being elected in the previous November, the first thing he and his majority Congress did was to rescind all drug laws at the federal level. I know it's difficult to imagine, but there used to hoards of federal goons breaking down people's doors and arresting people who were using drugs. After drug use became legal, most people stopped taking them as it wasn't daring and fun anymore. Some States of course still have their own drug laws, but there were no longer any federal drug laws. That really put a crimp in the party! Those drug enforcement people left town and were virtually unemployable anywhere else, even as policemen, because they were too violent.

I keep remembering! I'll bet you would find it hard to imagine that among the idiotic things the Washington Party crowd did was to make owning a gun illegal. No kidding! There was a huge amount of crime in America because of the illegal drugs, welfare, high taxes, unemployment, and bad neighborhoods. None of this exists any longer, but it certainly did 40 years ago, and people wanted to protect themselves from the criminals. Now it is difficult to imagine a household without a gun. An old man like me has a lot of memories. Memories of things that used to go on in America that sound like fairy tales now in 2024. These things were all the results of the famous Washington Party that drew people from all over America to have a great time at everyone else's expense.

The new STP administration had cut spending so much that one of the first Washington Party tables to be removed was the IRS table. That was the Internal Revenue Service for those of you who are too young to remember. Everyone used to have to pay taxes on their incomes. It actually happened. The IRS could take your home, land, car, or confiscate your bank account without having to answer to anyone. It was so bad that you were actually guilty until you proved yourself innocent! This was eliminated by the year 1998, because the federal government had grown so small it didn't need any money to operate other than the current one half of one percent tax on everything purchased.

There used to be an entire set of complicated courts known as "federal courts". That was abolished in 1999 as they were unnecessary. Huge chunks of America used to be owned by the federal government. Hundreds of millions of acres were owned by Uncle Sam. In 1997, Congress put all federal lands up for bid. The money was used to pay off the remaining federal debt, and every citizen got a $3700 check. The only land kept were the national parks and the few remaining government buildings. No one was allowed to bid unless they were an American citizen living in America. Most "national forests", if you can imagine such a thing, were bought by timber companies who were appalled at the wholesale destruction and waste that had occurred on the former federally owned lands. The new owners immediately set about replanting the land and caring for it. Today, the scars caused by federal clear cutting and intentional fires are almost gone, thankfully.

Congress used to be able to mail things free! It was called "franking", and the Washington party used it to keep the same good old boys in office year after year. There was no single term limit like we have now. They actually used to get an enormous salary and were in Washington for many months a year with gargantuan staffs and powers. The two months Congress is in session each year now would have been unimaginable 40 years ago. Why there even used to be money that wasn't backed by anything! You couldn't redeem it for gold or silver. Would I kid you?

The Washington Party was a gigantic mutual infatuation between lawmakers, influence peddlers, do gooders, publicists, opinion takers, writers, broadcasters, suppliers, hangers on, and above all spenders. It went on unchecked for far too many years. That party almost ruined America. It concentrated power and money in Washington and environs in such a way as it is difficult to describe. Now in 2024, even I can hardly remember that horror. The power concentration of the Washington Party and its bureaucracies was a threat to the entire world, not just America. Thank the STPers that began its ruination in 1992! The Liberty Party we have today is a direct offshoot of the old STP Party. I see America as it is today, a free, united, strife free, economically sound Republic with few divisions, but 40 short years ago it was broke, the largest debtor nation in the world, had huge amounts of crime, segregation, hatred, terrible taxes, and almost total power originating from Washington D.C.. The words "power" and "official" were big words then, but are not used any longer with regard to government like they used to be. When that party was broken up for good, America came out of the shadows and became what it is now; proud, strong, and the envy of the world. I hope these memories help everyone to understand how close we came to total self destruction thanks to that gigantic, almost indescribably corrupt Washington Party.

CONCLUSION

If there can possibly be a "conclusion" to the previous 90 chapters, it is that there is far more to say, but time and space is limited. We are at a crossroads. America was the light of the world for 200 years, but she is fading fast. Her decline is caused by overpowering government, welfare, and bureaucracy, which has caused the ruination of every single civilization in history.

I am not certain we haven't gone past the point of no return. With far too many Americans unable or unwilling to think, read, reason, and act, that point may be passed already. With so many Americans getting mythical "benefits", and checks from government, it is unlikely they will ever vote against it. A check from the government is analogous to a wild animal drinking its own blood after being wounded. A delicious meal that will result in death. Americans are drinking their own vital essence with each handout, welfare check, program, or "help" from Washington. The equivalent of a farmer eating his seed corn, or a cold person burning the siding off his house to keep warm. Short term comfort, but eventual death. As illogical as drilling a hole in the bottom of a leaking boat to let the water out. Americans are drinking their own blood, and becoming weaker with each taste.

We are witnessing a virtual duplication of the fall of ancient Rome. In Rome, the welfare system got so out of hand that to keep the recipients amused, Christians were thrown to the lions. Today, the producers are robbed and destroyed in order to give handouts to the non producers in the name of altruism, equality, and civil rights. In reality it is self destruction voted into law by ruthless politicians such as Teddy Kennedy and others of his liberal ilk.

Like other concerned writers, I wish there were a magic set of words or sentences that would cause America to rise up and throw the rascals out. We could then return to productivity, wealth, and happiness. Is this set of chapters the magic set of words? Or is it just another futile attempt to get through the smoke and mirrors that has too long passed for knowledge. I tried!

Thanks for reading!

Don Stott